'Quite simply, I love this book. Thank yc  probing insight into how organizational a often to the detriment of the human beings the shadow side of exhortations to become boundless energy, the book questions whose aspirational health talk. By critically examini colonize our way of thinking about the hum ... ...iat it should" be capable of, the book will cause me to pause whenever I find myself thinking "I'm not hacking it" because I feel justifiably weary!'

**Dr Donna Ladkin, Professor of Leadership and Ethics,**
**Antioch University, USA**

'In this book Tomkins and Pritchard use the lens of metaphor to consider how constructions of both "organization" and "health" relate to each other, and the implications of this for organizations and those who work in them. They reconsider the core metaphors of organization-as-machine and organization-as-organism, building on Morgan's seminal work in *Images of Organization*, before exploring a series of other discourses such as "Family", "Reinvention" and "Cyberspace". Through thoughtful, critical analysis of the research literature and examples from their own practice, the authors show how the metaphors that shape discourses of organization and health can either help or hinder attempts to enhance health in the workplace. A lively, engaging text that I would recommend to researchers and practitioners alike.'

**Dr Nigel King, Professor in Applied Psychology,**
**University of Huddersfield, UK**

# HEALTH AT WORK

Engaging with some of the most debated topics in contemporary organizations, *Health at Work: Critical Perspectives* presents a critical, contingent view of the healthy employee and the very notion of organizational health. Drawing on expressions such as 'blowing a fuse', 'cracking under pressure' or 'health MOT', this book suggests that meanings of workplace health vary depending on how we frame the underlying purpose and function of organization.

*Health at Work* takes some of the most powerful and taken-for-granted discourses of organization and explores what each might mean for the construction of the healthy employee. Not only does it offer a fresh and challenging approach to the topic of health at work, it also examines several core topics at the heart of contemporary research and practice, including technology, innovation, ageing and emotions.

This book makes a timely contribution to debates about well-being at work, relevant to practitioners, policy-makers and designers of workplace health interventions, as well as academics and students. This book will be illuminating reading for students and scholars across management studies, occupational health and organizational psychology.

**Dr Leah Tomkins** is Senior Lecturer in Organization and Leadership Studies at the Open University, UK.

**Dr Katrina Pritchard** is Professor in the School of Management at the University of Swansea, UK.

Leah and Katrina first met in the 1980s, when they began their careers in the world of management consulting. They worked on developing strategies of organizational health for their clients, using an implicit model of the healthy employee focused on optimal performance, consistency with organizational values and non-resistance to change. Since leaving the corporate world for academia, they have developed a more sceptical view of health at work, and endeavour to distinguish between the rhetoric of institutional health messages and the lived experience of the human beings that such rhetoric often ignores.

# Critical Approaches to Health

Series Editors: Kerry Chamberlain & Antonia Lyons

The Routledge *Critical Approaches to Health* series aims to present critical, inter-disciplinary books around psychological, social and cultural issues related to health. Each volume in the series provides a critical approach to a particular issue or important topic, and is of interest and relevance to students and practitioners across the social sciences. The series is produced in association with the International Society of Critical Health Psychology (ISCHP).

*For more information about this series, please visit: www.routledge.com/Critical-Approaches-to-Health/book-series/CRITHEA*

# HEALTH AT WORK

## Critical Perspectives

*Leah Tomkins and Katrina Pritchard*

Routledge
Taylor & Francis Group

LONDON AND NEW YORK

First published 2020
by Routledge
2 Park Square, Milton Park, Abingdon, Oxon OX14 4RN

and by Routledge
52 Vanderbilt Avenue, New York, NY 10017

*Routledge is an imprint of the Taylor & Francis Group, an informa business*

© 2020 Leah Tomkins and Katrina Pritchard

*British Library Cataloguing-in-Publication Data*
A catalogue record for this book is available from the British Library

*Library of Congress Cataloging-in-Publication Data*
A catalog record has been requested for this book

ISBN: 978-0-8153-8388-8 (hbk)
ISBN: 978-0-8153-8393-2 (pbk)
ISBN: 978-1-351-20519-1 (ebk)

Typeset in Bembo
by Swales & Willis, Exeter, Devon, UK

# CONTENTS

# ACKNOWLEDGEMENTS

We would like to thank the editors of *Critical Approaches to Health*, Kerry Chamberlain and Antonia Lyons, for their invitation to contribute to this series, and for their encouragement and support throughout the process.

The ideas and motivations for this book result from a range of research collaborations and conversations with other people over a number of years.

Leah dedicates this book to Virginia Eatough, Birkbeck, University of London, and Simon Wright, for their encouragement of the notion that we can define our own meanings and metrics of well-being. She would also like to thank Jean Hartley at The Open University and our colleagues at the Metropolitan Police Service in London, for inspiring and challenging many of the ideas in Chapter 5 on learning.

Katrina would like to acknowledge her indebtedness to Gillian Symon, Royal Holloway, University of London, for their research collaboration which inspired Chapter 6 on technology, and Rebecca Whiting, Birkbeck, University of London, for their work together which is reflected in Chapter 4 on age.

# SERIES EDITOR PREFACE

## Critical Approaches to Health

Health is a major issue for people all around the world, and is fundamental to individual well-being, personal achievements and satisfaction, as well as to families, communities and societies. It is also embedded in social notions of participation and citizenship. Much has been written about health, from a variety of perspectives and disciplines, but a lot of this writing takes a biomedical and causally positivist approach to health matters, neglecting the historical, social and cultural contexts and environments within which health is experienced, understood and practiced. It is timely for a new series of books that offer critical, social science perspectives on important health topics.

The *Critical Approaches to Health* series aims to provide new critical writing on health by presenting critical, interdisciplinary and theoretical writing about health, where matters of health are framed quite broadly. The series seeks to include books that range across important health matters, including general health-related issues (such as gender and media), major social issues for health (such as medicalisation, obesity and palliative care), particular health concerns (such as pain, doctor-patient interaction, health services and health technologies), particular health problems (such as diabetes, autoimmune disease and medically unexplained illness), or health for specific groups of people (such as the health of migrants, the homeless and the aged) or combinations of these.

The series seeks above all to promote critical thought about health matters. By critical, we mean going beyond the critique of the topic and work in the field, to more general considerations of power and benefit, and in particular, to addressing concerns about whose understandings and interests are upheld and whose are marginalised by the approaches, findings and practices in these various domains of health. Such critical agendas involve reflections on what constitutes knowledge, how it is created, and how it is used. Accordingly, critical approaches consider epistemological and theoretical positioning, as well as issues of methodology and practice, and seek to examine how health is enmeshed within broader social relations and structures. Books within this series take up this challenge and seek to provide new insights and understandings by applying a critical agenda to their topics.

In the current book, *Health at Work: Critical Perspectives*, Leah Tomkins and Katrina Pritchard offer a new examination of the intersection between the complex worlds of organizations, paid work and health. They accomplish this by offering an insightful, and carefully argued, account of the discourses and metaphors that frame our understandings of health and well-being at work. As they argue, these framings are often tacit and unacknowledged, and yet have important consequences for shaping expectations and practices around both health and work. Consistent with much of the work in this field, the authors take a broad approach to health, conceptualising it as overall well-being throughout the text.

Influenced by Morgan's (2007) work on images of organization, the authors present a series of chapters that identify and discuss a range of influential core metaphors and related discourses of work − metaphors of the organization as machine, as organism, as family, as competitive, as a site for learning and reinvention, for technologizing and for politicising − and show how these have significance for issues of health and well-being. The authors take a strongly discursive approach to these discussions, illustrating how the way we understand organizations is heavily implicated in the ways we understand and shape the healthy (and unhealthy) employee or organizational member, and how these also shape the employee-organization relationship. These diverse discursive framings of work and organization infiltrate the way work can be, and is, conceptualised, organized and experienced, and this in turn shapes the varied and complex − and often contradictory − ways in which institutions and their employees construe various versions of health. Throughout the chapters, the authors revisit a small set of case studies derived from their own years of experience working in this field to concretely and convincingly illustrate their arguments.

Discourses are inevitably constitutive of social and institutional relations and subjectivities. For each of their core metaphors, the authors describe how understandings and practices of health are co-constituted with understandings and practices of the institution and its institutional power, and consider how these shape possibilities and limitations for subjectivity. The authors also provide insightful and detailed discussion of the clash of understandings that can arise from resulting mismatches between organizational discourse, health interventions, and health and well-being experiences.

In their closing chapter, the authors review the effects of these discourses of machine, organism, family, competition, reinvention, cyberspace and power on understandings of the healthy and unhealthy employee, and argue that these discourses, through the competing constructions of organizational functioning that they create, reproduce and legitimise, have significant implications for the design of well-being interventions. As they elegantly articulate, different metaphors imply quite different understandings of the need for intervention and change, and also of the kind of change actions that are required. They maintain that failure to understand the clash between different discourses and their framing of organizations, persons and health, underlies the failure of many workplace health and well-being interventions.

This book, with its creative, novel and comprehensive discussions of the complex ways in which organizations understand and create health and healthy workers, is an excellent addition to the *Critical Approaches to Health* series.

April 2019
Kerry Chamberlain and Antonia Lyons

# INTRODUCTION

## Constructions of health at work

In this introductory chapter, we outline the overall approach and main themes of the book, and start to explore the effects of metaphors, discourses and other framing devices on our understandings of health and well-being at work. Specifically, we:

- Argue that our often tacit assumptions about the nature and purpose of work shape, reflect and legitimise our understandings and expectations about individual and organizational health.
- Highlight the metaphorical basis of our understandings of health in common expressions such as 'cracking up', 'breaking down' and 'losing one's way'; and propose that this can have a very real and tangible effect on how we approach issues of individual, collective and institutional well-being.
- Suggest that one of the reasons why organizational health interventions fail is because of clashes of construction or mixing of metaphors, in which inconsistent and contradictory ideas about well-being are juxtaposed in particular initiatives, policies and messages.
- Introduce the case studies which we will use throughout the book to bring these discourses, metaphors and clashes of health construction to life.

### Constructing organizational experience

When we talk about our working lives, we reveal a great deal of information about our assumptions regarding the organizations and institutions which employ us – or indeed, relate to us in some other capacity, such as contractor, client or customer. For instance, when we express frustration that a project is 'running out of steam', or that what's missing is 'traction' for an initiative of 're-engineering', or that our skills are a little 'rusty', we are using language and concepts from mechanical engineering. In the process, we are suggesting, perhaps, that something about the way this organization operates makes us feel like cogs in the machine apparatus. As cogs, employees are expected to be efficient and reliable; they must work in precise compliance with the machine design and in perfect alignment with the other component parts with which they intersect.

By contrast, when we talk about project 'trajectories', or the need to get a piece of work 'back on track' and stop 'spinning our wheels', we are invoking the language and concepts of a journey. Such a journey could be by metaphorical land (we experience 'bumps in the road' or 'reach a crossroads'), by sea (a project has 'hit the rocks'), or by air (a business is 'taking off'), but all of these expressions invoke imagery and feelings which suggest that things are in motion. With this kind of language, our experiences of organization feel as if they have some sort of forward momentum, with a relatively well-defined destination, even if sometimes we stray off course or choose to take the odd detour. Our experiences of such journeys depend, of course, on whether we are the driver, captain or pilot in charge of navigating the course, or we are merely passengers, placing our faith in those at the helm to get us safely and sensibly to our destination.

Or alternatively, when we talk about 'laying the groundwork' for a decision, or the need to create an 'architecture' for our solutions, the 'scaffolding' for an initiative, or the 'collapse' of an argument, a different image of organizational life is invoked. This time, the notion of organization as a sort of building might come into view, and with it, impressions of solidity, structure, containment, etc. When we use this kind of language, we seem to be expressing a desire for strength and stability in our working worlds, where what matters most is having a solid foundation from which we can build. This imagery also suggests that our organizations envelop and hold us during working hours, and that we exit them both literally and figuratively at the end of the day, thereby reinforcing a sense of separation between 'work' and 'life' (as in the idea of a 'work/life balance').

Metaphors like the machine, the journey and the building feel so natural that we often take them for granted as self-evident and directly representative of reality. The most successful metaphors blur the distinction between literal and figurative ways of thinking and talking about both organizations and the people within them. As Lakoff and Johnson (2003) suggest, we tend to think of expressions such as 'he cracked under pressure' as quite literal, but one only has to compare the idea of 'cracking up' with the notion of 'breaking down' to sense the different sources of these images and their different implications for how we see the healthy, or in this case, unhealthy, human being. The first is based on a metaphor of the person as a brittle object, and suggests that poor health is a kind of heightened, maybe frenzied activity; whilst the second evokes an image of the person as a machine or machine-component, and suggests that poor health is related to a slowing down or dampening of activity.

Our experiences of organizational life are shot through with powerful metaphors and other forms of imagery, analogy and association. They ebb and flow in their usage, often overlapping, sometimes undermining each other; but importantly, they tend to escape our notice, because they feel so normal and natural. The three metaphors: organization-as-machine, organization-as-journey and organization-as-building are, of course, just some of the myriad ways of conceptualising our experiences of organization, many of which we will be exploring in this volume. Such metaphors are significant, because they are not just ways of giving colour to our talk about organizations, they are also ways of acting in and on them. They are particular constructions or discourses of organization, each of which highlights certain features of organizational life over others, and suggests certain courses of action, behaviour and intervention over others.

In this volume, we argue that our tacit assumptions about the nature and purpose of organization shape, reflect and legitimise our understandings and expectations about organizational health. In other words, we want to explore what we mean by organization in order to tease out what this might mean for the 'healthy employee' within that organization and, indeed, for the health of the organization itself. If we are talking about things from the perspective of the organization-as-machine, for instance, our expectations of health will differ from those which emerge if we are framing organizational life in terms of a journey. And, of course, the flipside is also true; the unhealthy worker is constructed differently if one is seeing organizational life in mechanistic versus journey-like terms. If we pause to reflect on the idea of an employee 'blowing a fuse' as opposed to 'losing his way', these two metaphors of machine versus journey come into view. Whilst this may initially seem to be mere linguistic adornment, we argue that such images both construct and reflect a much deeper sense of what health at work is all about. Our title for this book, *Health at Work*, therefore has a double meaning. It refers both to health in the context of the workplace and to the 'work' of discourse, metaphor, imagery and analogy in constructing how we understand and aspire to health.

Our approach is a little unusual for a book on health; our starting point is not with models or issues of health, but rather, with discourses of organization. Such discourses both underpin and mould our understandings of desirable and undesirable workplace practices – healthy and unhealthy experiences – but they are rarely explored or problematized within the literature on organizational health, especially the practitioner literature. In other words, we think the occupational and organizational health literature tends to underplay the ways in which the healthy (and unhealthy) organization and the healthy (and unhealthy) employee are discursively and ideologically co-constructed.

There are as many different ways of conceptualising health and illness (Hauser et al., 2017; Klein, 2010; Mishler, 1981; Shaw and Kauppinen, 2017) as there are different understandings of the human body (Synnott, 1992). The body can be conceived as a tomb, a temple, an enemy, a master, or a slave, all with different philosophical foundations and implications for how we understand health, illness and indeed, life and death. There can be no consensus on 'health' whilst there are so many different understandings of the human body as the site, source or recipient of health. Our work connects with this view of the body as socially and culturally constructed, and emphasises that these constructions are *institutional* too. Thus, the various understandings of, and approaches to, the body at work are the result of the different ways in which organization itself is conceived.

## Clashes of construction

Our approach is not just based on a theoretical interest in discourse and metaphor. It also has a very practical basis and purpose. We suspect that a failure to acknowledge the various discourses of organization might be contributing to the failure of so many organizational health interventions to produce their desired and promised outcomes. Whilst evaluating the effectiveness of organizational health interventions is always a complex business (Nielsen and Randall, 2015; Richardson and Rothstein, 2008), we believe that surfacing the underlying assumptions of organization on which they are based – often unconsciously – is an important contribution to the debate. In particular, we hope that our book will sensitise academics, students, practitioners and policy-makers to what Synnott (1992) calls 'clashes of construction', and to resulting mismatches between organizational discourse, health intervention and health experience.

Clashes between constructions of selfhood on the one hand and constructions of health, illness, treatment and prevention on the other, make themselves felt in many of our most complex and controversial health debates, often triggering deep and difficult existential questions. For instance, the practices of organ transplantation or blood transfusion make total sense from the perspective of the body-as-machine, where the component parts can be replaced when they break down, wear out or become obsolete. This has very practical consequences because, as Belk (1990) suggests, people are apparently more likely to donate their organs if their schema of the body is that of the machine (which can be upgraded or rebooted) or the garden (which can be harvested), than if they associate the body with the self or the soul. With the machine and garden metaphors, the body can be rearranged and refreshed without changing the essence of the person.

Organ transplantation and blood transfusion are, however, more difficult to accommodate from the perspective of the body-as-temple, that is, as embodiment of the divine. As McClendon et al. (2016) suggest, the view that one's body is a celestial manifestation helps to account for the ferocity of argument against premarital sex, drug use, body piercings and tattoos in a number of religions. Furthermore, if these behaviours are felt to be sinful or blasphemous, it is no wonder that the exchange of body parts or body fluids, even in situations of medical emergency, can be experienced as extremely problematic. For followers of religions which teach resurrection of the body as well as the soul, giving away one's organs – or being in receipt of a donated organ – might be felt to compromise the possibility of an afterlife (Hayward and Madill, 2003; Lauri, 2009).

The notion that parts of the body can be swapped in and out like machine components is also challenged by philosophers in the phenomenological-existentialist tradition, for whom the body is the site and source of the existential self (Gallagher and Zahavi, 2008; Moran, 2010). In Heidegger's (1962) famous phrase, the human condition is 'being-in-the-world' (*Dasein*), and because the body *is* our 'being-in-the-world', any description or experience of the body is simultaneously a description or experience of the world (Morris, 2010). As Merleau-Ponty (1945/1962)(p.117) explains, 'far from my body's being for me no more than a fragment of space, there would be no space at all for me if I had no body'. For Sartre, human consciousness is bodily consciousness, and it is consciousness of *this* body, as opposed to any other (Sartre, 2003). From this perspective, altering the make-up of our body means altering the make-up of our world and our fundamental sense of self.

The complex relationships between selfhood, health and sickness are also revealed in our different approaches to people with different illnesses. As Sontag (1978) famously argues, we have a very different image of the tuberculosis patient in contrast to the cancer patient. The former is cast as a sensitive outsider, almost too delicate and rarefied for this world, but with a heightened sense of individuality and insight; thus it is culturally almost inconceivable that the author, Franz Kafka, could have suffered from any other illness. In contrast, the cancer sufferer is all too often constructed as the victim of invasion and infiltration, with a diminished sense of selfhood, for 'cancer is the disease of the Other. Cancer proceeds by a science-fiction scenario: an invasion of "alien" or "mutant" cells, stronger than normal cells' (Sontag, 1978) (p.69). Different illness categorisations and assumptions both create and reflect different selves.

Turning to the workplace, we find that organizational spaces are rich in construction clashes, which are often mined for their entertainment value by people outside the profession or sector in question. One such example is the notion of human resources professionals as 'experience architects' in an international consulting firm (which we will introduce as one of our case studies later in this chapter). This invites attention, because it involves such an interesting juxtaposition of ideas. Being an architect implies conscious design, expertise and technique, and invokes the image of the building (as suggested earlier). However, employees' *experience* feels as if it is – or at least ought to be – something personal, private and related to one's most intimate sense of self (Tomkins and Eatough, 2013), not something fashioned by others. Being the target or recipient of 'experience architecture' from a human resources department begins to feel very strange, indeed. In a way, it turns the employee into a kind of Disneyland visitor, having one's working life designed, managed and orchestrated by others, with notions of 'fun' and 'entertainment' forced onto experiences that we might not normally choose to characterise as such.

In organization studies, such clashes of construction have been explored particularly successfully in relation to organizational change (Grant and Marshak, 2011; Heracleous and Jacobs, 2008; Sackmann, 1989). The stubborn persistence of 'process re-engineering' in the language of change management is testimony to the enduring power of the notion of organization-as-machine (see Chapter 1), but it is often accompanied by images and analogies which suggest something less machine-like, such as 'interweaving' the various 'strands' of a change programme, or creating 'the burning platform' from which one has to metaphorically jump, thereby accepting the jurisprudence-related 'case' for change. Different metaphors imply quite different perceptions of the need for change and the nature and style of change actions that will be required. Therefore, consistency across the discourses invoked in the conceptualisation and description of a change initiative can play a vital role in whether that initiative makes sense and garners support and momentum. As Marshak (1996) (p.155) suggests,

> When people say: 'If it ain't broke, don't fix it', they are undoubtedly speaking from a metaphoric field that implies the organization is a machine that should be repaired only when broken. Consequently, requests to 'get out of the box' (rethink premises) might be ignored simply because they are incoherent within the metaphoric framework of 'fixing a machine'.

It is hardly surprising, therefore, that when we bring these worlds together, i.e., when we juxtapose constructions of the healthy/unhealthy body with constructions of organization, we find many such clashes. For instance, we think that people often mock the expression 'health and safety', partly because of the contradictory expectations of employee experience and performance which underlie it. The expression can invoke an image of the out-of-touch bureaucracy, which is perceived as frequently preventing people from doing apparently common-sense things, particularly in the 'health and safety gone mad' version. It involves, perhaps, a tension between the sensible, productive worker on the one hand, and the officially 'safe' but potentially unproductive worker who is prevented from getting on with the job because of senseless bureaucracy, on the other. We are not, of course, suggesting that there is no place for health and safety in contemporary organizational life; more that the transference of health and safety regimes from inherently dangerous working environments, e.g., mining or construction, into less inherently dangerous, i.e., office-based environments, warrants critical reflection. If 'health' is associated with being prevented from carrying paper from a store room to a photocopier in order to finish printing out a report, it is hardly surprising if the idea gets equated with a certain kind of madness.

Pausing to reflect on the yoking of health to safety begins to suggest some of the power dynamics of organizational health, including the politics of the under-reporting of accidents and other incidents even in, indeed, especially in, the most safety-conscious of organizational environments (Zoller, 2003a). So much policy focus in this area revolves around safety (or rather, the control of the risk of unsafety) that notions of health and well-being become highly politicised, especially in so-called 'behavioural' health and safety regimes (Frederick and Lessin, 2000; Rost and Alvero, 2018), which focus attention on the safety consciousness of individual workers rather than the presence of potentially hazardous working conditions. In such 'behavioural' initiatives, the onus for a safe working environment is placed firmly in the hands of the individual employee, involving a particularly insidious identity politics, because, as Frederick and Lessin (2000) argue, nobody wants to become known as an 'unsafe worker'. When health is yoked to safety, it is perhaps no wonder that a very narrow definition of well-being at work emerges and, indeed, invites cynicism.

Another example of a construction clash that has recently attracted our attention involves 'mindfulness', which is currently very fashionable in corporate human resources and employee well-being circles. In the Buddhist tradition, mindfulness is associated with qualities such as stillness, reflection and contemplation, which can be cultivated and developed through regular meditation (Kabat-Zinn, 2015; Purser and Milillo, 2015). It is not easy to see how this might dovetail with other, more dominant features of organizational life, in which it is more often assumed that the path to success lies in being visibly productive, engaged and action-orientated (Murphy and Cooper, 2003; Simpson et al., 2002). Surely, the point of 'business' is 'busy-ness'? If employees are being mostly evaluated on their 'busy-ness', then an executive development course on 'mindfulness' might well feel as if it is giving mixed messages. Is the route to health and well-being mostly through meditation, reflection and calmness, or is it mostly through dynamism, action and energy?

This example highlights that construction clashes are often the consequence of disparate interests at work, and in particular, differences between individual and organizational perspectives. In this case, it begs the question of who is responsible for deciding that mindfulness is the best kind of intervention (as well as what is the underlying 'problem' for which mindfulness is the 'solution'?). Is it the individual, who is searching for more balance and serenity in his or her personal, as well as working life, or is it the human resources manager, who decides – on behalf of the organization – that mindfulness training for executives might be a cost-effective intervention, that is, a relatively 'quick fix', to enhance health, well-being and hence performance? Based on our own experiences of the corporate world, we would suggest that mindfulness training as an organizational intervention can backfire. It may be appealing for a human resources department to be seen to be following the latest trends in employee well-being, but if the people participating in such training engage deeply and reflectively with the Buddhist practices at the heart of mindfulness, they may well conclude that the path to greater well-being lies outside the organization rather than within it!

The politics of responsibility for health will be an important theme running throughout this book, and will be given particular elaboration in Chapter 7. This dovetails with organizational scholars' growing critique of our Western culture of neo-liberalism, and associated values of individualism and autonomy, which can be seen in policies and practices of privatisation, deregulation, free trade and reductions in government spending designed, *inter alia*, to boost private sector investment. For critical organizational scholars, neo-liberalism warrants scrutiny, because it shifts responsibility and blame for organizational success and failure onto the individual employee, often under the aegis of attractive-sounding programmes of employee 'empowerment' and 'engagement' (Aguiar and Herod, 2006; Bloom, 2017).

In the particular case of mindfulness, a neo-liberal politics of epistemology begins to emerge when we consider the sustained efforts to establish its correlates in neuroscience (Tang et al., 2015; Van Der Velden and Roepstorff, 2015). As Cederström and Spicer (2015) (p.24) suggest, in organizational mindfulness initiatives, we find a 'strange hybrid of Eastern spiritualism, self-help, neuroscience, techno-fetishism and postmodern business jargon, all delivered in a corporate-casual style ... We seamlessly move between ancient Tibetan wisdom and double-blind clinical trials with MRI scanners.' If mindfulness is based on *science*, then it must be OK, right? And if this is the science of the *brain*, that is, the essential and private property of the individual, then mindfulness at work must surely be something for which the individual is ultimately responsible, as well as to blame, if its purported benefits do not materialise?

Our critique here is not, of course, that mindfulness is 'bad for your health', but rather that organizational health practitioners (and those in a position to decline as well as accept their health recommendations) would do well to pause and reflect before embracing the latest fad in the health and well-being marketplace. As Marshak (1996) argues, it is often enough to just identify the different metaphors entwined in a proposal to become aware of the contradictions that might make successful implementation problematic; to expose the different interests at work and to identify alternative possibilities for action. Just because a wellness intervention is fashionable does not mean it will necessarily be any good for either individual or organizational health, and it could just conceivably do harm.

## Our approach in this book

As Metzl (2010) (p.1) suggests, 'health' is a term 'replete with value judgements, hierarchies and blind assumptions that speak as much about power and privilege as they do about well-being'. We would counter that 'organization' is a term which often masks its discursive and ideological foundations, and that teasing out its dynamics of power and privilege is important if we are to encourage more nuanced and more realistic expectations and practices of health at work. And just as advances in 'health' reshape the ways in which human beings relate to themselves and 'do not merely promise coping, nor even cure, but correction and enhancement of the kinds of persons we are or want to be' (Rose, 2007) (p.26), so we would add that advances in 'organization' create different possibilities for the kinds of persons we want and need to be at work; and that whether we experience them as healthy or unhealthy depends, to a large extent, on how we conceptualise the meaning and purpose of work.

With this in mind, we see this book as an attempt to make connections between two different disciplines and bodies of literature, linking those who explore the construction of organization with those who emphasise the social, cultural and ideological construction of health. Although our entry point is via the debates and concerns of organization studies (and related disciplines of management and leadership studies), readers will see complementarities between many of our arguments and parallel conversations in other volumes in this series on *Critical Approaches to Health*, written from different disciplinary perspectives.

On the whole, we ground our discussion in the world of 'organization', and we focus our attention on the healthy (and unhealthy) experiences of 'employees'. We acknowledge that changing patterns of work mean that not everyone works as an employee for an employer (as traditionally understood), and that developments in technology (see Chapter 6), as well as in society (see Chapters 3, 4 and 5), are ushering in new patterns of work and new possibilities for the economic and psychological relationship between individual and institution, including various forms of entrepreneurship, self-employment, freelancing and independent contracting. However, since one of our objectives is to highlight the influence of discourses of organization on human resources and organization development *policies*, we are basing our analysis primarily in the domain where such policies are most likely to be developed and applied, namely the world of organization-based employment.

With our interest in the power and ideology of discourse, we ground our theoretical discussions first and foremost in the work of critical organization studies, rather than other disciplines of the workplace, such as work psychology, occupational psychology, organizational behaviour or human resource management, although we acknowledge that these latter disciplines also encompass scholars who write from a critical perspective. Discourse and metaphor play a very significant role in critical organization studies, partly because 'organization' itself is so hard to pin down definitively. As many have asked, what precisely is organization studies the study *of?* The easiest answer is, perhaps, that organization studies is the study of concrete organizations, i.e., entities with recognisable structures, properties, missions and resources, both human and other. This definition results in research strategies of observing individual organizations as case studies or through comparative analysis, often with the goal of determining the most successful organizational type. Others, however, focus on organizing as an activity, rather than organization as an entity. Most famously, Weick (1979) explores the social psychology of organizing, suggesting that organizing is something which happens when two or more people act in concert, with or without formal structure or institutional affiliation. Organizational scholars' interest in metaphor is not surprising, therefore, given Morgan's (2007) argument that metaphor is especially useful, even necessary, at the embryonic stage of a discipline, when the precise nature of the phenomenon being studied is unclear and/ or contested.

In terms of terminology, we tend to use the notion of discourse/discourses to invoke and crystallise some of the most significant assumptions about organization and their implications for our constructions of health. Our reference to discourse bears a great deal of similarity to Morgan's (2007) (p.4) elaboration of metaphor as 'a way of thinking and a way of seeing', that is, as a way of structuring and ordering our understandings of things, which can open up constructive possibilities for thinking and seeing differently when we become aware of their partiality and contingency. We choose to talk mainly about discourses rather than metaphors, however, because we suspect there is an unfortunate lingering association between metaphor and linguistic embellishment; whereas we want to emphasise a more fundamental connection between the way we conceive organizations and the way we conceive the healthy employee or organizational member and their relationship with the organization. We use the expression 'discourse' to refer to particular constellations of ideas, assumptions, images, values and practices, which are ways of thinking and seeing, and indeed, ways of being. Often there *is* a root metaphor at the centre of the discursive constellation, i.e., a strong central image which reflects and anchors the core idea, and invites us to examine particular ideas and practices in relation to it. When we talk about 'discourses of reinvention' for instance (Chapter 5), this refers to a constellation of ideas, assumptions and values which include, but also problematize and extend, the core central metaphor of the organization-as-brain.

The connection between discourse and ways of being is a central concern in critical organization studies. In their now classic paper, Alvesson and Willmott (2002) talk about the regulation of identity as a vital manifestation of organizational control in contemporary workspaces. Organizations provide discursive templates and images for the type of person who is most useful and most desirable through mechanisms such as recruitment, induction, promotion, training and other forms of organizational communication and messaging; these become vehicles through which not only external behaviour, but also internal experiences, feelings and expectations are synchronised and normalised. In other words, discourses of organization are implicated in the regulation of employee subjectivity, often in the service of creating and honing the 'perfect employee'. When this 'perfect employee' is defined in relation to health, such identity construction can assume a powerful ethical force, as medical standards morph into moral ones. Health is entwined in notions of perfection, which unfold in relation to organizational needs which are both instrumental and moral. For instance, there is an interesting development from the medical statement that smoking is bad for one's health, to a short-hand version that smoking is just bad, and towards the idea that smokers are bad people (Brewis and Grey, 2008). In the contemporary organization, the 'perfect employee' is emphatically not a smoker!

The way we use the notion of discourse takes us beyond language and into the realm of practices, materialities, ethics and power. In organization studies, such a definition is often capitalised as Discourse so as to distinguish it from the study of purely linguistic phenomena (Fairhurst and Putnam, 2004). As critical organizational scholars, we owe a great debt to the work of Foucault (Burrell, 1988), who sees discourse as constitutive of social and institutional relations and subjects, and whose work directs our attention to 'discourses with a capital D – the stuff beyond the text functioning as a powerful ordering force' (Alvesson and Karreman, 2000) (p.1127). However, distinctions between discourse and Discourse are not the focus here. Our interest is in how particular discourses (as constellations of ideas, assumptions, practices, images and ontological possibilities) infiltrate the way work is conceptualised, organized and experienced, and what this means for the complex and often contradictory ways in which both institutions and their employees define health and its various alternatives. Although these definitions usually emerge in various forms of linguistic text, this is not always the case, and we understand discourse as encompassing non-linguistic 'text', including materiality, practice and visual imagery (Pritchard and Whiting, 2015). In other words, we are interested in discourse-as-materiality, as well as discourse-as-analogy – the 'is' as well as the 'as if'; and some of the discourses we explore in this book are more overtly 'metaphorical' than others.

Our greatest theoretical influence throughout the book is Foucault. Over the past three decades or so, Foucault has inspired an enormous body of work on management, organization and leadership, including studies of organizations as systems of surveillance (Sewell and Wilkinson, 1992); practices of recruitment and selection by human resources professionals (Townley, 1993); organization as spaces of identity formulation (Knights and Clarke, 2017); organizational humour (Huber and Brown, 2017) and self-constitution as a foundation for ethical leadership and well-being (Ladkin, 2018). Foucauldian analyses encourage us to see health management and health intervention as particular practices of power, and to question our taken-for-granted assumption that health in this context is automatically and necessarily a good thing. Indeed, for Foucauldian scholars, it is precisely when something appears to be unimpeachably good that we should challenge it (Haunschild, 2003).

Foucault's work is usually categorized into three main phases (Dreyfus and Rabinow, 1983). The first is his archaeological phase, where he analyses how knowledge comes to be accepted as such, especially in relation to accepted knowledge about sanity and health (Foucault, 1989a, 1989b). Foucault's argument is that our accepted classifications of health and unhealth (both 'mental' and 'physical') are largely established by so-called experts, that is, they are ideological constructions rather than biological givens. This interest in constructions of health is carried forward into his second, genealogical phase, where he examines the ways in which power, knowledge and the body are interrelated, and how populations can be disciplined through surveillance and normalising assessment processes, crystallised in the notion of 'bio-power' (Foucault, 1979). In this view, regimes of power no longer work by subjugation or force, but rather through regimes of self-discipline, in which people work on turning their selves and their bodies into what is considered 'normal' or 'acceptable'. In what has come to be known as his third phase, Foucault looked to philosophies of antiquity to explore how institutional and ideological norms can be challenged and a certain kind of personal freedom perhaps made possible (Foucault, 1986, 1997a, 1997b). In this later work, the earlier emphasis on the fashioning of sub-jectivity through disciplinary norms becomes infused with a certain optimism about the possibility of self-constitution as the sort of person one wants to be (Ladkin, 2018).

From a Foucauldian perspective, therefore, understandings and practices of health are co-constituted with understandings and practices of power, institution and the possibilities and limitations of subjectivity. We use Foucauldian ideas in relation to a range of topics and ideas in this book. In Chapter 3, for instance, we explore a Foucauldian politics of self-care and suggest that discourses of self-care are helping to turn the healthy life-style into an individual rather than an organizational or societal responsibility. In Chapter 4, we consider Foucauldian influences on connections between age and well-being, and the construction of health in terms of competitive performance and fitness. Also, we invoke Foucauldian philosophy in Chapter 5 to reflect on the relationship between health and learning, and the case of the neo-liberal learner-subject, who discip-lines him/herself into becoming a desirable and successful employee through a career- and life-long commitment to skills-refresh and self-reinvention.

Over the course of this book, therefore, we will argue that our understandings and experiences of workplace health are dependent on the discourses of organiza-tion which underpin them. This means that we offer no single or straightforward definition of health; instead, we allow particular meanings of health to emerge within their discursive, ideological and institutional framings, and suggest that it is these framings which affect whether, for instance, it is physical or psychological health which is at stake. By extension, we offer no simple definition of well-being, which is probably associated in most people's minds with a sense of health beyond the purely physical, incorporating psychological, emotional and even existential fac-tors. We acknowledge calls for greater definitional clarity for the concept of well-being, given how often and how loosely the concept is invoked in our institutional lives (e.g., Dodge et al., 2012; Forgeard et al., 2011). We argue, however, that any such clarification work will almost inevitably ignore the partiality, contingency and ideology with which certain aspects of well-being come to the fore, depending on the theoretical prism through which one is looking. Thus, we would suggest that well-being means something different depending on whether one's need for organizational identification and emotional security are the main priorities (see Chapter 3); whether one is at the start or towards the end of one's working life (see Chapter 4); whether one is investing time in skills-building because of job insecurity or job enrichment (see Chapter 5); and whose interests are at stake in defining it in such a way that particular interventions and solutions become self-evident (see Chapter 7).

Understandings of health and well-being may also differ depending on whether one is writing from an academic or a practitioner perspective. By this we mean that different professional interests may seek to work with a concept in different ways. Without wanting to over-simplify such differences, we both write from the perspective of practitioners-turned-academics (a peculiar version of the 'poacher-turned-game-keeper', or perhaps more appropriately, the 'game-keeper-turned-poacher'?), and we are reflexively aware of the differences between these two perspectives, especially in the question of dealing with complexity. Thus, for many academics, uncovering and exploring (without necessarily resolving) complexity is where the challenge and joy of academia lies; for many practitioners, on the other hand, complexity is a problem which needs to be resolved in order to produce and implement a practical programme of action. In short, definitions of abstract notions such as well-being depend on what one needs to *do* with the concept and which framings and metaphors one deploys (consciously or otherwise).

Just as we highlight the contingency and complexity of health and well-being, we also argue for the contingency and complexity of their opposites or alternatives. Earlier, we suggested that the idea of an employee 'blowing a fuse' versus 'losing his way' exposed the different metaphors of machine versus journey. Throughout this book (and summarised in Chapter 8), we will see how the most powerful discourses of organization produce different understandings of the *unhealthy* employee. In the two dominant discourses we examine in Chapters 1 and 2, for instance, the organization-as-machine and the organization-as-organism see both health and its alternatives very differently. Thus, with the machine metaphor, health is equated to a fully functioning machine component, and hence the unhealthy employee is effectively one who is *broken*. With the organism metaphor, where development, growth and adaptability are key, the unhealthy employee is more readily seen as one who is *stunted,* that is, as someone with unmet potential and/or who fails to adjust to changing organizational requirements. Earlier in this chapter, we touched on the interesting yoking of health to safety in the 'health and safety' discourse, which helps to cast the unhealthy employee as one who is *unsafe.* In other words, when talking about organizations, the opposite of health is not necessarily − perhaps not even usually − illness.

## The specific discourses at work

There are multiple ways of understanding and approaching organization through discourse and metaphor (Alvesson and Karreman, 2000; Alvesson and Spicer, 2010; Cornelissen et al., 2008; Koch and Deetz, 1981), both in theory and in practice (Weaver, 2015). Perhaps best known in organization studies is Morgan's (2007) work on the eight 'images of organization'. These images are ways of thinking and seeing, which have practical and political consequences for how we theorise, describe, order and behave in our working worlds, both in general terms and specifically in relation to health and well-being.

Morgan's eight images of organization are the machine; the organism; the brain; culture; the political system; the psychic prison; flux and transformation; and the instrument of domination. Each of these can be seen as a vehicle for a cluster of theories and ideas about organization, management and the workplace, as well as 'common sense' understandings of what institutionalised work is all about. In this book, we explore four of these images in depth – machine (Chapter 1), organism (Chapter 2), brain (Chapter 5) and political system (Chapter 7) – because we think these four have the most to say about the construction of organizational health. In addition, we present analyses of constructions which do not appear in Morgan's taxonomy, namely, discourses of family (Chapter 3) and competition (Chapter 4), as well as reflecting on how the characteristics of the industrial-age machine are morphing into a contemporary technologizing of health through developments in digitisation, robotics and artificial intelligence (Chapter 6).

Of course, Morgan's eight images are not the only ways in which organizational life has been, or could be, conceived. Other constructions of organization that readers may find intriguing include: organization-as-safari, with strategy-making likened to a journey of disorientated animals eventually moving towards a common space which is at once both open and bounded (Heracleous and Jacobs, 2008); organization-as-Wonderland, which demolishes fantasies of rationality and emphasises the paradoxical, the ridiculous and the just plain silly in organizations (McCabe, 2016); organization-as-ice-hotel, which juxtaposes the temporary and the permanent, the sustainable and the unsustainable (Pinto, 2016); organization-as-jazz-concert, which emphasises the notion of improvisation within agreed boundaries (Zack, 2000); organization-as-theatre, which sees things in terms of performance, role and stage management (Cornelissen, 2004); or even organization-as-vampire, with its constant need for fresh blood and its obsession with the new and the young (Riach and Kelly, 2015).

So, our aim with this book is basically two-fold. In Morgan's language (2007), we want to highlight both metaphors and metaphor, i.e., draw attention both to metaphors (as specific frames or prisms through which to view the world) and metaphor (as a way of thinking about the world which recognises that *any* perspective is partial, and that seeing one thing in terms of another is a fundamental part of how human understanding develops). Thus, we hope to sensitise readers to particular discourses of organization and their potential effects on how we conceive health, grounded in a discussion of some of the most important and challenging topics in contemporary organizational life. We also wish to sensitise readers to discursive influences more generally, and encourage an attunement to the presence of, and clashes between, work-related constructions beyond these particular examples, thereby fostering a critical engagement

with the ideological elements of health at work. Since all of us engage with
organization at some point in our lifetimes, whether school, family, employer or
state, we hope that this book will resonate across a range of institutional experiences and highlight some of the choices we have available for how we think
about, and act upon, our health.

## Our examples

Wherever we can, we try to bring our arguments to life using concrete, 'real-
world' examples from organizational life. Since we are interested both in the
healthy employee (that is, the experiential subject of health and the target of
health interventions), and in the organizational practices aimed at health (that is,
the rationale and design of health interventions), our examples include both
employee-talk and official-talk, and are designed to suggest some of the ways in
which these interact, co-constitute and sometimes clash.

Some of these examples come from our own empirical research, where we have
interviewed people at work as part of our academic studies into workplace experiences across a range of different sectors, industries and functions. Other examples
come from our ethnographic observations, where we have spotted instances of
interesting health language, practice and policy in our consultancy work, including
things that we would suggest are clashes of construction. More informally, we have
also paid attention to the ways in which our friends, colleagues and students talk
about their organizational experiences of health (and its alternatives), and in particular, the ways in which new – and sometimes surprising – images and expressions
come to life and gain a foothold in corporate rhetoric and everyday work-talk.

Because of confidentiality agreements with most of the organizations and individuals concerned, we are not always able to use these research data directly and
explicitly. It is also very difficult to secure copyright agreement from corporate
lawyers to reproduce company material, even when it is already available in the
public domain on company websites and other advertising spaces. As a result, we
have decided to create three fictitious case studies which we will use throughout
the book. These are amalgams or composites of the real organizations we have
come across, worked with and worked for. We have reworked them to preserve
the anonymity of the specific organizations and people concerned. These cases are
therefore designed to give a feel for the sort of organizational health-talk to which
we are referring, without explicitly associating this talk with any particular company, institution or individual. Our three case studies are as follows:

### AnOther Consulting

A large international management consultancy firm which prides itself on offering state of the art employment practices and innovations, as well as being an
'Employer of Choice', whilst maintaining a strong focus on excellence of
performance and delivery.

## *Department X*

A UK central government department which is striving to incorporate attitudes of 'customer service' and 'stakeholder engagement' into the cultural and budgetary regime of the UK public sector. *Department X* is working towards 'best practice' in relation to diversity, inclusion, fairness, etc., in its employee well-being initiatives.

## *Guilty Pleasures!*

A hip and trendy food and drinks manufacturer and distributor, with a range of goods and services targeted specifically at health and well-being. Seen as an example of British entrepreneurial excellence, *Guilty Pleasures!* has recently been sold to a large multinational food and drinks conglomerate.

We intersperse these three fictitious case studies with other examples, including personal reflections from our own experiences of health at work and other vignettes and illustrations from organizational practice.

# 1

# EFFICIENCY AND HEALTH

## Discourses of the machine

In this chapter, we focus on the first of the two most dominant metaphors of institution, namely the organization-as-machine. We consider some of the ways in which mechanistic constructions of organizational experience have a powerful, often taken-for-granted influence on our assumptions and understandings of health and well-being. Specifically, we:

- Reflect on how notions of the well-functioning organization and the well-functioning employee have been shaped by the qualities of the well-functioning machine, so much so that human experience and performance are shot through with issues of efficiency, reliability, predictability and consistency.
- Consider the resulting construction of organizational health as an implicitly mechanistic injunction to 'fix it!', with binary assumptions of health/unhealth akin to the on/off switch on a machine.
- Propose that much of the mainstream literature on occupational health, in particular, operates with such mechanistic underpinnings, with a resultant focus on fixing physical and/or psychological breakdown, rather than actively promoting well-being.
- Argue that mechanistic constructions of both organization and the human body in post-Enlightenment Western thought imply that all problems are fixable with the right diagnostic expertise and efforts of re-engineering.
- Share some personal reflections from our own corporate experiences as diagnosticians, fixers and re-engineers.
- Suggest some of the ways in which the machine can be resisted or subverted, thereby paving the way towards other metaphors in the remainder of the book which set themselves up in direct opposition to mechanistic constructions of both individual and organizational health.

## The organization-as-machine

As we outlined in the Introduction, there are multiple ways of understanding and approaching organization through discourse and metaphor (Alvesson and Karreman, 2000; Alvesson and Spicer, 2010; Cornelissen et al., 2008). Morgan's (2007) seminal work on the images of organization is a useful point of departure for us here, because the first two of his eight metaphors – the machine (this chapter) and the organism (Chapter 2) – are arguably the master discourses of organization (Grant and Oswick, 1996). They both represent and reveal the most firmly embedded assumptions about the purpose and dynamics of organization and their effects on the constitution of individual and organizational health.

The contrasting notions of organization-as-machine and organization-as-organism have dominated organizational theory and practice over the past century or so. Each has very different implications for how we understand what it means for organizations and the people who work for them to be and stay healthy, and for the difficult, but crucial, question of who is responsible for this health. These differences can be crystallised as the distinction between efficiency and effectiveness – a pairing that comes extremely easily, almost automatically, in organizational conversations when we look for ways to summarise what successful organizational functioning comprises. To unpack the effects of these taken-for-granted assumptions on health, we focus in this chapter on the notion of efficiency and discourses of the machine.

Mechanistic assumptions underpin a great deal of classic management theory, such as Taylor's principles of scientific management and the notion of 'one best way' of organizing (Taylor, 1914). Mechanisation infuses Weber's (1946) discussion of bureaucracy, where bureaucracy standardises and regulates the business of administration in the same way that the machine standardises and regulates the business of production. Both the well-oiled bureaucracy and the well-oiled machine have specific components allocated to specific tasks, and their success is measured primarily against criteria of efficiency, reliability, predictability and consistency. As Morgan (2007) (p.13) suggests,

> The mechanistic mode of thought has shaped our most basic conceptions of what organization is all about. For example, when we talk about organization we usually have in mind a state of orderly relations between clearly defined parts that have some determinate order. Although the image may not be explicit, we are talking about a set of mechanical relations. We talk about organizations as if they were machines, and as a consequence we tend to expect them to operate as machines: in a routinized, efficient, reliable and predictable way.

Many of the things we take for granted about organization have elements of this mechanistic approach, such as the standard depiction of a business in the shape of an organization chart, showing hierarchy, reporting relationships and specialisations, in which everyone has an allocated place, purpose and set of interfaces. Indeed, bureaucracy is proving remarkably resilient as the default organization type. In response to those who claim that the death of bureaucracy with all its 'red tape' is nigh (e.g., Bennis, 1967; Hamel, 2014), other scholars argue that bureaucracy persists as the base model for organization because it protects us from arbitrary power and patronage (Du Gay, 2000) and has adapted well to the demands of contemporary neo-liberalism (Graeber, 2015; Hanlon, 2016).

In the mechanistic mode of organization, there is little interest in the outside environment, whether it be customers, clients, consumers or any other external stakeholders. Instead, design and management effort is directed towards how well the machine runs internally. In a sense, therefore, any theory of the workplace which emphasises endogenous qualities of efficiency, reliability, consistency, etc., reveals the influence of the underlying metaphor of the organization-as-machine. The machine metaphor gives us a view of organization as a largely closed system, in which the organizational dynamic revolves around qualities of autonomy, self-reliance and self-reference (Morgan, 2007). Several influential theories derive from this depiction of organization as closed system, including models based on notions of *autopoiesis* or self-generation (Maturana and Varela, 1980) and self-organization (Ostrom, 1990).

From this perspective, it is not just the organization itself which is seen as machine-like. Mechanistic qualities and values spread to the organization's employees, too. In other words, human beings are expected to behave as if they were component parts of the machine. Thus, the individual employee is measured and assessed in terms of performance, productivity and reliability, and these expectations are laid out in contracts, systems and standards of performance management and professional development, which are designed to be applied consistently across all members of a function or department, adjusted for the specifics of individual grades or seniorities. In other words, the 'perfect employee' is maximally productive and efficient, but also relatively easily replaced – the perfectly-tuned cog in the wheel. There is no room for inconsistencies or idiosyncrasies, for each employee-cog needs to comply with the machine design and align perfectly with the other cogs in the machine apparatus – a little like fitting in as a piece in a jigsaw puzzle.

It is not just the 'perfect employee' who is seen in machine-like terms, for mechanisation has infused notions of the ideal leader, too. For instance, the metaphor of the leader as cyborg shines a spotlight on the type of leader who is characterised by almost super-human dedication, perfectionism, reliability and an absolutely tireless energy. As Muhr (2011) (p.153) puts it, 'a cyborg leader holds the ability to keep working on a continuous basis, almost like a machine that does not need breaks … It is almost as if they have an unlimited source of battery power, which never reaches low levels'. Cyborgs – both real and metaphorical – embody many of the ideas and qualities of the base metaphor of the machine and, in the process, come to blur the boundaries between human and machine (Nyberg, 2009; Parker, 1998). Moreover, their presence is not limited to the realm of science fiction; Muhr (2011) argues that the effects of the cyborg can be felt in many popular organization and management works, especially those which emphasise superiority, excellence and a succeed-at-all-costs mentality. By associating the qualities of Duracell bunny-style energy with business success, the metaphor of the cyborg creates a virtue out of humans behaving like long-life batteries. Such associations extend beyond the corporate world and enter the political realm, too. For instance, it is interesting to reflect on US president Donald Trump's persistent accusations that his Democrat rival, Hillary Clinton, lacked stamina and energy, whereas his own health and ability to push through was considered to be 'astonishingly excellent' (McCartney, 2016; McGranahan, 2017). Consciously or otherwise, Trump seems to have made very canny use of the leader as cyborg.

As we outlined in the Introduction, discourses exert not just a top-down, managerialist influence on how people behave in organizational life; they also exert their influence on how people feel about their work and their role in an organization, becoming absorbed into the employees' ways of being and sense of self. With the machine metaphor, in particular, mechanistic expressions such as 'blowing a fuse', being 'a little rusty' and 'running out of steam' have a forcible and enduring impact because they seem to equate to how people actually *feel* about their relationship with the organization and working life. Thus, discourses shape and regulate people's 'insides', not just their external actions and behaviour (Alvesson and Willmott, 2002; Collinson, 2003; Ezzamel et al., 2001; Knights and Willmott, 1989).

## Mechanistic constructions of the healthy employee: 'Fix it!'

When we apply these mechanistic constructions of organization to the domain of health, we find what we call the 'fix it!' mentality, with the organization cast as 'corporeal garage' (McGillivray, 2005). If the ideal employee is healthy in the sense of the perfectly functioning cog, then the undesirable, i.e., unhealthy, employee is the broken or malfunctioning machine part which needs to be fixed or, if it cannot be fixed, replaced. There is a simple binary divide between the healthy and the unhealthy employee; one is either 'fit for work' or not, just as the switch on a machine is either on or off. As the vignette below suggests (Box 1.1), the binary nature of such constructions of fitness can affect how they are perceived and received in practice.

---

### BOX 1.1 VIGNETTE: FAILURE OF 'FIT FOR WORK'

In 2014, the UK government's Department for Work and Pensions introduced legislation under the heading 'Fit for Work'. This initiative was designed to support employers to manage sickness absence in the workplace through a range of measures, including free referral for occupational health assessments for employees who had reached, or whose General

Practitioners (GPs) expected them to reach, four continuous weeks of sickness absence.

In 2018, the service was scrapped because of low referral rates, amid apparent scepticism amongst employers, employee representative bodies and health professionals about its viability and usefulness. Whilst not changing their assessment that levels of sickness absence are a serious problem for UK organizations, the British government has now pledged to explore other ways to tackle the issue, including considering how changes to the ways in which doctors fill out 'sick notes' – now refashioned as 'fit notes' – might support more effective return-to-work conversations with patients.

There are, of course, many possible explanations for the failure of the UK government's 'Fit for Work' initiative. Commentators have highlighted a chronic shortage of qualified occupational health assessors, and a failure to invest enough resources in publicity for the new service. Adding to this list of very feasible explanations, we would suggest that this binary 'fit' versus 'not fit' construction simply does not resonate with most people's subjective experiences of health – whether their own health or that of others whom they encounter as patients, clients or other kinds of referral. Unlike the industrial machinery from which this language and symbolism derives, our health does not usually operate with an on/off switch.

In passing, we note that the notion of 'fit' versus 'not fit' for work is reminiscent of another popular piece of organizational rhetoric, the idea that something or someone is (or is not) 'fit for purpose'. This has become one of the most frequently heard organizational excuses to crystallise and simplify why something has gone wrong, inviting a radical, all-or-nothing kind of organizational recovery. If something is deemed 'not fit for purpose', it is simply beyond the scope of what can be repaired. The fact that it is also increasingly mocked by comedians and political commentators suggests a level of awareness, we would suggest, that it merits exposure for the tensions of its construction. There is something dehumanising indeed about the idea that a human being is 'not fit for purpose' (Cutcliffe, 2000; Nolan, 2015).

Health scholars argue that such mechanistic, binary assumptions reveal the origins of the occupational and organizational health literature in the fields of preventative medicine, epidemiology and engineering, in which the emphasis is on preventing and repairing breakages and breakdowns (Quick et al., 2007). Within this mechanistic paradigm, a great deal of the occupational health literature focuses on how to maximise employee productivity; manage absenteeism and other sources of non-productivity; avoid risks, mistakes, accidents and hazards; and comply with health and safety and employment legislation (Schultz and Edington, 2007; Smedley et al., 2013). It is mechanistic in orientation, in part because it relies on creating clear and discrete health 'issues' so that specialist interventions can be targeted, effectively 'chunking up' employees' lived experience. Much of it examines the down-side of organizational life, such as burn-out, psychiatric disorder, bullying, substance abuse, etc. It also tends to be orientated towards 'quick fixes', that is, towards providing enough repair to allow employees to get back to work, but without really focusing on any longer term change or health reorientation. The focus is not so much on health, but on avoiding and managing unhealth, because unhealth is inimical to successful organizational functioning (Macik-Frey et al., 2007).

We referred in the Introduction to important parallels between discourses of organization and the social, cultural and ideological construction of health, self-hood and the body. Perhaps the most striking of these parallels is this connection between the organization-as-machine and the notion of the body-as-machine. A mechanistic approach has dominated understandings of embodiment over the past couple of hundred years, and is often traced back to Descartes' comparison of the human body to a clock, which works without a mind (Descartes, 1641). With the rise of Enlightenment thinking, mechanistic understandings of health and medicine became entwined with a broader mechanistic, scientific and positivist outlook on life itself, summarised as 'emphasising the search for invisible (to the senses) causative mechanisms, an analysis of phenomena into their component parts, the use of quantitative methods and physical measurement in research, and an objective stance toward phenomena' (Osherson and AmaraSingham, 1981) (p.223).

With this mechanistic understanding comes an assumption that all problems can be fixed if we apply the right combination of cause and effect, and allocate the right specialists to their treatment. As Sontag (1978) argues, we live in an era when medicine's central premise is that all diseases can be cured, and anything which is not fully and scientifically understood, and therefore fixable, is 'felt to be morally, if not literally, contagious' (Sontag, 1978) (p.6). In the parallel track of constructions of organization, we find a similar and powerful set of assumptions about the workplace: all (or at least, most) problems can be fixed, just as long as we diagnose them accurately and apply the right kinds of expertise to their resolution. And if we fail to fix them, the organization will eventually break down or become obsolete with a not-dissimilar sense of professional, even moral, failure.

The army of consultants, coaches and other kinds of professional expert we find in the contemporary organization speaks to the residual power of the machine discourse, and its emphasis on compartmentalisation, specialisation and repair. It is interesting to reflect on how, and with what effect, the language and practice of 'organizational diagnosis' has come to be taken-for-granted as a crystallisation of what it is that these experts and consultants actually do (Kahn, 2015; Lucas, 1987). Both body and organization are analysed into their component parts and engineered towards improved functioning. With such causal and compartmentalising ideas at work, no wonder the dominant injunction in organizational and occupational health is 'fix it!'. As the vignette below illustrates (Box 1.2), our own professional experiences have been heavily infused by such assumptions, imagery and analogy.

## BOX 1.2 PERSONAL REFLECTIONS: CONSULTANTS AS DIAGNOSTICIANS AND FIXERS

As we have worked on this book, the two of us have been revisiting our own experiences in our former careers as management consultants. When looking through examples of presentations and reports given to clients, we have been struck by how often – and how unconsciously – we used to draw on the language of 'diagnosis' to describe a default process of deconstructing the client organization into its component parts, usually into some combination of so-called 'hard' and 'soft' factors, such as Weisbord's (1976) 'purposes, relationships, leadership, structure, mechanisms, rewards' or the famous McKinsey (see Bryan, 2008) 7-S framework of 'strategy, structure, systems, shared values, skills, style, staff'.

Similar instincts underpinned much of our consultancy work on 'organizational health', too. We can both find examples of consultancy reports which 'diagnose' the issue of 'health' against inventories or indices, where it can be measured and reported against using predominantly questionnaire-based tools. Furthermore, we have become more reflexively aware of how successfully management consultants and other professional experts both expose and reinforce a 'fix it!' mentality through the language of 'tools' and 'tool-kits'. We suggest that the automaticity of the notion of 'tool-kit' in contemporary organizational practice and methodology is a considerable discursive achievement for the organization-as-machine.

A mechanistic approach to the body and the self is perhaps the most insidious of the metaphors of health in contemporary Western life – insidious, because it usually slips past us unnoticed. It is much easier to detect the constructions of health from traditions other than our own, because their very strangeness draws attention to the contingency of their construction. As Osherson and AmaraSingham (1981) suggest, we notice the metaphor of the river in ancient Egyptian medicine with its preoccupation with the body's 'floods' and 'droughts', and we can appreciate that this is just one way of understanding health with certain emphases and implications.

In contrast, when we think about health in terms of causal mechanisms such as stressors, and in terms of the isolation of different component ailments to treat, we are more likely to assume that this is a relatively accurate reflection of how the body truly functions. Thus, in our constructions of both physical and emotional health, the 'fix it!' model often slips past us unnoticed; we are much more likely to describe an employee's health problem in terms of 'break-down' or 'stress' than in terms of 'floods' or 'droughts', and to assume that these are accurate representations of reality.

We will return to the topic of stress, stressors and stress management in Chapter 7, where we reflect on the way in which the overall concept of 'organizational health' has come to accommodate (and sometimes blur) institutional and individual levels of analysis. This is a significant issue, because it creates a tension between something which is seen as caused by the environment, yet down to the individual employee to manage. For the time being, we will simply proffer that the emphasis on causality in the stress literature suggests to us aspects of the mechanistic discourse, but this is made more complex – and successful stress management intervention is thus more problematic – because of the emphasis on individual responsibility for identifying, addressing and controlling it. Of course, the politics of individual responsibility for health goes beyond the issue of stress; it is one of the main themes running throughout this book, and something which we consider in more detail in the next chapter.

## Possibilities for subversion

As we highlighted earlier, discourses are said to exert both a top-down, managerialist control on how people behave in organizations and a bottom-up, experiential influence in the sense that people absorb these ideas and their associated values into their most intimate sense of themselves. However, this process of discourse absorption – or 'identity work', as it is often labelled in critical organization studies (Brown, 2017; Watson, 2008) – is not automatically geared towards satisfying objectives of managerial or systemic control. Discourses can be resisted and reworked as well as appropriated and integrated into one's sense of self. Identity regulation is not *necessarily* effective in increasing employee commitment, identification or loyalty, and may instead contribute to employee cynicism or be a catalyst for resistance, especially if the discourses in question are interpreted 'as intrusive, "bullshit" or hype' (Alvesson and Willmott, 2002) (p.622).

Thus, some mechanistic concepts may infiltrate employees' taken-for-granted understandings of who they are at work, whilst other elements may be resisted as being too incongruous with their broader sense of personal or professional identity. For instance, in Ezzamel et al.'s (2001) classic study of identity regulation and resistance, factory workers developed their own version of 'working like clockwork', which allowed them both to hit their targets efficiently and consistently, and to preserve a sense of independence and idiosyncrasy over their working patterns – to the enormous frustration of the change management consultants who were charged with 're-engineering' them. These workers managed to 'stop the clock' when it suited them, and to make it tick to a different, more personalised, rhythm.

Elsewhere in the organization studies literature, the dynamics of subversion and resistance are theorised from a psychoanalytic perspective, that is, as fantasies which unfold as constellations of emotions and desires (Bloom, 2016; Stein, 2016). As Gabriel (1995) (p.479) suggests, fantasy involves a 'symbolic refashioning of official organizational practices in the interest of pleasure, allowing a temporary supremacy of emotion over rationality and of uncontrol over control'. Of particular relevance to us here is that many of the most common fantasies of organization seem to involve the relationship between the individual employee and The System; in other words, they reveal the enduring power of the organization-as-machine and the seemingly irrepressible instinct of human beings to go up against it.

Common narratives of the individual versus the machine include identity constructions of the hero, who manages to beat The System; of the heroic survivor, who refuses to be beaten by The System; and of victim, who becomes a casualty of The System. Gabriel (1995) recounts stories of human shrewdness and plain 'common sense' winning the day over The System when, for instance, simple work-arounds with literal and metaphorical post-it notes achieve what complex machinery apparently cannot. Organizational narratives of the ongoing battle between human beings and inhuman machines involve considerable paradox and subversion, for:

> Such stories reverse the classic scenario of the *deus ex machina*. Instead of the god from the machine coming to solve the problems of the erring humans, an ordinary person with wits comes to the rescue of expensive, arrogant and disagreeable hardware.
>
> *(Gabriel, 1995) (p.485)*

This does not, however, lessen the power of the machine; if anything, the fact that it stimulates resistance indicates the machine's authority. The stronger the metaphor, the more it will inspire human beings to go up against it, and define themselves in relation to it.

Moreover, the machine itself is not always quite as solid and immutable as it might at first appear. As we move away from the factory production line as the source of the machine metaphor and towards more contemporary forms of mechanisation, we find that different kinds of machines can behave differently, even idiosyncratically. With on-line virtual assistants, for instance, avatars come to represent the ultimate 'perfect employee', with their superhuman levels of effort, concentration and patience (Gustavsson and Czarniawska, 2004). The avatar is the healthy employee *par excellence*; it never gets ill, never breaks down and never feels depressed. If we shift from avatars to cyborgs, however, we find that the machine starts to become less reliable and less predictable. In other words, the employee as cyborg may have endless stamina and hence maximum efficiency, but it also has the capacity to revolt (Muhr, 2011; Parker, 1998). In the anthropomorphising of the machine, the balance of power and control could tip either way for, as Czarniawska and Gustavsson (2008) (p.679) put it, 'cyborgs stand for new worlds and new organizations, in the (happy) endings they become more human; in the (unhappy) endings they revert to their mechanic characters'.

We will return to the mechanisation of organizational experience and discourses of cyberspace in Chapter 6, where we consider the ways in which developments in technology are challenging, complicating and changing our understandings and expectations of health. Whilst it is easy to assume that mechanistic approaches belong to a more industrial age, when manual labour and factory-working were more commonplace than they are today (at least in the West), the influence of discourses of the machine is probably as significant now as it ever was. As our machines and technologies develop, so too do our mechanistic constructions of health at work. Traditionally, discourses of the machine have involved a strong intertwining of health, efficiency and hence compliance and conformity; in the future, however, such connections may well be loosened and potentially replaced with understandings of health which are more infused with notions of resistance and freedom. Like the unpredictable cyborg, the healthy employee could well go rogue.

## Final thoughts on organization-as-machine

As Morgan (2007) (p.5) explains, when we look at organizations through the prism of any one of his (or indeed, any other) metaphors, we automatically force other aspects into the background, for:

> Metaphor is inherently paradoxical. It can create powerful insights that also become distortions, as the way of seeing created through a metaphor becomes a way of *not* seeing.

To make explicit what has been mostly implicit in this discussion so far, the main criticism levelled at the organization-as-machine is that it neglects human factors. By emphasising design, structure, rationality, efficiency, deconstruction and control, the organization-as-machine casts human beings as system components, with on/off, fit/not-fit switches and compartmentalised health issues which can be fixed as soon as they are definitionally ring-fenced and their causality determined.

As we touched on with strategies and fantasies of resistance to The System, however, the living, breathing human beings who populate our organizations do not always behave or experience things in mechanistic ways – they (we) do not always perform or persist like the Duracell bunny. The organization-as-machine leaves a huge gap for other ways of conceptualising and theorising organizational experience which reflect the up-side rather than the down-side of human endeavour, including our capacity for growth, meaning and beauty. The dominance of mechanisation on our understandings of working life is unquestionable, but it is not the only prism through which we might approach the question of human functioning and human well-being at work, and it is important that we remain alert to the power and politics of its construction. For, as Gergen (1992) (p.207) famously suggests, there are other ways of viewing the working world, and we should ask ourselves why these do not take such a hold of our imagination:

Why do we find it so congenial to speak of organizations as structures but not as clouds, systems, but not songs, weak or strong but not tender or passionate? Is it because organizations physically resemble one but not the other, that we somehow discern through the clamorous hurly burly something that is structural, but not cloudlike, systematic rather than rhapsodic, strong but not tender? ... No, there is little sense to be made of the assumption that organization theories are read off the world as it is.

As we move forward into the other metaphors and discourses we have selected for this book, we will start to explore alternative ways in which our understandings of organizational experience – both healthy and otherwise – might be framed. This begins with our next chapter, where we shift our attention from efficiency to effectiveness, from the machine to the organism.

# 2

# EFFECTIVENESS AND HEALTH

## Discourses of organism

In this chapter, we consider the second of the dominant metaphors of institution – the notion of organization-as-organism. This metaphor underpins a great deal of both theoretical and practitioner work in the domains of human relations, human resource management, organizational development, and the more humanistic approaches to organizational change. Specifically, we:

- Reflect on the implications of seeing both organization and health in terms of effectiveness, adaptability and growth, in contrast to the efficiency and reliability criteria of the machine (Chapter 1).
- Propose that discourses of organism shift attention towards a positive concern for health, rather than the repair of malfunction, both at the level of the individual human being and at the level of the organization.
- Introduce the heuristic that health through the prism of the organismic metaphor is an injunction to 'flourish!' rather than the more mechanistic notion of 'fix it!'.
- Consider how discourses of organism give health and well-being an aesthetic dimension, concerned with beauty, growth, and the achievement of potential, not just functionality.
- Start to explore and problematize the question of responsibility for health – a central theme of the book.
- Introduce and start to challenge the assumption of synergy between individual and organizational health.

## From efficiency to effectiveness

As we saw in Chapter 1, organizational discussions often juxtapose notions of efficiency with notions of effectiveness. Efficiency reflects and reinforces assumptions and qualities of mechanisation and systematisation, whilst effectiveness demands a somewhat different take on what it means for organizations and the people within them to be, feel, and function well. When we ask ourselves whether something or someone is *effective*, we tend to mean something like: Are they making a difference? Are they contributing something beyond just the basics? In other words, we mean more than just: Are they doing their job? We mean: Are they doing their job *well*?

To explore this effectiveness dimension of organizational life, we turn to nature, biology, and evolution, rather than mechanical engineering or science. Thus, the second of the dominant discourses sees organization as a living eco-system, existing in a wider environment to which it needs to adapt and adjust to both survive and thrive. As Morgan (2007) (p.33) explains,

> As we look around the organizational world we begin to see that it is possible to identify different species of organization in different kinds of environments. Just as we find polar bears in arctic regions, camels in deserts, and alligators in swamps, we notice that certain species of organization are better 'adapted' to specific environmental conditions than others.

Expressions which suggest the power of the organismic metaphor in everyday work-talk include ideas which 'come to fruition', 'cross-fertilise', or indeed 'wither on the vine'; the need to 'plant the seeds' of a proposal in people's minds; and the organization of people, initiatives, and activities into 'cells' or 'pods'. A specifically evolutionary take on the nature of organizations can be seen in the notion of the 'survival of the fittest' in relation to both organizations and employees, and the frequent use of the label 'dinosaur' for those who seem out of touch with the way a company, industry or sector is 'evolving' (Hayes, 2016; Lawler and Galbraith, 1994).

Discourses of organism have had an enormous influence on both theory and practice in organizations. For instance, contingency models (Burns and Stalker, 1961; Lawrence and Lorsch, 1967) emphasise that organizations are open systems which need careful guiding to adapt to changes in their external environment. Unlike the closed-system, mechanistic approach, in which there is assumed to be a universally applicable 'blueprint' for organizing, the contingency-orientated organismic discourse focuses on the need to understand the particulars of one's environment and adapt accordingly. Therefore, issues such as fit, flexibility, responsiveness, and agility become matters of crucial strategic and operational importance.

One of the reasons for the enduring success of this discourse is that it can account for a range of different organizational types, including the bureaucracy which is held to be the definitive manifestation of the organization-as-machine. As Morgan (2007) suggests, through the overall meta-prism of the living organism, bureaucracy makes sense as the most suitable response to environments that are stable or protected in some way, where strategy formulation spans, say, five or ten years, and the appetite for risk and experimentation is minimal. In contrast, organizations which operate in more fluid environments, and with a higher tolerance of risk and inclination for experimentation, need to move more quickly and deftly than the bureaucracy will allow; so different species of organization will be required for these more dynamic ecological conditions. Thus, it is more likely that government and other public sector bodies will take the form of the bureaucracy; whereas start-ups and other entrepreneurial entities will reach for other, less rigid formulations, such as 'adhocracy' (Mintzberg and McHugh, 1985), in which control and cross-reference mechanisms are brought in on an as-needed, non-permanent basis, or 'ambidexterity', in which a corporation organizes itself deliberately to pursue contradictory goals simultaneously (Parikh, 2016).

From the organismic perspective, both organizations and the people within them are seen as having *needs*, which must be satisfied if they are to thrive. In other words, organization is not so much a technical or structural challenge as a motivational and developmental one. The classic human psychology projects of the mid-20th century can be argued to reflect this shift from mechanistic to organismic principles. These include the famous Hawthorne Studies (Mayo, 1949), which suggest that human participants in organizational processes are more motivated to perform well if they feel flattered to be given special attention, and get a sense that there is something interesting or important in the work itself. In a related vein, Maslow's well-known hierarchy of needs (Maslow, 1943) suggests that organizational life must satisfy 'higher order' human needs, such as self-actualisation, aesthetics, and meaning, not just the basic needs of remuneration and primal levels of physiological safety. Although such ideas may seem self-evident to us now, these studies were ground-breaking in highlighting that organizations rely not just on efficiency and reliability to be successful, but on human motivations, aspirations, inspirations, and desires as well. Thus, discourses of organism are strongly implicated in the establishment of the human relations movement (Bruce, 2006), and the creation of the disciplines of human resource management (Hendry and Pettigrew, 1990) and organizational development (Foster, 2016).

## Organismic constructions of the healthy employee: Flourish!

By highlighting the presence and significance of human factors, including 'higher order' needs, the organization-as-organism (living, breathing, thriving, growing, etc.) paves the way for a positive concern for health, rather than the more defensive concern for the prevention or repair of unhealth, i.e., mechanistic malfunction – both at the level of the individual human being and at the level of the organization itself (Broekstra, 1996; Morgan, 2007). After all, we do not usually think about a machine being healthy, unless we stretch the metaphor to its very extreme and start to anthropomorphise; but health is absolutely central to, perhaps even synonymous with, our understanding of what it means for an organism (of any type) to be alive. With the organization-as-organism, therefore, health is associated with the opportunity and incentive to adapt, grow, and reach one's full potential. This is what we think of as the 'flourish!' approach to health at work.

Within contemporary organization studies, such flourishing is reflected most obviously in the work of positive organizational scholarship (Kelly and Cameron, 2017; Nilsson, 2015) and positive organizational behaviour (Koutsoumari and Antoniou, 2016; Nelson and Cooper, 2007), both associated with positive psychology (Seligman and Csikszentmihalyi, 2000). A useful summary of the positive approach is 'the study of that which is positive, flourishing, and life-giving in organizations' (Cameron and Caza, 2004) (p.731). Positive organizational scholars argue for a move away from an emphasis on the *costs* of occupational health measures towards seeing them as *investments*, which are designed to bring out the best from an organization's human assets (Bakker and Schaufeli, 2008).

From this perspective, health and well-being are not just utilitarian means-to-an-end (i.e., useful in support of, but subordinate to, the overall goal of successful organizational functioning), but are also considered important ends in themselves (Wright, 2003). Thus, issues of health at work are conceptualised in terms of personal growth and the search for authentic, meaningful, and empowering experiences in the workplace (Macik-Frey et al., 2007). Health is no longer a matter of fixing problems and breakdowns, but rather, an ongoing process of meaning-making and the fulfilment of potential, grounded in a more holistic notion of selfhood. The healthy employee is one who is engaged in continuous growth and development, rather than defined in terms of the binary state of health/unhealth as per the on/off switch of the machine.

The organization-as-organism also gives health an aesthetic dimension. The connection between health, nature, and aesthetics relates not only to those aspects of the environment that enhance the quality of our workplace experiences, such as plants and other ways to bring nature into the workspace (Smith and Pitt, 2009; Veitch, 2011). It also refers ontologically to the way in which an aesthetic requirement infiltrates employees' sense of self. If health and well-being are considered to be desirable goals in themselves, rather than simply a route to improved organizational functioning (Wright, 2003), then in the metaphorical garden or field, the healthy employee is as much a flower as a vegetable. Thus, health involves projecting a certain image of vitality, growth-potential, and attractiveness. Just like a flower display, health is something *on show* – to be appreciated and admired by others (Huzzard and Spoelstra, 2011).

## Critical reflections: Who or what is supposed to be flourishing?

In the vignette below (Box 2.1), we see an example of the organismic metaphor at work. The naturalness of the language of this pretty typical advert speaks to the success and ubiquity of discourses of organism, with their emphasis on the need for time and space to grow.

---

### BOX 2.1  CASE STUDY: A RECRUITMENT ADVERT FROM *ANOTHER CONSULTING*

Stuck in a rut? No room to grow?

Here at *AnOther Consulting*, we understand that everyone needs space to develop their skills and follow their passions. So, wherever you're from, and whoever you are, we'll recognise your contribution as one of a kind, and we'll create the conditions for you to thrive.

We have worked hard to cultivate a culture of personal fulfilment, where people feel valued, nurtured and confident to be themselves. This is what our clients value most, because they know that the advice they get from us comes from an authentic place.

For us, the equation is simple: Employee well-being = client satisfaction!

So join us, and *be* the person you want to become!

For more information, see the Our People: Our Growth tab on the *AnOther Consulting* website.

---

This advert may feel a little exaggerated and 'over the top', but it probably does not strike us as very unusual or inappropriate. The appeal of the organismic discourse is in part connected to its unimpeachable – but also vague – associations between health, growth, empowerment, fulfilment, authenticity, and transformation. As Huzzard and Spoelstra (2011) suggest, this language is full of empty signifiers, much like the term 'excellence', that is, it sounds absolutely wonderful, but is often close to meaningless when one scratches beneath the surface.

Moreover, there is a dark side to the organization-as-organism because, if growth and flourishing are to be encouraged and enabled, practices of pruning, weeding, cutting back, staking out, etc., are also required (Sackmann, 1989). And if the mantra is the evolutionary 'survival of the fittest', that is all very well for those species who adapt and thrive, but what about other species who die out? In other words, the organization-as-organism conveys and legitimises a certain amount of ruthless managerialism behind its surface rhetoric of growth and fulfilment. Not all employees will ever be equally valuable organizationally; and it is in the interests of management, usually supported by human resources, to distinguish between the healthy and desirable employees who are flowers to be cultivated and put on display, and those who do not adapt so successfully and are therefore weeds to be scythed down.

We have probably now become so accustomed to the organismic discourse that we take it for granted that we need organizational development to nurture healthy employees and healthy organizations. We would, therefore, encourage readers to question such taken-for-granted assumptions, and to reflect critically on whose interests they really serve. Indeed, we think that organizational health scholarship from the 'flourish!' perspective tends to be a little blind to its own ideology, that is, to the ways in which this discourse is just as historically contingent and politically charged as the machine discourse it is thought to supersede. An emphasis on growth and self-fulfilment certainly *sounds* more humane than a mechanistic concern for efficiency and reliability, but we wonder whether it is not a kind of therapeutic fiction (Ciulla, 2004) which serves the interests of corporate stakeholders first and foremost, and only incidentally, accidentally, and inconsistently leads to any true health benefits for employees (Doughty and Rinehart, 2004; Fineman, 2006).

Across the literatures we have mentioned, i.e., traditional contingency theory, the literature on human resource management, organization development, and contemporary positive organizational scholarship/behaviour accounts, there is a crucial assumption of a synergy between individual and organizational health. It is posited that the healthy employee will develop and grow in tandem with the healthy organization's development and growth. Indeed, ever since the introduction of the construct of 'organizational health' in classic works by Bennis (1962) and Herzberg (1974), there has been a tacit assumption in much of the literature that the two levels of health are positively correlated (Brache, 2001) – an assumption which was illustrated in the vignette of the recruitment advert (Box 2.1), where *AnOther Consulting* laid out their equation of employee well-being = client satisfaction, i.e., individual health = organizational health.

Such assumptions of synergy lean heavily on the language of organic growth and flourishing, and a cross-fertilisation of benefits, advantages, and goods at both micro/individual and macro/organizational levels. Thus, there is a great deal of faith that 'from healthy leaders and healthy individuals grow healthy organizations' (Quick et al., 2007) (p.190), and that a key question for organizational development is 'what can organizations do to attract and keep creative, dedicated, and thriving employees who make organizations flourish?' (Bakker and Schaufeli, 2008) (p.147). An intertwining of individual and organizational health is reflected in an approach referred to as 'integral health management' (Zwetsloot and Pot, 2004), which is said to produce a 'win–win' situation for both the organization and its employees. In integral health management, there are said to be seven strategic priorities for organizational development, which Zwetsloot and Pot (2004) (p.115) summarise as:

> (1) Health as a strategic company interest; (2) the realization of a healthy primary process; (3) a safe and sound physical (work) environment; (4) an inspiring social (work) environment; (5) vital people; (6) a sound relationship with the immediate organizational environment and local community, and (7) healthy products and/or services.

Readers will draw their own conclusions as to whether this is a genuinely enlightened crystallisation of organizational mission or an instance of the empty signifiers to which discourses of organism and health *qua* growth are especially vulnerable (Huzzard and Spoelstra, 2011). The point we wish to emphasise is that, if we stop and reflect a little on the organismic discourse, we might well conclude that the anthropomorphising of the 'organization' (by giving it the attribute of 'health') is just as bizarre as thinking that a machine could experience 'health'. The construct of 'organizational health' is now firmly established in corporate rhetoric and policy, so we do not usually pause to ask ourselves what it is within or about the 'organization' – beyond the people who work for it – that might be seen as creatures who can experience 'health'. Surely we cannot mean that an organization's buildings, or processes, or intellectual property can be 'healthy', except as some sort of euphemism or consultancy-speak? Indeed, the more we reflect on the corporate rhetoric of organizational health, the less it seems to concern human beings. Instead, it seems to have more to do with macro-level organizational issues, such as performance, market-alignment, client-retention, and strategic capability. This is an issue to which we return, and in greater depth, in Chapter 7.

Perhaps the most significant implication of this discourse for critical understandings of health is the way in which it helps to shift responsibility for health onto the individual employee – a theme running through this book, and developed most explicitly in Chapter 7. The rhetoric of employee health and well-being often draws on notions of empowerment and the space to strive to realise one's full potential. However, with empowerment come agency and responsibility, and the vocabulary of growth morphs into the injunction to manage self-growth. As the body increasingly becomes the target of self-optimisation and we push past what used to be considered natural, biological limitations (Rose, 2007), so the healthy employee is increasingly focused on self-optimisation in the service of pushing past previously accepted expectations of performance. Both in and out of work, health is increasingly an issue of self-construction, self-correction, and self-perfection. The quest for health and well-being means searching for the key with which to unlock one's own inner potential – as suggested in the vignette below from our case study organization, *Guilty Pleasures!* (Box 2.2).

## BOX 2.2 CASE STUDY: A FLYER FOR AN EXECUTIVE DEVELOPMENT PROGRAMME AT *GUILTY PLEASURES!*

Be the Author of Your Own Story!

*Programme Objectives:*
This programme explores how you can unlock your potential to maximise your opportunities and impact at work. It is designed to help you shift from thinking of 'training' as something you have to attend every now and then, towards a mentality of continuous professional development or CPD.

*Target Audience:*
This programme is aimed at managers and aspiring managers who need to examine and maximise their own potential in the business as they look to progress in their careers.

*Key Topics:*
The meaning of personal growth; developing inner and outer confidence; uncovering unhelpful and unhealthy habits; understanding goals to achieve results; leading with authenticity.

Whilst seemingly quite benign and liberating, such associations between well-being, success, self-optimisation and self-fulfilment create a burden for the individual which can be quite difficult to bear. Unlocking one's potential sounds enticing, but failure to locate the key can lead to feelings of guilt and shame, and 'to get rid of these persistent emotions of guilt we turn to ardent self-management' (Cederström and Spicer, 2015) (p.46). Such projects of self-management can involve a heady mix of contradictory experiences, being simultaneously self-obsessive and self-effacing, full of both self-adoration and self-harm, both self-love and self-hate. Ultimately and ironically, 'flourish!' can become almost as mechanistic as 'fix-it!', turning the human *being* into the human *project*. As Cederström and Spicer (2017) (p.331) urge, perhaps we should consider whether so much work on self-optimisation actually takes us *away* from health, in the sense that:

> I was not sure what was left of 'me' here. Much of what had been achieved had come through renouncing my own self. Had I willingly turned myself into a machine? [Like the athlete who] pushed himself to keep running and said to himself: I'm not a human. I'm a piece of machinery. I don't need to feel a thing. Just forge on ahead.

## Final thoughts on the dominant discourses

The notion of both organization and employee as living eco-systems with the capability to grow and thrive if their potential can be harnessed is a very attractive one. It is woven into the very fabric of our contemporary understandings of organization, and thus deeply embedded in our assumptions about organizational health. Over the course of this book, we will see elements of this 'flourish!' approach infiltrate a range of paradigms, models, and practices. For instance, we will return to the notion of self-optimisation in Chapter 3, where we problematize the way in which the idea of the caring organization merges with notions of self-care to reinforce a sense of health as the responsibility of the individual. The notion of growth and self-optimisation will also feature in Chapter 4, where it is linked to discourses of competitive performance, and to tensions between maturity and vigour in the context of an ageing workforce. The politics of self-development and self-enhancement will also be examined in Chapter 5, where we consider the popular concept of the 'learning organization' and the health implications of its implicit command to keep working on perfecting and reinventing oneself.

For the time being, we will pause our discussion of the organization-as-organism, that is, as a creature whose very *existence* depends on its health, with the suggestion that, for many scholars and practitioners, it seems difficult to imagine how else we *could* conceive organizations (Morgan, 2007). The organismic image of organization has established itself so powerfully that it is now almost inconceivable that the classical management theorists could have paid so little attention to the influence of the environment, or believed in one-size-fits-all principles of management worthy of universal application. But it is precisely when a metaphor or discourse feels inevitable that we should be most alert to the politics of its construction. As Morgan (2007) proposes, there is a real danger of this organismic metaphor becoming an ideology, with normative guidelines for shaping practice; and when this ideology is so entwined with issues of *personal* responsibility for *organizational* flourishing, the costs on human health and well-being merit critical examination.

We have opened our book with this overview of the two dominant discourses of organization-as-machine (Chapter 1) and organization-as-organism (this chapter) to sensitise readers both to constructions of organizational health in general, and to the presence and influence of the two master metaphors in particular. In a sense, this juxtaposition between machine and organism seems to map onto a differentiation between the traditional view of occupational 'health', as the prevention and response to accidents and illness, and the repair of breakdowns, and the more contemporary-feeling notion of 'well-being', which incorporates psychological and existential welfare as well as the purely physiological. This is, of course, a simplification, but we think it is a useful heuristic, nonetheless.

In detecting a basic binary mapping of constructions of organizational health, our approach dovetails with Allender et al. (2006), who propose a contrast between health-as-safety and health-as-lifestyle. In this view, health-as-safety is grounded in employees' relationship with the physical environment of the workplace, and is reinforced by legislation and technical expertise; whereas health-as-lifestyle blurs the boundaries between organization and home, and is reinforced by a broader set of cultural norms, expectations and dietary/fitness expertise. The two constructions are sustained by emphasising different kinds of threat. Thus, health-as-safety sees workplace hazards as the main threat to health; whereas health-as-lifestyle conceives attitudes and behaviours as the main threat. These clashing discourses construct the individual employee in very different ways. With health-as-safety, the individual is infantilised, but protected from harm; whereas with health-as-lifestyle, the individual experiences intrusion, but with the prospect of motivation and greater self-confidence. We think Allender and colleagues' analysis is very illuminating, notwithstanding that we ourselves see a paradoxical contradiction even *within* the notion of 'health and safety' (see our Introduction), and not just between health-as-safety and health-as-lifestyle.

Like Allender et al. (2006), we argue that construction clash is more than just a conceptual or linguistic matter. In practical terms, it sends out mixed messages to employees, which can be disturbing and demotivating. We conclude with an example of such apparently mixed messages from our own research (Box 2.3). We think this vignette reveals something of a clash of construction between engineered efficiency versus personal growth – between machine (Chapter 1) and organism (Chapter 2) – between 'fix it!' and 'flourish!'.

---

**BOX 2.3  CASE STUDY: EXCERPT FROM A DISCUSSION WITH A HUMAN RESOURCES MANAGER AT *ANOTHER CONSULTING***

I can give you an example of something that really didn't sit right. Yoga, free yoga classes that [a senior partner] got very excited by, thinking that was a really good thing for us to offer to staff, you know, that would be popular and, you know, good for recruitment and retention, but not cost us too much to put on.

I mean, it was a great idea in theory. I like yoga myself. And I always feel better after a yoga class, you know, that time to breathe, and move, and also just, you know, switch off a bit. But the way *we* did it was hilarious – I mean 'hilarious' not as in funny, but as in ridiculous. We had to offer yoga 'The *AnOther Consulting* Way'. So, you know, 're-engineered' to within an inch of its life! Like, the classes were scheduled for people's lunchtimes, one at 12, a second one at 1pm, you know, so that people had a choice between the two. But it was, like, so regimented. So, by the clock and by the rules. It was more like a military parade than a yoga class.

It was completely mixed messages, I thought, you know, being healthy is all great, but as long as it can fit into a 55 minute lunch hour! And you know, you can relax, and find space to reconnect with your inner self, and find peace, and what-not, but only if you can fit that into 55 minutes! And I heard that the teacher was only allowed to teach certain moves, or pos-tures. There were some moves that weren't allowed because they were too risky, or needed too much equipment, and apparently the teacher wasn't allowed to do them because of 'health and safety'!

And you know, the classes weren't anywhere near as successful as we'd hoped they would be. There was something really odd about trying to con-trol and regiment something that should've been just much more relaxed. I think, on reflection, it would have been much better just to let people find their own thing, their own way to be healthy, or not healthy, or just what-ever they want to do for themselves, really. I think there is a limit to what we ought to be 're-engineering'!

# 3

# CARE AND HEALTH

## Discourses of family

In this chapter, we explore interconnections between experiences of health and constructions of organization as a family unit, where relationships are conceptualised in terms of kinship, and well-being is enveloped in feelings of belonging. Specifically, we:

- Propose that the metaphor of organization-as-family triggers fantasies and expectations of being the recipient of care.
- Argue that, through the prism of care, health and well-being are defined in terms of quality of relationship and feelings of specialness, safety and belonging.
- Suggest that this can invoke powerful emotions, both positive and negative, whether the organization-as-family is an explicit, deliberate marketing strategy or a more unconscious appeal to the family as the base template for *all* our experiences of institution.
- Consider the growing influence of care on organizational conversations, practices and policies, not least because an ageing population creates more employees who are also 'carers'.
- Reflect critically on associations between care, dependency and unreliability, which can create and reinforce an unhealthy power imbalance in organizational relations.
- Explore the ways in which well-being is increasingly enveloped in the notion of self-care, which makes it a matter of the individual's lifestyle choices.
- Suggest that through a Foucauldian prism of self-care, well-being can be experienced in illness as much as in health.

## The organization-as-family

As suggested in the invitation on social media from our case study *Guilty Pleasures!* (Box 3.1), organizations can construct themselves as a family, not only for their employees, but also for a broader range of stakeholders, including current and potential customers. Whether used as an internal or external communication strategy, an appeal to the idea of the family unit can be extremely powerful, evoking emotions such as the desire to feel 'at home', be looked after and feel safe. In effect, it triggers associations between well-being and belonging.

---

### BOX 3.1  CASE STUDY: ADVERT ON SOCIAL MEDIA FROM *GUILTY PLEASURES!*

Welcome to the *Guilty Pleasures!* family.

This is just our way of reaching out to like-minded people, inviting you to join the *Guilty Pleasures!* family.

Sign up, and we'll email you with special offers and the chance to win lots of yummy food and drinks. We'll also invite you to special family get-togethers, where you can meet lots of other family members and get to taste our new lines.

Sound good?

Click here to join our family.

---

Connecting institutional experience with what it means to be in a family is not without its risks as an organizational strategy. As Smith and Eisenberg (1987) report, when the Walt Disney Company consciously cultivated the notion of their employees belonging to the Disney family, it fostered a culture of warmth and informality which, initially at least, spread in a positive way to relations between employees and customers. However, it also led to Disneyland employees expecting other benefits of family membership, such as unconditional loyalty, favouritism and regular treats, such as the annual party known as the 'family picnic'. When economic pressures led to the need for cut-backs, employees reported feelings of deep personal betrayal: 'Accustomed to thinking of themselves as different and special, it was unthinkable to bring Disneyland employees in line with other amusement parks' (Smith and Eisenberg, 1987) (p.375). Subjecting people to the threat, let alone the reality, of job cuts was no way to treat one's family.

In the fictitious *Guilty Pleasures!* and real Disneyland examples, the appeal to discourses of the family is a deliberate and conscious marketing and employee engagement strategy. However, the notion of family can make itself felt at an unconscious level, too. This is the focus of psychoanalytic organizational theory, which sees the origins of our relationship with both organization in general

(Schwartz, 1992) and leaders in particular (Gabriel, 1997, 2015) in our formative childhood experiences: just as we idealise and identify with our parents in our early years, so we idealise and identify with our surrogate parents in our working careers, that is, our employers, managers and other authority figures (Schwartz, 1992). As Gabriel (1997) suggests, many of our most powerful hopes and expectations of organizational authority have their basis in familial fantasy, and we project onto leaders both the strength which we once attributed to our father and the unity and comfort which once tied us to our mother. From a psychoanalytic perspective, it is the emotional force of these associations that explains why we tend to think of organizational leaders in very black or white terms, that is, as either sinners or saints. With leaders, just as with family members, it is not calm, collected rational thought which leads the way, but visceral fears, hopes, anxieties and associations.

## Theories and expectations of care

Gabriel (1997, 2015) identifies four core fantasies that employees have about their leaders: omnipotence, legitimacy, availability and care. The first two are associated with the archetype of the father. Thus, the organizational leader is required and assumed to be powerful, strong, fearless and capable of performing miracles, as well as having a legitimate claim to power, whether based on achievement, expertise, or the circumstances of his or her recruitment to the leadership position. Fathers and leaders are similarly projected as being able and willing to take charge of the situation, with unchallenged qualifications of authority and legitimacy if their respective 'family units' are to survive and thrive. In organizational theory, these two aspects of masculinity find their way into a range of heroic models of leadership, which continue to dominate popular understandings of leadership, despite coming under sustained fire from critical organization and leadership scholars (Collinson et al., 2018; Tourish, 2013).

Representing the maternal side of the archetypal family, organizational leaders are expected to be available and accessible, even if their appearances in person constitute special occasions. Not showing up in times of trouble is one of the most fatal mistakes a leader can make, because it creates a serious dent in employees' feelings of safety, security and sense of affiliation. And finally – and most significantly for this particular discussion of health and well-being – leaders are expected by their employees to *care*, not in a general, abstract sense, but in a very personal, individualised way. As Gabriel (2015) (p.322) proposes:

> Caring outweighs any other consideration regarding the moral obligations of leaders in the eyes of their followers. A leader may be strong, may be legitimate, may be competent but, if she is seen as not caring, she is likely to be viewed as a failing leader.

From this perspective, the notion of care plays a crucial role in employees' expectations and experiences of health and well-being at work. These are grounded in the sense that leaders and other authority figures are *genuinely* concerned with one's well-being and prepared to go above and beyond the call of duty to secure it (Gabriel, 2015). Moreover, associations with the family highlight an expectation of favouritism. As employees, we not only expect a genuine concern for our well-being; we also imagine that our needs and desires will be known and understood, and that we will be given preferential acknowledgement over those who do not belong to this particular family unit. With the organization-as-family, therefore, psychological and emotional aspects of health and well-being come to the fore: being well both involves and relies on feeling that figures of authority both care *for* us and care *about* us – an important elaboration and differentiation for many care scholars (Barnes, 2006; Dalley, 1996). As recipients of care, we get the sense, however unconsciously, that we are somehow special. From a psychoanalytic perspective, therefore, the healthy employee is a kind of favoured child, confident because of the provision of a safe and loving psychological home.

Psychoanalysis is not the only theoretical tradition interested in the connections between care and well-being at work. The positive organizational scholarship community also sees care as one of its central concerns. For scholars in this tradition, care and the related concept of compassion have been associated with enhanced workplace self-esteem (McAllister and Bigley, 2002), organizational commitment (Lilius et al., 2012), organizational performance (Cameron et al., 2003), organizational productivity (Kroth and Keeler, 2009) and organizational resilience (Boyatzis et al., 2006). Underpinning much of this literature is a definition of care as an empathic response to the pain and suffering of others (Dutton et al., 2006). As Madden et al. (2012) suggest, the caring organization is one which demonstrates compassion and concern in the face of both an individual crisis, such as an employee's loss of a family member, and collective crisis, such as the effects of the terrorist attacks of 9/11 on the organizations directly caught up in them.

In positive organizational scholarship, care is usually constructed as a response to unusual rather than everyday events (Dutton et al., 2002). It involves standing back from the pressures of 'business as usual' to acknowledge that the priorities of work must (occasionally) give way to the priorities of the human beings who are undergoing loss, shock and/or bereavement. Seen this way, care is defined in relation to feelings of pity, sympathy and kindness in the face of exceptional circumstances. This has a surprising effect on constructions of health, because it triggers associations with the reactive repair of specific occasions of unhealth, rather than the proactive, positive nurturing of an ongoing sense of health – which is an interesting departure from our usual association of positive scholarship with flourishing (i.e., the organism) rather than fixing (i.e., the machine).

Not only does this view of care locate health and well-being in the context of special circumstances, it also seems to play into the hands of those who would criticise theories and models of the human factors of organization for their emphasis on the 'soft' or the 'pink and fluffy' (and hence not the stuff of serious organizational theory or practice). Increasingly, critical scholars working with philosophies of care (Ciulla, 2009; Gardiner, 2018; Ladkin, 2018; Tomkins and Simpson, 2015) take pains to emphasise that care is not about prioritising the cuddly side of organizational life, but instead, often involves taking tough decisions on behalf of colleagues, subordinates or others. Thus, care may cast the employee as one whose well-being derives from feelings of belonging, but this is not the same as having one's every wish or whim granted, or being shielded from the more difficult aspects of working life. Indeed, scholars such as Ciulla (2009) are trying to rescue the notion of care from being drowned in associations with niceness, suggesting that if care means love, it is more often than not a tough love.

In addition to these philosophical, psychoanalytic and positive perspectives, care is the focus of a powerful body of feminist literature on the ethics of care (Gilligan, 1982; Held, 2018; Liedtka, 1996; Noddings, 2003; Tronto, 1993). This literature sees care in terms of moral orientation; it unfolds in a relational process which is closely associated with female maturation, rather than the abstract, rules-based process which is more usually associated with male development. In contrast to the masculine ethics of justice, a feminine ethics of care does not see human well-being in terms of binary rights and wrongs or goods and bads. Instead, well-being is something we work on and work towards, not something we switch on and off like a machine. Moreover, this work is relational and grounded in everyday experience, that is, embedded in enduring relationships, not just linked to the people we consult or lean on in times of trouble (Lawrence and Maitlis, 2012). For care ethicists, therefore, health is as much a social as an individual matter.

By claiming health and well-being as a social issue, however, care ethicists are not suggesting that it belongs to the public as opposed to the private domain. Indeed, their claim is the very opposite, namely, that an ethics of care helps to reinforce the value of the private, not as something different from, but rather something constitutive of, the public. This mounts a challenge to the traditional division of our lives into work versus family (promulgated in notions such as 'work/life balance' and 'work/life boundary'), in which the family or life side is systematically devalued (Ernst Kossek et al., 2010). As Engster and Hamington (2015) (p.1) explain, 'in care ethics, the center of moral action is shifted from interactions amongst citizens in the public forum and marketplace to personal relationships'.

With care ethics, therefore, we should look to our personal lives for data on how we might thrive at work. As Tomkins and Simpson (2018) suggest, there are important parallels between the things we instinctively do in our private relationships and the approaches we adopt with colleagues and subordinates at work, especially in relation to the question of how – and how much – to intervene to sort things out when people around us get into trouble. Through the prism of care ethics, our personal lives and our private relationships become the site and the source of understanding for what happens in the workplace, alerting us to the force of the emotional undercurrents in both spaces. Becoming more aware of these parallels might make us more alert to 'the choices that are available to us in *all* our relationships, and to what might be at stake in the decisions we make' (Tomkins and Simpson, 2018) (p.99). This reinforces the discourse of organization-as-family: if our most important templates for well-being are grounded in our personal relationships, then the fundamental blueprint for these is that of the family, both real and imagined.

In their various ways, these theoretical traditions all associate health and well-being with relationship, and with feelings of belonging, protection and nurturing. Whether or not this is explicitly connected to constructions of organization-as-family depends on the specific theoretical affiliations of scholars writing in this space. Nonetheless, care is emerging as one of the most powerful discursive influences on contemporary understandings of organization (Cameron et al., 2003; Lawrence and Maitlis, 2012; Madden et al., 2012). This is not least because of the growing awareness of the numbers of 'carers' in our labour-force, that is, employees who juggle paid work with unpaid, informal care, usually for a family member (Lloyd, 2006). The implications of the demographics of an ageing population for our understandings of health will also be considered in Chapter 4 on the connections between age and health. Our point here is that the presence of 'carers' (whether or not they would use that moniker for themselves) is one of several factors contributing to the growing influence of care on our organizational conversations, policies and practices.

## *Critical reflections on care*

Constructions of care bring about a range of challenges and controversies for both organizational and individual well-being. Caring leaders, compassionate organizations, support for 'carers', etc., may sound humanistic and enlightened (who would not rather work for an organization in which people care, rather than one where they do not?), but critical organization scholars have suggested a more sinister underbelly to such discourses of care. By its very nature, they argue, care is associated with issues of dependency, which means that care reinforces an unhealthy power imbalance in organizational life.

For instance, Munro and Thanem (2018) (p.55) argue that the infiltration of care ethics into organizational life 'actualizes a sense of pastoral care that is deeply invested with power ... Today the priest has been replaced by the figure of the manager-leader in current expressions of pastoral care'. In such an actualization, employee well-being involves having one's needs and desires anticipated and met (or refused) by others. The individual employee is cast as someone in need of care, that is, as dependent and therefore weak, inadequate or inferior in some way. And if the organization-as-family constructs the healthy employee as a sort of secure and favoured child, as we suggested earlier, this critical edge turns that child into a kind of adolescent, who is favoured only as long as he or she behaves, and whose attempts at independence can be read as teenage stroppiness – something which both families and other institutions find notoriously difficult to navigate. From this perspective, the notion of care reinforces a kind of unhealth, which is defined in terms of the inequality, even exploitation, that results from relationships of asymmetry (Kittay and Feder, 2002; Munro and Thanem, 2018).

Moreover, we suggest that a focus on care helps to surface one of those clashes of construction we described in our Introduction. From an experiential perspective, care does not always fit easily with other understandings of organizational life, and in particular, with the dominant discourse of organization-as-machine. In other words, employees do not always feel comfortable when issues of care or associations with family are invoked, whether or not this is done deliberately. Tomkins and Eatough (2014) suggest that employee discomfort with discourses of care may be because care conjures up associations with unreliability, even stigma, and it feels safer in organizational life to be associated with professionalism and competence than neediness and dependency. The reliable employee is usually felt to be a safer subject position than the unreliable employee, irrespective of whether this unreliability comes about for worthy reasons. Thus, the more an organization's internal and external marketing emphases care and caring, the more complex the feelings triggered by this construction clash will be.

In a sense, discourses of care cast an especially harsh spotlight on differences between our *actual* experiences of organization and our sense of how things *ought* to be, if only we worked for a better employer, or were better skilled, better managed or better motivated ourselves. As Schwartz (1992) illustrates, when talking about the realities of organizational experience, most people describe a world of chaos, drama, emotion and stress, rather than a mechanistic world in which things run like clockwork; and yet, when it comes to strategies for self-improvement and success, Schwartz's own students 'wanted to know the techniques for managing clockworks' (Schwartz, 1992) (p.8), which were akin to 'an article of faith' (ibid.). In a world of clockworks (real or imagined), it is no wonder that a concept such as care is felt to be problematic. Care evokes neediness, emotion, messiness, vulnerability and dependency, and it challenges the idea that business needs can and must always come first.

Reflecting on these issues gives us a sense of the clash between the logic of the machine on the one hand, and the human factors of organization on the other – indeed, perhaps between the masculine and the feminine, and/or between an ethics of justice and an ethics of care. And with this clash comes a growing suspicion that the health and well-being of the organization may not be entirely synergistic with the health and well-being of the individual employee – a topic which we explore in some depth in Chapter 7. If organizational health revolves around efficiency, delivery and just getting on with it, and individual health unfolds in and through relationship, belonging and feeling 'at home', no wonder the world of work can be such an unsettling and contradictory space, and health and well-being so hard to achieve.

## From care to self-care

Whether as a reaction against the power asymmetry and dependency-associations of care discourses, or because of a more general influence of neo-liberalism on our understandings of organization, there is another important way in which care is shaping our approach to health and well-being, namely, an increasing reference to the notion of 'self-care'. The idea of self-care was almost unheard of in the workplace a few years ago, except in the context of looks and appearance, where it was mostly used as a criticism of women who were deemed to be lacking in it. Now, however, the rhetoric of self-care features quite prominently in organizational life, and in our relations with institutions generally (see also Lupton, 2018, in this series). Take a look at the following vignette from our case study, *AnOther Consulting* (Box 3.2). It talks about the need for self-care throughout the year, and not just 'blue Monday' (typically the third Monday in January, and allegedly the most depressing day of the year, in the Northern Hemisphere, that is).

---

**BOX 3.2 CASE STUDY: WEBSITE POST FROM THE EMPLOYEE WELL-BEING DIRECTOR OF *ANOTHER CONSULTING***

There's a real risk that 'Blue Monday' trivialises the problem of well-being at work. It implies that extra attention should be focused on just one day per year and that we just need to 'pull ourselves together' to get past this particularly difficult time. It ignores the fact that what we really need is consistent self-care to sustain us throughout the year.

Of course, this time of year may be especially hard, with people feeling they may have over-indulged financially and lifestyle-wise over Christmas, and spent more time with the extended family than they usually do at other times of the year. All of this can contribute to feelings of depression in January, when it is still cold and dark, but without the fairy lights and Santa stockings to lift our spirits.

This means that we all need to invest in proper self-care. Here are some tips which should help you to take care of yourself at any time of the year:

- Try to remember to eat healthy foods. I know this can be difficult when you're working hard and late, and the only food available is that sandwich with the curled up bread in the canteen. But too many days on the trot eating fast food is not going to help with self-care.
- Exercise is a god-send for self-care! Even if you can't manage any treks through the countryside, try to remember to take shorter walks whenever you can. Think about using the stairs, rather than the lift. And maybe get off the tube one stop too soon and walk the final stretch home?

- Never underestimate the power of a good night's sleep. Sleep helps to restore our energy and resilience levels. Put your tablet or smart phone away at least thirty minutes before you go to bed, so that your body system has a chance to get ready to enjoy the gift of sleep.
- Don't be too hard on yourself! Beating yourself up all the time is not good for self-care! Try to think of things not as failures but as opportunities for learning. There will always be a next time to get things right!

Within contemporary organizational theory, the notion of self-care is most regularly associated with the philosophy of Foucault. In Foucault's so-called third phase (Dreyfus and Rabinow, 1983), he looked to philosophies of antiquity to explore how institutional and ideological norms can be challenged and a certain kind of personal freedom made possible (Foucault, 1986, 1997a). Central to his argument is the notion of self-care, and he traces variants of this idea – both continuities and discontinuities – from Socrates and Plato, through the Stoics, Cynics and Epicureans, through the advent of Christianity and towards contemporary notions of the self. Our modern interpretations of the classics, Foucault argues, have emphasised the importance of self-knowledge over a more fundamental principle and practice of self-care. Whilst the specific elements and emphases vary across different philosophical schools and across the centuries, Foucault suggests a number of core themes in antiquity's view of self-care. These include commitment to critical self-reflection, a careful scrutiny of opinions and claims to truth – both one's own and those of others – the unlearning of bad habits and the cultivation of courage to speak out and speak up. As Foucault explains (1997a) (p.95), 'in all of ancient philosophy the care of the self was considered as both a duty and a technique, a basic obligation and a set of carefully worked-out procedures'.

In many of the classical variants of self-care, there is an explicit connection with health, because care of the self means that 'one must become the doctor of oneself' (Foucault, 1997b) (p.235). Through the prism of self-care, health and well-being are grounded in rigorous self-reflection, self-analysis and self-correction, and are intimately entwined with questions of ethics and responsibility (Ladkin, 2018). Unhealth is explicitly attributed to the unexamined life, unchallenged opinion and unreformed practice (Nehamas, 1998). From this perspective, health and unhealth are located in the soul as much as the body or the mind.

The idea of the family gets a gender twist in the classical notion of self-care. Unlike psychoanalytical organizational theory, which sees care as linked to fantasies of the mother, it is the father who plays the crucial role in philosophies of self-care. Whilst this emphasis may, of course, be an effect of historical gender inequality, rather than an inherent psychic need (as psychoanalysts would have it), it is seen as the Socratic father's (or older brother's) duty to care for his sons by teaching them how to care for themselves (Nehamas, 1998; Tilleczek, 2014). Indeed, without wanting to simplify things to the point of trivialisation, seeing this distinction through the prism of gender helps to illuminate an interesting difference between care and self-care. Most interpretations of care involve meeting another person's needs, with the carer more experienced, more able or more qualified to help those who lack such experience, ability or qualifications (although this is not without its controversies; see for instance, Tronto, 1993; Walmsley, 1993). Socratic self-care suggests a different way of responding to the needs of others, which involves encouraging others to take care of their *own* needs. When translated into the rhetoric of contemporary organizations, therefore, self-care becomes a strategy of enablement and empowerment as much as self-discipline and self-reflection.

There is debate amongst both classicists and Foucauldian scholars about the ultimate purpose of the ethics of self-care (Boyle, 2012), that is, whether self-care is fundamentally a personal project of self-improvement and self-preservation (Nehamas, 1998) or a more political project geared towards becoming useful in public and institutional life (Foucault, 1997b). For our present purposes, it is enough to suggest that these two are not necessarily in opposition, highlighting, for instance, that both Socratic and Foucauldian treatments discuss the significance of controlling one's own desires so that they do not harm or disadvantage others, thereby playing an important private and public role (Foucault, 1997c; Tilleczek, 2014).

It is important to emphasise that Foucault does not advocate for self-care as a kind of narcissistic self-obsession (although he has certainly been misinterpreted this way). His work encourages a deep and continual critical scrutiny of one's motives and actions, through which one might constitute one's own way of being (including one's own way of being both healthy and unhealthy), not rediscover some kind of true, essential self as if it were something lying dormant within us all along. As he explains:

> In the Californian cult of the self, one is supposed to discover one's true self, to separate it from that which might obscure or alienate it, to decipher its truth thanks to psychological or psychoanalytic science, which is supposed to be able to tell you what your true self is. Therefore, not only do I not identify this ancient culture of the self with what you might call the Californian cult of the self, I think they are diametrically opposed.
>
> *(Foucault, 1997c) (p.271)*

In emphasising self-care as self-constitution rather than self-discovery, Foucault, like his ancient forebears, gives well-being an ethical edge. When health is enmeshed with the Socratic, Platonic and Foucauldian care of the self, it is *work,* not leisure.

## Critical reflections on self-care

In contemporary discourses of self-care, there is a tendency to associate an ethics of care with the kind of Californian self-obsession and self-coddling, against which Foucault warns (Ladkin, 2018). Indeed, constructions of self-care as self-obsession fit almost seamlessly with what Cederström and Spicer (2015) (p.6) call the 'wellness syndrome', which is 'based on an assumption about the individual as someone who is autonomous, potent, strong-willed and relentlessly striving to improve herself'. The organizational employee who engages properly in self-care is both a product and a project of lifestyle and ideology.

Somewhere in the translation from philosophy to organizational rhetoric, a number of key features of self-care have been lost, or at least, distorted. Thus, when we reflect on how our contemporary understandings of health are shaped by notions of self-care, we do not usually mean the Socratic rigours of self-scrutiny or the Foucauldian injunction to turn oneself into the sort of person who can model a different way of living and speak up when things are wrong. We have lost the sense of paradox of Foucauldian self-care, in particular, whereby well-being can be enveloped in 'illness' as much as in 'health', as the 'healthy' self is one who tells his/her *own* story in the 'practice of reclaiming a voice that bodily trauma and institutional treatment have caused to be silenced' (Frank, 1998) (p.336). Thus, the cancer patient or the aids patient might be seen as 'healthy' as she/he eschews the normal patient identities that those illnesses confer (Sontag, 1978), creating a paradox of health-within-illness, or indeed, ill-ness-within-health. Foucauldian self-care is complex, however, for efforts to distinguish between 'healthy', i.e., liberating, self-constitution and less healthy, i.e., compliant, 'technologies of the self' are likely to remain frustrated (Frank, 1998).

These days, we have almost totally lost the classical idea that self-care involves teaching or modelling a way of living and a kind of work for others, and that it is more about struggle than about enjoyment. In short, philosophical notions of self-care have been stripped of their relational quality. Instead, the corporate rhetoric of self-care is now more likely to make us think, 'me, me, me!' As the Guardian newspaper journalist Arwa Mehdawi (2017) suggests, contemporary use of the notion of self-care involves acts of relaxation and *privilege;* and 'rather than being a route to social change, self-care has become a destination in itself'.

Not only does this realisation of self-care emphasise lifestyle and evoke privilege, it also involves a profound shift of responsibility for health away from the organization and onto the individual. As we suggest in the vignette below (Box 3.3), when organizations and institutions emphasise self-care, it is hard to resist the interpretation that what they are really saying (at least in part) is, 'look after your own health, so that we don't have to look after it for you'.

## BOX 3.3 VIGNETTE: POSTER ANNOUNCEMENT AT A LOCAL HEALTH SERVICES PROVIDER

Announcing Self-Care Week 2019!

Self-care is about keeping yourself fit and healthy. It means understanding what you can do to look after yourself, when a pharmacist can help, and when you need to get advice from your GP [general practitioner] or another health professional.

If you have a long-term condition, self-care is about coming to terms with the condition and adapting so that you can live with it.

Embrace self-care for life!

Organizations which draw on the rhetoric of self-care may sound very modern and in tune with the *Zeitgeist*, but the implications for the question of responsibility are more unsettling. If the individual employee is empowered to care for him or herself, there is nobody else to blame if health remains elusive. Our health becomes a matter of lifestyle choice, and if we choose not to devote adequate time and resources to perfecting ourselves, we are left with a profound sense of guilt and inadequacy. Within this neo-liberal understanding of organizational life, any failure of care for the self triggers a punitive self-loathing, in which 'stress, anxiety and feelings of depression are not seen as a creation of the external work environment. Instead, they are a creation of your own lazy and unfocused mental habits' (Cederström and Spicer, 2015) (p.25). Through the rhetoric of self-care, organizations become facilitators of employees' efforts at self-enhancement, fostering dissatisfaction with their previous selves in order to work harder to become the 'perfect employee'. In effect, 'the work ethic has been replaced by the work-out ethic' (Cederström and Spicer, 2015) (p.40). This, surely, lets organizations off the hook.

## Final thoughts on discourses of care and the family

As we reflect on notions of care and self-care, we see a range of ways in which apparently humane, people-orientated concepts can get interpreted in ways which serve the health of the organization perhaps more than the health of the human beings who work in and for them. Thus, critical scholars problematize discourses of care for their construction of employee dependency, inequality, inferiority and hence exploitation, and self-care for the way it permits an abrogation of responsibility on the part of the institution. Either way, health becomes intertwined with issues of power and questions of responsibility, leading to relationships between people and organizations that we might well decide are pretty *unhealthy*.

We hasten to add that we are not against either care or self-care. Both ideas have the potential to enhance our experiences of the workplace, not least because they remind us of the importance of relationships for our feelings of well-being. But as we argue with all the topics in this book, a key challenge in contemporary organizational health is to understand the discursive underpinnings and the practical, political and psychological implications of even the most apparently benign and well-intentioned organizational health messages. Discourses of care are amongst the most ideologically appealing of our current constructions of organizational life. This means that we should be especially alert to the ways in which they can distort, rather than support, what it means to be 'healthy'.

Both care and self-care trigger powerful associations with the discourse of organization-as-family, and with the complex emotions that feelings of belonging and their flipside, the fear of rejection, can evoke (Rosenblatt and Albert, 1990). Through this prism, the role of the individual employee is cast in a variety of ways, including cosseted child, rebellious adolescent, or young adult in training to become self-sufficient. Whether via care and the mother, or self-care and the father or older brother, the family is a powerful base metaphor for our understandings of organizational life. As our actual families have become more fractured and less containing, we have reached more towards our surrogate organizational families to grant (or deny) us the possibility of grounding our well-being in feelings of safety, security and belonging (Bauman and May, 2014; Schwartz, 1992). We have come a long way from the cold logic of the machine.

# 4

# AGE AND HEALTH

## Discourses of competition

In this chapter, we explore how discourses of competitive performance construct work-as-sport, leading to particular understandings of health and fitness for both people and organizations. Specifically, we:

- Unpack some of the ways in which discourses of competition position the fit employee, drawing on studies of both work-as-sport and sport-as-work.
- Explore relations between health, performance, fitness and age, and highlight the discursive tensions that emerge between younger and older employees in relation to well-being at work.
- Consider how the concern with demographic change highlights ageing as an issue of global significance, focusing on the fear of the implications of an ageing workforce.
- Examine the recent move to deploying generational labels (such as the oft-maligned Millennial or the selfish Baby Boomer) as a way of crystallising health and lifestyle attitudes, capabilities, expectations, and problems.
- Review how a life course perspective can inform understandings of health and age, particularly as related to the start and end of working life.

## The idea of 'healthy' competition

Competition is, of course, central to capitalist economies. Over the past half century or so, discourses of competition have infused all forms of organizational and institutional life. 'Healthy' competition has become a well-known mantra that pertains to an idealised state of a neo-liberal economy, in which rival organizations strive to 'come out on top' while still playing (or appearing to play) by the 'rules of the game'. These broader understandings of 'healthy' competition provide an important contextual backdrop for the consideration of age and health that is the main focus of this chapter. However, we also draw on competition in a sporting sense, recognizing that the business of sport has become significantly more organized and commercialised in recent times. Relatedly, sporting metaphors are commonly deployed at work, and increasingly organizational leaders are encouraged to seek inspiration on the winning ways for 'the field of play'.

A discursive framing of competitive relationships between organizations translates into beliefs about how those working within organizations should behave in order to succeed. In this way, understandings of both individual and team sporting endeavour carry forward into our expectations of the healthy, or indeed athletic, employee at work. Competition is a highly flexible discourse and sporting competition even more so, not least because the specific attributes vary depending on the particular sporting discipline: the marathon runner, the heavyweight boxer, and the ice skater may have vastly different physical attributes and capabilities. However, there are strong common threads of physicality, commitment, and discipline that run across all sporting endeavours and relate to competitive advantage. Such threads emphasise meritocracy in competitive sport and can be directly transferred to organizational life. Thus, it is widely taken for granted that those employees who combine commitment, hard work, and talent will rise to stand on the top of the metaphorical podium. Within this constellation of discourses, health and well-being both contribute to, and result from, performative success.

From these understandings, it is a relatively straightforward move to consider the 'corporate athlete' (Loehr and Schwartz, 2001) (p.122), where experiences of coaching professional athletes towards optimal levels of performance are applied to help leaders to develop:

> Supportive or secondary competencies, among them endurance, strength, flexibility, self-control, and focus. Increasing capacity at all levels allows athletes and executives alike to bring their talents and skills to full ignition and to sustain high performance over time.

This development of individual capacities requires individual commitment. Where there is competition, it becomes natural to assume that those who invest the most effort will be the most successful. Adopting the idea of the sporting competition alongside more commercial interpretations at work offers a means by which organizations can position themselves positively as an agent for change and as promoting health and well-being more broadly.

Age is critical to such discourses of competition because of our enduring associations of fitness and energy with youth, while connecting frailty and decline with the effects of ageing. Elsewhere in this series, Stephens and Breheny (2018) discuss how notions of successful ageing which emphasise the importance of keeping fit and active are discursively constrained by the more dominant biomedical models of ageing as one of decreasing physical and mental performance, of illness and deterioration.

However, the performance aspect of sporting competition offers a more complex positioning regarding age and experience. The energetic young sportsperson might be considered a rising star, but has she had enough experience in which to hone her skills and understand what it takes to succeed? She may not be tough enough for the competition and there is a risk of peaking too soon with a subsequent, often dramatic, fall from grace. Those who make it through these early years may mature into 'champions', but it will not be long before speculation about retirement or being 'past it' begins, especially if there is a dip in form. Such assumptions about performance are easily translated to the workplace and may therefore impact workers of all ages.

## Competitive constructions of the 'healthy employee'

Within competitive discourses that draw on sport, the employee is constructed as a 'corporate athlete', and success at work is achieved via peak performance. Such discourses build on assumptions about physical and mental fitness, applied to maximum effect, either individually or collaboratively, within the 'rules of the game'. Results are based on talent, effort, and training. Within this section, we draw on understandings of both work-as-sport and sport-as-work to explore the 'healthy employee'. However, we deliberately distinguish between health and fitness, given the performance associations in competitive sport with the latter. To succeed in sport, it is not enough to be healthy (although this is of course necessary); rather, one must also demonstrate the appropriate level of fitness for the occasion. In short, one must be an athlete, and performance must be athletic (Coupland, 2015).

In the context of athletic performance, while ill-health is problematic, it is injury and incapacity (either physical or mental) which are the most serious obstacles to sporting success. Crucially then, the athletic employee must be sufficiently mentally tough to withstand the pressures of competition, and the rollercoaster of its highs and lows. Many contemporary discussions of well-being at work identify such resilience as essential for both employee and organizational success (King et al., 2016).

In many such discussions, the emphasis is also clearly on the individual body, even though these bodies may be assembled into teams for broader organizational success. With sporting ambition, nothing is left to chance; rather, the athletic body is a highly managed and regulated body (Coupland, 2015). So, too, the athletic employee must be kept 'in shape', through exercise, healthy eating and other related health practices. This is the primary responsibility of the sportsperson (the employee), but it is also down to the coach (the manager) and the team (the organization). Here, notions of synergy between individual and organization, which are common to discourses of human resource management and neo-liberalism, are reinforced, since both the athletic employee and the athletic organization are held to benefit from a mutually supportive relationship.

An emphasis on the management and regulation of the body can be found in notions of both work-as-sport and sport-as-work. In her study of rugby players, for instance, Coupland (2015) (p.802) observes that 'the government of the body is a collective enterprise, where other organizational members are performing a potentially panoptical environment that subjects the player to surveillance', thereby highlighting the Foucauldian notion of bio-power (see also Chapter 7). This emphasis on surveillance and regulation suggests some of the ways in which power/knowledge are embedded in our everyday actions and understandings of our bodies, their capabilities and the actions we might take to enhance their performance (Kelly et al., 2007). Surveillance is, of course, not limited to sporting organizations and is of increasing relevance across a wide range of workplaces (Lupton, 2018).

Relatedly, research has started to explore how employees' engagement in sport and talk about fitness at work are increasingly linked to notions of being a healthy employee. That is to say, healthy competition is no longer simply a useful analogy; rather, looking after your body outside work, being fit and demonstrating sporting achievement are all becoming an important means of showing desirable work characteristics, of becoming the ideal 'corporate athlete'. Work on the body via engagement in sport shows a commitment to ensuring that one is fit for work (including de-stressing). It also offers valuable networking opportunities, and gives access to the detailed technical discourses of certain (desirable) sports that can be used effectively at work (Costas et al., 2016).

So far, this discussion of the sporting and athletic employee is a generic one. The introduction of age, however, serves to highlight critical assumptions that are often associated with athletic and competitive performance. We see direct discursive clashes between quick thinking, active, creative 'potentiality' (Taylor et al., 2010) of youth and vigour (Shraga and Shirom, 2009), versus the wisdom, thoughtfulness and experience of age, with associated implications for their management. For the purposes of this chapter, we can start to position age in relation to these assumptions. For example, we may consider young employees as physically robust, easier to train and more likely to bounce back from a knock. On the other hand, older workers are perceived as fragile and on an unstoppable trajectory towards exit. Age-related stereotypes can play a significant role; indeed, Spedale (2018) explores how exits for older workers can be constructed and experienced like death, with associated grieving. Such bodily analogies are also found in Riach and Kelly (2015), who explore the ways in which 'fresh' young workers are seen as the essential lifeblood of an organization, while older workers become positioned as essential 'sacrificial objects' in the organization's pursuit of immortality. Thus, the perfect 'corporate athlete' is young enough to be strong and vibrant, but (just) old enough to be robust and experienced.

## The demographic 'time bomb' and the risk of the older employee

The term 'time bomb' has been coined to highlight the changing demographic trends that are having broad societal, economic and health effects. Simply put, this refers to the increased life expectancy of a population coinciding with a reduced birth rate: the old are getting older and increasingly represent a larger share of the population. Japan is a well-known example of the 'time bomb', with 2018 census figures showing people over 65 accounting for nearly 28% of the population (Japan Times, 2018). Global demographic change is, of course, a complex picture, yet the dominant perception is of an ageing population and, by extension, an ageing workforce. Life expectancy is a crucial part of this demographic picture. According to World Health Organisation (WHO, 2018a) figures, in 2016 the average life expectancy (irrespective of gender) was 72 years, but this varied from a somewhat shocking 52.9 in Lesotho, to 82 in Switzerland and 83 in Japan.

Critically, however, the main issue for societies and organizations is not simply how long we are likely to live, but the more complex issue of how long we are likely to live *well*. WHO suggests that globally this healthy life expectancy is eight years lower than overall life expectancy (WHO, 2018b). Importantly, opinion is divided as to whether healthy life expectancy will continue to increase, even in countries at the upper end of the scale. However, as Börsch-Supan (2013) highlights, perceptions of frailty and decline still dominate the way in which ageing and the elderly are viewed, particularly in most Western cultures. We can, for example, contrast the way in which the use of the word 'elderly' conjures up somewhat different images than the term 'Elder', which has more positive associations with a respected contribution (Bianchi, 2011).

More broadly, and somewhat contrastingly, however, our understandings of markets are also changing: the 'grey pound' and 'silver surfer' are terms used to denote the increasing influence of older consumers. Yet, while such consumerism might construct the older person as active, most organizations are more concerned about changes to workforce demographic composition. Where labelling of an older worker can begin as early as 50, this clearly influences the perception of a large proportion of many workforces (Whiting and Pritchard, 2018). In the UK, for instance, unemployment statistics have historically only included individuals aged up to 64, after which age individuals are assumed to have entered retirement and to be supported financially by receipt of the state pension.

Perhaps this fear of the ageing workforce accounts for Acemoglu and Restrepo (2017) finding that those countries ageing the fastest are at the forefront of the adoption of new technologies, specifically robots. Where 'fresh blood' (Riach and Kelly, 2015) is in especially short supply, investment in alternative technologies is seen as the only means of negating the impact of an ageing workforce. This is a particular concern in areas of manual work, where health issues – and hence performance – are more problematic (POSTNOTE, 2011). For example, in relation to construction, Eaves et al. (2016) (p.10) note that 'injury and ill health are often expected to come with the job', but their research finds that those over the age of 50 report fewer acute issues compared to younger construction workers. A difference in reporting practices for different age groups might be a significant factor here; older workers may be reluctant to highlight issues, whereas younger workers may raise issues more readily (Eaves et al., 2016).

While Eaves et al. (2016) argue that older workers might be reluctant to draw attention to health-related issues, other studies present cases of younger workers being held responsible and blamed for their own inexperience in relation to accidents. For example, Price and McDonald (2016) propose that perceptions of immaturity are often held to be the cause of accidents at work – an assumption that places responsibility firmly with the individual young person. This connects with our discussion in the Introduction of the politicisation of health and safety, and the undesirability of the construction of the employee as an 'unsafe worker'.

The picture becomes more complex when one looks at the evidence related to productivity at work. Reports such as those by the International Longevity Centre or ILC-UK (Franklin, 2018) highlight that ageing is shown to have both negative and positive effects on productivity. This is due, in part, to the complexity of measuring productivity at all, never mind identifying potential age-related differences. This report questions the assumption that productivity should increase continually over a working life, recognising that for a variety of reasons, a productivity ceiling might exist. This notion is also considered by Börsch-Supan (2013), who suggests that differences between younger and older workers generally even out when measuring productivity, whilst also reinforcing concerns with measurement practices. The ILC-UK report goes on to say:

> We can speculate that rising life expectancy could help to negate this impact by shifting the productivity curve to the right and thereby raising the peak productivity age. Lifelong learning and retraining could also result in changes to the gradient of the curve. For instance, it may help to slow the speed of decline in productivity growth as people supplement old and potentially obsolete skills with new ones. An important question is the extent to which retraining and life-long learning can sustain productivity growth over the lifecycle. Similar points could be made regarding investment in health and healthy ageing – which may also prolong the slowdown.
>
> *(Franklin, 2018) (p.12)*

Moreover, the report highlights that the number of workers over the age of 70 is still such a small number that it makes any statistical generalisation problematic, highlighting the difficulties of isolating age as a factor:

> Across English local authorities, the level of health and education is strongly correlated with workforce productivity. Raising the level of education and health of the population will therefore remain key drivers of workforce productivity irrespective of age.
>
> *(Franklin, 2018) (p.4)*

Our concern here is not solely with the reality or the scale of demographic change, but with the presentation of risk and disaster that accompanies an ageing population. Organizations perceive older workers to be a risk to their competitive positioning, compromising the possibility of 'organizational health'. Discourses of the demographic 'time bomb' have been around for some time. Bytheway (1994) (p.53) cites the 1949 Royal Commission as highlighting a similar concern that 'a society in which the proportion of young people is diminishing will become dangerously unprogressive', and suggests that this re-emerges as a sense of rising panic in news coverage during the 1980s. This panic persists in headlines today, which often include phrases such as 'ready to explode …', 'tick, tick, tick' and the notion of having to 'defuse' a tricky situation. These confirm the presence of this 'bomb' as potentially heralding a catastrophe. The disaster of demographic change is established as being out of control, affecting states, societies and organizations. In competitive terms, this becomes a lose-lose situation. Clearing up and doing the best one can to limit the damage is all that can be expected. This construction establishes ageing itself as disastrous, and the old and elderly as fundamentally problematic. In this way, understandings of overall demographic change can be personalised to individual older people, and indeed older employees, who are then cast as a burden – the very opposite of the 'perfect employee'.

While there are many aspects of this risk construction of demographic change, the overwhelming association of ageing with poor health and dependency has broader ramifications for our understandings of older workers. As Börsch-Supan (2013) (p.6) states, 'the common exaggeration of the diminished function of older persons is due in part to archaic views of the elderly'. Yet these archaic views are present in many assumptions about the capability and performance of older employees. While younger employees may be depicted as risky because of their lack of experience, this risk is usually seen to be less significant than the problem of the older employee. Ageing will, after all, help the younger worker to gain the necessary experience, but it is problematic once you are labelled as 'old'.

A further concern is that concentrating on age appears to divert attention away from other pertinent factors that impact health and the ability to work, particularly those related to all forms of social and cultural capital (Brown, 1995). The emphasis is on how individuals can effectively delay their ageing, or ideally avoid it altogether, to continue to lead productive lives (Stephens and Breheny, 2018). Within these debates, negative understandings of ageing mean that it becomes normal for older people to find it difficult to obtain or retain positions within organizations. Therefore, new constructions of appropriate identities are promoted to offer a solution for older people to remain competitive, productive and independent. For example, Whiting and Pritchard (2018) explore the ways in which a neo-liberal entrepreneurialism is increasingly positioned as an ideal solution for people who need to earn money. They review the emergence of a new group labelled 'Wearies', which stands for 'Working, Entrepreneurial and Active Retirees' (Friends Life & The Future Foundation, 2011). Of course, the irony of this acronym is that it positions this group in such a way that denies access to the very identity it is said to promote (Whiting and Pritchard, 2018).

From this discussion we can see that discourses of competition frame perceptions about demographic change and the implications for organizations. An older workforce is presented as inherently problematic and potentially damaging in terms of both organizations' and societies' competitive standing. Below we explore how this becomes positioned as potentially 'unhealthy' competition between generations.

## Generations and intergenerational working

Generational and intergenerational well-being has emerged as a critical aspect of debates around age and work. A generational cohort is usually defined by years of birth and related to a set of significant or meaningful circumstances, such that those born during the specified time span are believed to share similar experiences, particularly during formative years. This idea of a generational cohort originates in sociology and from work by Mannheim (1927/1952) and Bourdieu (1993), who both draw attention to the need to explicate what might otherwise be taken-for-granted influences that cross other forms of categorisation (such as social and economic status, for example).

Shared experiences are considered to exert a significant influence on individual characteristics within particular generational cohorts (Twenge, 2014). They are not theorised as simplistic differences between the young and old, but as distinct cohort effects. For instance, it is expected that a 20 year old in 2019 – let's call him Tom – would, according to some measures, feel and behave differently to how a 20 year old did in 1980 – let's call him Tim. Each individual is said to carry these cohort effects with them throughout their lives, shaping future experiences and behaviours. Therefore, in 2058 when Tom is 59, he will continue to exhibit different behaviours due to his membership of a particular generational cohort, and these will be different from Tim at the same age in 2019. In other words, cohort effects are theorised differently from age effects. On the one hand, it seems obvious that there are differences between our parents' and grandparents' generations across a vast range of factors. Yet on the other hand, we are often aware of the similarities across the generations in terms of age-related perspectives. Thus, the interrelation of age and cohort effects is extremely complex.

Twenge and Campbell (2010) highlight that a recent generation in the USA demonstrates significant differences in certain personality traits (particularly narcissism), an increase in mental health problems, and a decline in community participation when measured against previous cohorts at a similar age. They suggest that 'the preponderance of the evidence paints a very consistent picture of increased individualism and the traits related to it (materialism, narcissism, self-esteem, lack of trust)' (Twenge and Campbell, 2010) (p.86), and assign these characteristics to a group described as 'Generation Me'. This work highlights a start date for this generation (1980), but not an end date. Members of this generational cohort are depicted as possessing particular traits and exhibiting certain behaviours that are distinct from previous generations. Collectively, these traits and behaviours, along with the label assigned to the cohort, represent a very powerful construction of how we might expect a member of this generation to behave both generally, and specifically in relation to both work and health.

Twenge (2013) also recognises other labels for this 'Generation Me' cohort, specifically Generation Y and Millennials, as all referring to those born after 1980. In addition to the variety of names, there are definitional issues around the boundaries of these generations, especially since transition points to subsequent generations are left unspecified. Pritchard and Whiting (2014) note that some set the transitional point as early as 1994/5 (Cogin, 2012), whilst others suggest the transition to a subsequent generation did not occur until the early 2000s (Sullivan et al., 2009). A recent New York Times article (Bromwich, 2018) even ran a naming poll for the members of the generation following the Millennials, as no consistent label has yet emerged, although the terms iGen and Generation Z are both used regularly within the popular press.

Aside from these not inconsiderable definitional issues, there are further methodological concerns regarding cohort research, which include the datasets used, the assumptions made about the indicators measured and behavioural outcomes, factors controlled for, and the generalisation across cohorts and geographical boundaries (Deal et al., 2010; Parry and Urwin, 2011). Despite these concerns, however, some researchers take generational characteristics and groups as an assumed given, going on to consider their implications for work and values (Meriac et al., 2010). Significantly, further confusion arises when 'generation' is simply used as a shorthand for 'age', for example, when the term 'Millennial' is used to refer to young workers. This conflation of age and generation causes significant problems for those seeking to statistically explore the difference and/or interaction between age and cohort effects.

As the vignette below suggests (Box 4.1), practitioner-orientated research has been quick to capitalise on the idea of generation-derived characteristics (Logan, 2008), and the implications for managers and human resources professionals, who might then need advice, training and support in how to approach the motivation, support and supervision of these individuals differently in order to generate organizational competitive advantage.

---

**BOX 4.1 CASE STUDY: MARKETING FOR *ANOTHER CONSULTING* EXECUTIVE DEVELOPMENT SERVICES**

A new generation has arrived in the workplace!

Are you ready for Generation iPossible?

Our extensive survey of those aged 22–25 already in work has revealed that this is the new generation of entrepreneurial, ethical and egotistical young-sters. If you assume you can manage and motivate the iPossibles as easily as previous employees, think again!

Join our exclusive executive training programme to discover solutions that will ensure you get the best out of this generation's professionals. We can offer you unique insights into the challenges your organization will face, and we can help your existing and mature employees to step up to the mark.

Intergenerational working is here to stay: can you learn how to play and win at the only new game that counts?

---

As suggested in the vignette, it is not simply the specifics of a new generation at work that is presented as a challenge for organizations, rather the prospect of mixed or multi-generational workplaces is also positioned as a risk that must be overcome. For example, Knight (2014) (p.1) poses questions to 'the boss' that need to be addressed to support healthy multi-generational working:

> How should you relate to employees of different age groups? How do you motivate someone much older or much younger than you? And finally: what can you do to encourage employees of different generations to share their knowledge?

Although this is presented as a review of multi-generational working, the discussion about age groups conflates age and cohort effects. It also naturalises differences in age as inherently problematic for competitive advantage. Indeed, it would be possible to remove all age-related commentary from this quote and still highlight significant challenges for organizational leaders relating to relationship management, motivation, and knowledge sharing which exist in many contemporary organizations.

To some extent, the same generational discourses are found at both societal and organizational levels. A number of commentators blame members of particular generations (usually Baby Boomers) for the current problems of younger generations (e.g., Willetts, 2010). The cohort characteristics embedded in older generations are seen to be creating the contexts for the development and characteristics of future cohorts. Specifically, the selfishness of the Baby Boomers is said to be sabotaging the chances for health and success (usually defined in material terms) of the Millennials and subsequent generations (Pritchard and Whiting, 2014).

Competitive discourses feature strongly here, as older generations have created an 'unequal playing field' with regards to critical measures of capitalist success, particularly career status and home ownership, and thus have a knock-on effect on various measures of well-being and health. An emerging approach is to adopt practices based on intergenerativity or intergenerationality, which focus on creating communities by bringing generations together to improve mutual understanding, while also engaging in practical projects, including those focused specifically on physical and emotional well-being; for instance, attempts to tackle issues of loneliness across age groups (e.g., Generations Working Together).

In respect to employment, however, there is a particular concern about the so-called 'lump of labour fallacy'. This posits that there is a fixed number of jobs that can be supported by the economy at any point in time, and that if older workers of a particular generation work for longer there will be fewer jobs available for the next generation (Börsch-Supan, 2013). While appealing from a 'common sense' perspective, this has been shown to be false, and indeed the reverse may be true, since more jobs are generated via economically active older citizens (Börsch-Supan, 2013).

When looking at the research on the health of Millennials, Deal et al. (2010) highlight concerns regarding both incidence and understandings of obesity amongst this cohort in the USA. This suggests that specific points of difference regarding health may, indeed, be worthy of further exploration, but without the broad generalisation and labelling that accompanies many generational debates. An example of a more focused study is Virtanen et al. (2016), which investigates different cohorts' experience of youth unemployment under varying economic conditions. Importantly, this research is clear about the cohorts under investigation, and there is no attempt to 'fit' these within a broader generational cohort or apply a generational label. Moreover, this geographically-bounded study looks at a very particular variance in the economy. It concludes that there are increased long-term impacts on mental health, in particular, for the cohort experiencing recession at the time when they were making the transition from education to employment.

Generational competition has become a well-established discourse, often overlapping and confusing many debates about age and health at work. While there remains concern with generalising about attitudes and behaviours across cohorts, some focused research on links with health and health behaviours seems to offer potential insights related to work. However, the broader focus on competition as a critical problem sets the scene for a focus on interventions around generations at work. These position leaders and managers as in control of problematic worker characteristics ascribed to generation and/or age and therefore have the potential to cause more issues than they resolve (Scheuer and Mills, 2017).

## Health and the changing life course

In contrast to the focus on age-related characteristics at a particular chronological point, a life course perspective draws attention to our understandings of the 'norms' by which we might expect people to progress through different life stages. This is a well-known, but highly variable perspective within the broader field of health studies, and usefully highlights some of the ways in which we think about health in relation to movement and transitions (Alwin, 2012; Brydsten et al., 2016).

In terms of movement, traditional perspectives highlight career progress as key, at least up to a certain point at which 'peak performance' is reached, after which an inevitable decline sets in. In terms of transitions, we have expectations about the typical types of transition and norms in relation to the age at which these are experienced. Any discussion of life course in relation to age and ageing is thus linked to our previous topics of demographic change and generations. Demographic changes are seen to impact life courses both directly (due to, for example, the large size of cohorts at later stages of the life course) and indirectly (due to policy changes around issues such as education and retirement, which result from increasing/decreasing age cohort size).

The life course perspective opens up a range of potential areas for investigation in regard to ageing and health. For example, Mortimer (2009) highlights the increasing range of pathways from education to work so that transitions are increasingly complex and lengthy. This new reality contrasts with previous understandings of a relatively clear-cut and straightforward transition (subject to economic variability). This is perceived to be contributing to health concerns (particularly mental health concerns), where old stereotypes persist and are held up as ideal – an ideal that many find impossible to achieve. More broadly, a concern with 'solving' youth unemployment has been a policy priority, and is implicated in these more complex transitions. For example, within the UK, the statistical identification of a group labelled NEETs (those classified as Not in Employment, Education or Training) (Furlong, 2006) has been implicated in changes to both educational and employment policy, so that the problem of this group could be said to be solved. Indeed, it is suggested that the NEET label hides the complexity of educational and work positioning that is simply the reality for many people during these transitional stages. Here it seems possible to suggest that presenting simplified transitions and problematizing those who do not fit this narrative might have direct health implications. Research highlights that transitions are most problematic for those already vulnerable via a wide range of measures (including health and economic), with some contesting the discourse of transition itself (Shildrick and MacDonald, 2007). Thus, the construction of transitional norms has significant implications for work exclusion, which can perpetuate across the life course and relate to health concerns (Cieslik and Pollock, 2017). The notion of being 'in the game' or competitive at all may be taken for granted, but it is inherently problematic for some.

We have already highlighted that understandings of retirement have undergone a significant change in recent times. This is having a major impact at the other 'end' of the life course. In particular, this has been influenced by the emergence of what has been termed the 'successful ageing' discourse (Stephens and Breheny, 2018), which invokes ideals of activity, autonomy, and personal responsibility

(Whiting and Pritchard, 2018). Successful ageing is part of a wider neo-liberal ideology, which we summarised in the Introduction as emphasising individual responsibility for health, lifestyle, and well-being (Braedley and Luxton, 2010). Retirement as an aspirational consumer lifestyle has thus been superseded by discourses promoting longer working lives (Rudman and Molke, 2009).

However, this creates particular challenges for those experiencing transitions to retirement (Stenholm et al., 2016). Life course perspectives highlight how individuals 'carry forward' earlier experiences, particularly of transitions. They may then experience a mismatch or conflict in relating their own previous experiences to new realities. For those who experience health issues, this creates particular difficulties. Many studies show that individuals with a history of health problems tend to retire at a younger age (e.g., Feldman, 1994). Moreover, when a person experiences poor health, he or she is significantly more likely to have trouble in the transition to retirement, with a subsequent knock-on effect on health, creating something of a vicious circle. To compound this further, difficult transitions to retirement are often associated with an increase in overtly unhealthy behaviours, such as higher levels of alcohol consumption (Perreira and Sloan, 2002) or smoking (Henkens et al., 2008). This is not inevitable, however, and there is contradictory research that suggests that retirement from work can have a positive impact on psychological health and well-being (van der Heide et al., 2016).

A further concern is the relationship between biological transitions and the life course. Recognising this as also an opportunity to introduce matters of gender, we now focus on issues specifically experienced by women. While women's increasing presence in the workforce is no longer the topic of debate, women's *competitiveness* in the work arena continues to provoke controversy.

Barely mentioned in public until recently, a particular concern for women is the impact of the menopause and its presentation as both an individual and organizational health issue. One aspect of this concern is, of course, the direct impact, as nearly 25% of women experience serious symptoms that affect their ability to work effectively (Brewis et al., 2017). However, very few organizations have specific policies in place, despite the fact that UK employers can be accused of discrimination if they do not take into account the problems that menopausal women might encounter at work (Wynne Evans and Zarb, 2018). There are now more working women of menopausal age than ever before, yet interestingly women employees report fewer symptoms, especially those at managerial grades (Jack et al., 2016). The key word here may be 'report' for, as Jack et al. (2016) (p.93) suggest, there is perhaps a 'fear that making menopause a broadly visible topic in the workplace may generate negative or derisory responses'.

As with the discussions of generational norms above, life course norms can easily become stereotypes by which we judge individuals or groups. A classic example is the differentiation between male and female life courses, which can easily be assumed to be associated with personal relationships, an inevitability of childbearing, and a tacit heteronormativity. Unsurprisingly then, there is similarly gendered advice to address workplace challenges, such as the need for women to 'lean in' (Sandberg, 2013) and, of course, take personal responsibility for any resulting health implications. Indeed, the idea of the appropriate body at work is said to be especially challenging for women since, as Gill (2008) (p.42) observes, physical appearance has become the 'primary source of women's capital'. Relatedly, women are said to be more likely to experience ageism at work (Duncan and Loretto, 2004). The menopause is, of course, a normal biological transition, yet it remains a problematic term. For example, the Deputy Governor of the Bank of England (BBC, 2018) referred to the UK economy as 'menopausal', suggesting it was a term to describe economies that were 'past their peak, and no longer so potent', though he quickly retracted and apologised for this description (Issac, 2018). This highlights the vulnerability of older women workers to stereotyping as 'codgers in cardigans' (Colley, 2013) (p.327).

In short, life course perspectives can lead to normative assumptions about health and work, particularly associations with understandings of transitions. If applied sensitively, however, the potential to understanding multiple, interconnecting narratives of age, health and work has much to offer, and provides opportunities for nuanced critique of the potent discourses of age, vitality, and competition.

## Final thoughts on competition, age and health

We began this chapter with a consideration of the way in which discourses of competition frame understandings of the healthy employee as a 'corporate athlete'. Managing personal and corporate athleticism at work requires careful consideration of short-term needs and longer-term performance – consideration that is heavily influenced by our assumptions about the capabilities of both the youthful and the ageing body.

The value of a particular body or bodies to the organization may well affect institutional decision-making. After all, the organization must assemble the team most likely to beat the competition, with victory often suggested as the only means of securing future opportunity, prosperity, and security for all employees. Indeed, in discussing neo-liberal ideology, Braedley and Luxton (2010) (p.8) suggest that this merely entitles individuals to compete, since competition is a natural force for good, but is not concerned with any right to 'start from the same starting line, with the same equipment or at the sound of the same gun'. Contemporary discourses of competitive performativity confer the right to vie for certain outcomes (including enhanced opportunities for health and well-being), but not the right to these outcomes themselves. Alternatively, as Kelly et al. (2007) suggest, the management of the body to peak fitness can be constructed as an opportunity open to all, should they decide to invest the effort. It is critical, therefore, that this opportunity be seen as available to people of all ages, so that they can be encouraged to participate (and generate personal and organizational benefits). This is also reflected in broader constructions of successful ageing (Rudman and Molke, 2009), which rely, in part, on the individual's own commitment to health and fitness to ensure they do not become a burden to the state.

It is important to note that the relationship is not one way; just as we can see work-as-sport, we can also see sport-as-work. A complex recursive relationship exists that reinforces the discursive positioning of the 'corporate athlete' in both business and sport (Weinberg and McDermott, 2002), for instance, via sponsorship, venue, and team ownership, and an overall emphasis on professionalization. As the distinctions become increasingly blurred, the 'corporate athlete' positioning becomes normalised, and the recursive relationship between organization and sport reinforce the naturalness of these discourses. This is perhaps somewhat ironic, as in sport itself the very notion of 'healthy' competition has recently become stigmatised. High profile concerns about performance enhancement (for example, within cycling; Cycling Weekly, n.d., and across Russian sport, Ingle, 2018) have exposed the ideals of fair sporting competition to new scrutiny.

A further apparent irony is that this emphasis on employee fitness is increasing at a time when the physicality of much work is reduced (World Bank, 2014), and we are being warned of the risks of our sedentary lifestyles and their link to issues such as obesity. The 'corporate athlete' must, therefore, increasingly turn to activities outside their employment to demonstrate fitness. Such engagement in physical activity outside work, in what might be seen as leisure pursuits, is not available to all, not least due to the financial and time commitments involved. As Kelly et al. (2007) suggest, this has led to some companies launching their own corporate fitness programmes, in which individuals are encouraged to engage for their own (and the company's) benefit. Many such programmes approach the notion of fitness from a broad, and sometimes much less competitive perspective and blend fitness with health, mindfulness, and related well-being approaches. Here, barriers to participation are seemingly removed, and any resistance becomes difficult to justify; after all, we should all have a self-interest in maintaining and improving our health. Moreover, the healthy body is idealised as an attractive and popular body. The positioning of the employee in relation to the sportsperson 'portrays the fit and thin body as not only healthy, but also beautiful and sexy. The unfit body is ugly, unsexy, and unpopular' (Pylypa, 1998) (p.25). Judgement of success is not only under the managerial gaze, but is enabled more widely through the constant scrutiny of the fit and healthy bodily appearance (Knoppers, 2011).

This positioning connects many themes within this chapter, as the employee, old or young, and whatever their gender identification, must, at the very least, be seen to *make an effort*. Furthermore, the sheer range of available health and fitness possibilities provides the potential for any individual who wishes to make the effort to become a successful 'corporate athlete'. For organizations, the uniting thread of individual commitment to achieve meritocratic success does not depend on the particular sporting contest. The sporting employee is constructed as the cooperative employee who abides by the 'rules of the game' (Cudd, 2007).

In exploring the demographic 'time bomb', generations and the life course in more detail, it becomes apparent that one of the critical challenges in discussing age is that our ability to step back from its effects is limited by our own personal deep associations with chronology as a natural organizing mechanism. Age is an everyday label to which we have been subjected since childhood. Age is recorded via most of the administrative processes we encounter and is a constant theme in the media and in our multiple other experiences of institution. Via the metaphor of competition, age and fitness become co-located and embodied, yet there remains a tension between the promise of youth and the reliability of the seasoned performer, balanced precariously during the ambiguity of middle age.

# 5

# LEARNING AND HEALTH

## Discourses of reinvention

In this chapter, we explore some of the ways in which issues of health and well-being have become entwined with both individual and organizational learning. Specifically, we:

- Interrogate the assumption that learning is automatically or necessarily good for us.
- Introduce the metaphor of organization-as-brain, highlighting how many of the most desirable characteristics of organization (intelligence, inventiveness, connectivity, flexibility, etc.) take the brain and its capacity to learn as their implicit blueprint.
- Suggest that a prioritisation of organizational learning constructs the 'perfect employee' as someone committed to ongoing self-development and self-reinvention.
- Explore interrelations between learning and well-being, suggesting both that learning enhances well-being (learning enough to be well) and that well-being enhances learning (being well enough to learn).
- Reflect on how an emphasis on learning casts the individual as an agent of his or her own employability, and hence responsible for the health benefits that continuous employment produces.
- Consider the emotional costs of discourses of learning and reinvention, such as feelings of guilt, shame and a sense that one is never quite good enough.
- Reflect on how individualised responsibility for both learning and well-being casts popular organizational tools, such as personal development plans (PDPs), in a different light.

## The organization-as-brain and the significance of organizational learning

Organizations can be likened to brains in terms of their capacity to receive, process, retain and generate knowledge and information. The human brain is capable of responding incredibly quickly and creatively to an ever-changing set of stimuli and demands, and of generating entirely new repertoires of thought and behaviour as it adapts (Garud and Kotha, 1994). It is not hard to see why the qualities of the well-functioning brain should have been so enthusiastically transposed onto the well-functioning organization; both are marked by intelligence, flexibility, speed, connectivity, resilience, self-organization and the capacity for invention and reinvention. Popular management expressions such as 'corporate consciousness' (Campion and Palmer, 1996), the 'corporate mind' (Hampden-Turner, 1990), 'corporate imagination' (Hamel and Prahalad, 1991) and 'organizational intelligence' (Liebowitz, 1999) suggest the power of this metaphor to shape and reflect our understanding of the well-functioning organization.

The brain provides a powerful blueprint for capabilities which both include and exceed the logical and computational, such as judgment and intuition (Claxton et al., 2015; Sadler-Smith, 2016). For instance, it inspires work on the integration of creative 'right brain' capabilities with more rational, analytical 'left brain' proficiencies (Ford and Gioia, 2000; Leonard and Straus, 1997; Mintzberg, 1976). The notion that both organizations and individuals have two different qualities of brainpower, based on the biology of two brain hemispheres, has a strong intuitive resonance. We frequently find arguments in popular management literature that the key to success lies in 'putting the whole organization's brain to work', that is, in finding ways to take advantage of both analytical and intuitive capabilities. For instance, Herrmann and Herrmann-Nehdi (2015) (p.9) suggest that 'certain modes of thinking will increasingly dominate an organization as it matures unless the leadership applies Whole Brain Thinking to consciously cultivate and encourage the breadth of thinking that is necessary for ongoing success'.

The most significant aspect of the brain metaphor is that it emphasises the importance of *learning*. The brain's plasticity, that is, its ability to reorganize itself by forming new pathways between neurons, provides an ideal template for the notion that both organizations and employees can form new connections between ideas, opportunities and practices – in short, that functioning well involves and requires reinvention. Indeed, the language of plasticity is now being applied explicitly to organizational types that are able to adjust, change and innovate rapidly and seemingly spontaneously (Alqithami and Hexmoor, 2014; Levinthal and Marino, 2015).

In a sense, this emphasis on plasticity and reinvention is a development of the organization-as-organism discourse (Chapter 2), in that it focuses on the need to change and adapt rather than sticking to the rigid blueprint of the organization-as-industrial machine (Chapter 1). The key distinction between the organism and the brain metaphors is that, whereas the organismic approach emphasises the need to adjust in response to changes in the environment, the brain metaphor depicts a more internally-generated, spontaneous, self-organizing dynamic. The organism 'learns' reactively, that is, in the face of specific requirements and stimuli; whereas the brain 'learns' proactively, in that learning is what it is designed to do and keep doing. As Senge (2006) explains, the contemporary learning organization must do more than just adapt and survive; it must also generate new ideas, new connections and new ways of working. In other words, innovation and continuous self-renewal are the very hallmarks of the organization-as-brain.

Much of the work in this area has focused on the constructs of 'organizational learning' (Argyris, 1992; Argyris and Schön, 1978) and 'the learning organization' (Burgoyne et al., 1994; Senge, 2006). Although there has been much debate about the relationship between these two terms, the most common way to differentiate between them is by saying that the former refers to certain types of activity that take place within an organization, whereas the latter is a particular entity or type of organization in and of itself (Tsang, 1997). The former is more likely to be the focus of academic work in this space, and hence more exploratory and/or critical, whereas the latter is more likely to be appealing to practitioners, and hence possibly more performative (Easterby-Smith and Lyles, 2011). Both organizational learning and the learning organization have considerable currency in organizational conversations, and their popularity has resulted in the emergence of a 'learning perspective' as one of the dominant paradigms in contemporary organizational research and practice (Bapuji and Crossan, 2004). As the vignette below (Box 5.1) suggests, such dominance is reflected in the ease with which learning and continuous self-renewal have come to be seen as priorities for both organizations and the people within them.

---

### BOX 5.1 CASE STUDY: EXCERPT FROM AN INTERVIEW WITH A SENIOR PARTNER AT *ANOTHER CONSULTING*

So, you asked me what I think is the key to business success. In the past, I might have said something different. But right now, I am going to say 'learning'. But not learning in the sense of collecting impressive-sounding qualifications. More learning in terms of being passionate about rising to the challenge of working in this globalised, tech-enabled world, where overnight, things change and demand us to change with them. I think many people in business feel they're going to be left behind if they don't invest in serious self-renewal to make sure their skills are fresh. You know, that awful feeling of embarrassment when the new crop of graduates come in, and they talk about things and you have no idea what they are talking about?! Well, avoiding that feeling is high up my own list of priorities! And you know, it's interesting, isn't it, that Zuckerberg – well, perhaps not him, because he is having quite a hard time of it right now, but let's say a range of the major tech entrepreneurs – they don't have degrees, they don't have

> MBAs from swanky business schools. What they have is a different kind of learning. Learning is in their DNA ... kind of. You know, they seem hard wired to kind of mould themselves into who their businesses need them to be. They are serious learners!

Through the prism of the brain metaphor, therefore, the individual employee is constructed and evaluated in terms of his or her willingness and ability to learn. The qualities we associate with the human brain at its best, namely, intelligence, flexibility, inventiveness, self-organization and proactive networking, are core attributes of the 'perfect employee', and these are marshalled and put to work through programmes, cultures and attitudes of learning. This commitment to learning is more than just the specific response to a particular 'training need' at a single point in time. Instead, employees – indeed, all members of society – are increasingly expected to engage in 'life-long learning', where both personal and professional development are a continuous focus over one's entire adult life, including past the point of formal retirement (Berglund, 2008; Mantie, 2012; Nicoll and Fejes, 2008), occupying a powerful presence in discourses of 'healthy ageing' (Stephens and Breheny, 2018). As the *AnOther Consulting* partner in the previous vignette illustrates, the 'learning perspective' implies that what organizations and institutions value most is people invested in serious self-renewal and self-reinvention.

## Connections between learning and well-being

In much of the rhetoric on contemporary organizations, anything containing 'learning' as a suffix or prefix is now automatically assumed to be a positive thing. In many of the organizations we have encountered, corporate materials promote a 'learning culture' as a space of opportunity, experimentation and discovery; corporate conversations encourage the development and demonstration of a 'learning mindset' as the route to personal success and collective innovation; and line managers and human resources professionals use artefacts, such as 'learning contracts' and 'personal development plans', to structure (and soften) performance management conversations – a topic to which we return later in the chapter.

In the literature, too, learning is almost inevitably cast in positive, uplifting terms. For Senge (2006), the learning organization inspires people to find meaning, self-fulfilment and happiness in one's work. Indeed, Kofman and Senge (1993) crystallise the differences between bureaucratic and learning organizations by suggesting that the latter are a place of wonder and joy. From a more critical perspective, Contu et al. (2003) (p.933) suggest that 'learning discourse seems to have become constituted as truth: it is unproblematically assumed that learning, like vitamins and stopping smoking, is *a good thing*'. As this quote suggests, learning has been put into the basket of things assumed to be inherently and unequivocally good for one's health.

## *Learning enhances well-being*

Because learning is generally held to be 'a good thing', it is hardly surprising that arguments have been made for a positive connection between learning and well-being. This is especially prevalent in the literature on 'life-long learning', where an ongoing commitment to learning, especially amongst older citizens, has been associated with enhanced well-being (Jenkins and Mostafa, 2015; Merriam and Kee, 2014). This is a topic of increasing interest to social policy makers, since an ageing population means that people are living much longer post retirement than in previous generations – a matter which is considered in some depth in Chapter 4 on the connections between health and age, and elsewhere in this series in the context of discourses of 'healthy ageing' (Stephens and Breheny, 2018).

In the literature on adult learning, positive correlations have been traced between learning and well-being, both in a direct sense (e.g., learning increases people's positive feelings about themselves and their lives, and their uptake of positive health behaviours, such as better diets and regular exercise) and in a more indirect sense (e.g., learning increases the likelihood of good earnings, and hence facilitates a more comfortable and healthy lifestyle) (Field, 2009). Jenkins and Mostafa (2015) report that good health amongst older citizens is strongly related to participation in social learning activities, such as art classes and book clubs, suggesting that there is something significant about the health benefits of the relational and interpersonal aspects of the learning experience, as much as the content of the learning *per se*.

Within the domain of the organization, the effects of learning on well-being are of considerable interest in the context of Continuous Professional Development (CPD) – a particular manifestation of life-long learning in organizational contexts. CPD is something of an umbrella concept, which connects a range of ideas and practices, including professional education, personal development and career advancement (Kennedy, 2014). Increasingly, CPD has become part of the regulatory fabric of organizational life, having 'turned from acts engaged in by professionals for their own satisfaction to a systematized and codified set of activities that has consequences for their continued registration, and in many cases, their right to practice their profession' (Boud and Hager, 2012) (p.17). The commitment to ongoing CPD has profound implications for the politics of identity construction (Mackay, 2017; Mulvey, 2013) for, whilst participating in CPD may be a regulatory requirement, individual enthusiasm for the ethos of CPD as an opportunity for growth, self-improvement and self-reconstruction is also a personal choice. The successful employee sees dedication to learning and regular skills-refresh as one of the keys to that success; and by implication, one of the keys to well-being.

The connections between CPD and well-being are of interest to researchers working across a range of sectors. In the health sector, for instance, Hugill et al. (2018) trace positive health benefits of CPD, defined as enjoyment of improved supervisor-supervisee relationships, enhanced levels of motivation, and more effective provision and use of constructive feedback. In the education sector, Lofthouse and Thomas (2017) emphasise the significance of participation in the design of

CPD, suggesting that well-being unfolds in collaborative partnerships designed to support individual learning plans and highlighting the health benefits of learning relationships. Mulvey (2013) suggests that CPD amongst professionals might have a positive impact on well-being in a more existential sense, namely, as a way of helping professionals move past periods of mid-career crisis and self-doubt. In short, there is strong support for the notion that learning has a beneficial effect on how people feel about themselves, their careers, the value of their contribution, and the quality of their relationships with others.

## Well-being enhances learning

There is another way in which the relationship between learning and well-being might be seen as a positive thing for organizational functioning, which involves a reversal of the direction of influence. As well as arguments that learning enhances well-being, it is possible that well-being might enhance learning, that is, that both individual and organizational learning can only take place if people are well – in the sense of feeling confident, safe and secure at work. This argument emerges in the literature on barriers to organizational learning, and the question of why both organizations and employees often fail to learn. With organizations investing increasingly heavily in programmes and technologies of knowledge management, the question of why so many of these initiatives fail to deliver – and why the same organizational mistakes seem to be made over and over again – is of growing concern, especially since failure seems to be the most likely outcome, even when such initiatives are reasonably well resourced and sponsored by organizational leaders (Storey and Barnett, 2000; Syed, 2015).

The complexities of the relationships between learning and well-being are of great interest to scholars of emotion in organizations, especially those writing from a psychoanalytic perspective. Writers in this space emphasise that the psychology of learning is one of emotional upheaval, disturbance and disruption, in which anxiety both promotes and discourages learning (Vince and Martin, 1993). Anxiety can promote learning when people are motivated to work through and resolve the discomfort that feelings of uncertainty and not-knowing evoke. It can discourage learning, on the other hand, when such feelings of uncertainty and not-knowing threaten to become overwhelming. When this happens, people instinctively resort to defensiveness, because it is easier to deny than to confront the feelings of discomfort of not knowing or not understanding something. If employees are unable to contain their feelings of uncertainty or unsafety, they are more likely to resist learning, whether actively in 'fight' or more passively in 'flight'. The excessively or persistently insecure employee is thus not emotionally 'well enough to learn', for when we buttress ourselves against anxiety through defences, denials and avoidances, we engage in what Vince and Martin (1993) (p.210) call 'willing ignorance'.

In many organizational experiences, there is an important connection between barriers to learning and the threat and avoidance of blame. The notion of the 'blame culture' is something one hears frequently in people's descriptions of their working lives, and in particular, their fear of the conse-quences of making and admitting to mistakes (Edmondson, 2011; Resodi-hardjo et al., 2016; Weaver, 1986). The fear of being blamed for things going wrong can mean that employees behave with greater caution and con-servatism in the interests of self-protection. This is likely to have an adverse effect on learning, because both the fear and the reality of blame undermine the ability and willingness of leaders and employees to engage in processes of critical reflection and dialogue, through which constructive, open and hence 'healthy' communication about the *systemic* causes of mistakes and failures might lead to genuine organizational improvement (Vince and Saleem, 2004). With a 'blame culture', therefore, it is the organization, not just the individ-ual, which is not 'well enough to learn'.

## Towards a 'healthier' kind of learning

In the psychoanalytical literature on organization, a picture emerges of a poten-tially more productive relationship between well-being and learning, with both concepts co-constructed in terms of emotional resilience. Here, well-being is not associated with the 'management' i.e., suppression or avoidance, of difficult emo-tions in order to try to be happy or calm all the time. Instead, well-being unfolds in the experience of learning how to acknowledge and contain such difficult emo-tions. It means accepting that it is unrealistic to want to be happy or calm all the time, just as it is unrealistic to think that one will always know what to do in organizational practice, or that a lesson, once learned, will never need to be learned again. This kind of emotional learning involves adjusting to the pressures, imperfections and inevitable failures of organizational life, rather than learning as the acquisition of knowledge via planned development programmes, which focus on explicit content designed overtly to support organizational objectives.

The distinction between different kinds, or qualities, of learning is interesting for an analysis of both organization and health through the lens of metaphor. The 'common sense' idea that learning involves the acquisition and transfer of know-ledge gives learning a concrete tangibility, as if it is a thing that can be possessed. This is entirely consistent with the overall metaphor of organization-as-brain, whereby knowledge and learning are construed as being located and contained in the head (Boud and Hager, 2012; Hager and Hodkinson, 2009). Challenging the tangibility of learning allows us to shift its dynamics, taking it out of the meta-phorical head and into a broader range of experiences and practices, where it can emerge in dialogue, feelings and bodily sensations, often theorised in terms of 'experiential learning' (Kolb, 2014; Strati, 2007; Tomkins and Ulus, 2016).

Learning to live with the experiences of failure and disappointment is no mean feat, however. Much of the rhetoric of organizational life hinges on what Vince (2002a) (p.1192) calls the 'politics of imagined stability', which promotes a vision of control and coherence in which rationality, rather than emotion, is assumed to be the key organizing principle. Believing in such a vision protects employees from the potential destructiveness that acknowledging things like failure, weakness, mediocrity and disappointment might unleash; but, from a psychoanalytic perspective, this vision is fantasy, not reality (Gabriel, 1999; Vince and Saleem, 2004). A healthy attitude to organization requires resilience, therefore, to acknowledge both fantasy and reality and try to distinguish between them.

This kind of emotional resilience is not the same as 'emotional intelligence' (Goleman et al., 2013), a concept which has both supporters and critics in roughly equal measure (and which we sometimes use in our consultancy conversations, notwithstanding some conceptual discomfort, simply because it resonates with practitioners and can be used to establish a degree of common ground). Writing from a critical perspective, Fineman (2004), for instance, suggests that the construct of 'emotional intelligence' represents an attempt to *tame* emotion in the interests of the corporate bottom-line, distinguishing between 'high' emotions which are desirable and worthy and 'low' emotions which are inimical to healthy organizational functioning. As Gabriel and Griffiths (2002) suggest, 'high' emotions which might help the organization include hope, excitement and pride, whereas 'low' emotions which are considered unhelpful include anger, disgust and envy. Thus, 'emotional intelligence enthusiasts, while claiming to liberate emotion, seek to subordinate it to reason and in particular the instrumental reason of business and organizations' (Gabriel and Griffiths, 2002) (p.216). Encouraging employees and leaders, in particular, to work on improving their 'emotional intelligence' invokes the metaphor of the brain through the concept of intelligence, but it might be argued to be an instrument of organizational compliance rather than emotional resilience or genuine well-being.

From a psychoanalytical perspective, learning to engage with the more difficult, and perhaps less attractive, emotions is an important aspect of both individual and organizational well-being. Clancy et al. (2012) argue that the experience of disappointment, in particular, is a vital source of learning. Rather than the traditional view of disappointment as a negative, i.e., 'unhealthy' emotion that needs to be repressed and controlled to prevent it from harming both individual and collective morale, they argue that disappointment reflects a mature, more balanced, and hence healthier view of organizational realities. Disappointment is thus a crucial component in the experience of moving past primal, over-simplified splitting between good and bad – a core feature of the narcissistic organization with its heroes and villains (Schwartz, 1992). As Clancy et al. (2012) (p.528) suggest:

> One reason why the expression 'blame culture' is such a widespread description of organizational experience is not only to do with an impulse to protect oneself (or the members of a group) by projecting failure onto others. It is also about the inability to integrate failure within the organization.

Engaging with disappointment – both individually and collectively – might help organizations to soften the dynamics of blame and anxiety and their often negative, defensive effects on both learning and well-being. Learning to tolerate and survive disappointment may, therefore, be part of what is needed to create healthier, more productive and more resilient organizational cultures.

Of course, the notion of resilience conjures up the politics as well as the emotions of organizational life. To navigate the politics of organization, successful employees assess which aspects of learning will serve their interests best, including deciding when to make their learning overt, e.g., by sharing their 'lessons learned' and examples of 'best practice' with others, and when to maintain a lower profile. Thus, not all learning is necessarily productive or conducive to organizational improvement, for 'learning to cover your back is important learning' (Vince and Saleem, 2004) (p.137), especially when things are not going to plan and there is a danger (real or imagined) of censure and scapegoating. As the following vignette suggests (Box 5.2), the successful employee therefore calculates when to construct him/herself as a 'learner', and when to draw on alternative discursive repertoires, such as an 'expert'.

---

**BOX 5.2 CASE STUDY: EXCERPT FROM A RESEARCH INTER-VIEW ON ORGANIZATIONAL LEARNING WITH AN EMPLOYEE AT *DEPARTMENT X***

Well, every few years or so, this place gets very into the idea of organizational learning. And the consultants come in, and you academics come in, and we are all supposed to, kind of, develop the 'learning mindset'. And we are all supposed to become, what do they call it, 'knowledge-brokers'. And we are all meant to share examples of best practice, and post, you know, on the intranet, the things that have happened, and gone well, and also what hasn't perhaps gone quite so well [laughs], and what we can all learn from all this stuff, so that we don't have to re-invent the wheel all the time, blah, blah. But it isn't quite as simple as that, because, you know, who's to say that what I think is best practice, another department isn't going to pick on and say that's a matter for disciplinary, you know! What happens if the learning that I am supposed to have got out of it isn't the right kind of thing, and gets me into trouble! And you know, this culture of innovation that we are meant to be encouraging; I don't know. It doesn't feel very innovative. In my own mind, I now have two tests whenever I consider sharing something on the intranet, you know, the knowledge portal thing. One: is it a good idea that others might benefit from? Two: is it safe to admit to it, or am I going to get into trouble? If it doesn't pass both those tests, then frankly, I'm going to stay quiet.

---

Furthermore, cues for learning can sometimes encourage people to learn and reinforce unhelpful and/or unhealthy practices. For instance, superstitious learning may occur when the subjective experience of learning is compelling but misleading, i.e., the connections between actions and outcomes, or cause and effect, are fragile, random or simply inaccurate (Levitt and March, 1988), such as subjectively associating breakthrough on a task with allowing oneself a cigarette break. Superstitious learning may happen when routines are considered 'best practice', not because they are demonstrably 'best', but because they have become associated with success or with the avoidance of failure and the reduction of risk. With superstitious learning, both people and organizations become committed to a particular set of routines, but these arise relatively arbitrarily, rather than as the product of systematic, evidence-based learning (Nystrom and Starbuck, 1984).

Such complexities notwithstanding, if the arguments for at least a degree of positive co-constitution between learning and well-being are valid, then encouraging employees' receptiveness to learning, as well as giving them time and space for learning, ought to surely be the target of organizational well-being initiatives. From this perspective, the more secure employees are – both emotionally *and* politically – the more able and willing they will be to overcome their defensiveness and access the benefits that learning is said to provide. Employee well-being is thus not just an appealing objective in its own right, it is a prerequisite for the successful learning organization, with its competitively advantageous ethos of innovation, flexibility, self-reinvention and sustainability (Senge, 2006).

## Critical reflections on learning and well-being

Emerging from the discussion above is a sense that the nature of the relationship between learning and well-being depends, to a great extent, on how we define well-being. In the section on learning enhancing well-being (learning enough to be well), it mostly meant feelings of self-fulfilment, growth and purpose, whereas in the following section on well-being enhancing learning (being well enough to learn), its meaning revolved around overcoming anxiety, defensiveness and the fear of blame. This discussion highlights, therefore, that well-being is a very broad concept, involving feelings, experiences, commitments, levels of institutional performance and participation, and quality of relationships with others, *inter alia* (Grant et al., 2007). Such breadth of meaning serves a purpose, of course. The literature on life-long learning, in particular, often blurs the distinction between individual well-being and what Merriam and Kee (2014) call 'community well-being'. In other words, the efforts an individual makes with training and other forms of self-reinvention are associated at least as much with not being a burden to others as they are with feeling good about oneself (Brookfield, 2012).

Such issues take us into the territory of the politics of learning. Thus, critical scholars challenge the ways in which learning has become so established as an unimpeachably 'good thing', whether in the corporate context of the 'learning organization' (Senge, 2006) or more broadly in constructs of the 'learning society' (Hughes and Tight, 1995) and the 'learning economy' (Lundvall and Johnson, 1994). Within the context of neo-liberalism, learning is constructed as a key ingredient for success in modern society, which requires individual and collective flexibility to respond to the challenges of our knowledge-driven 'age of information'. A sustained commitment to learning (often framed as up-skilling, re-skilling or skills-refreshing) is seen as a necessary response to the social and economic pressures of an increasingly globalised world. As Berglund (2008) (p.138) suggests, 'lifelong learning seems to be regarded as something of a miracle cure to whatever disease society might suffer, a kind of educational Viagra to create potent citizens for the so-called learning society'. In other words, the learning society is the healthy society.

The implications of such intertwining of learning and health are profound. Critical management scholars problematize the ways in which employees within 'learning organizations' and 'learning societies' are socialised into highly individualist subject positions, responsible for mobilising and motivating their own learning in the face of whatever organizational and societal demands are thrown at them. As Contu et al. (2003) (p.945) suggest:

> Learning discourse offers points of identifications for subjects of/at work to understand themselves as 'learners', as responsible agents of their own employability. The fulcrum of learning discourse is the transformation of subjects. In this sense, the accent of learning discourse is relentlessly individualistic and individualising.

As agents of their own employability, charged with relentless learning in order to realise the benefits of material and psychological security, employees are thus also the agents of their own well-being: 'Healthy individuals subject themselves to the logic of the learning society and become active and capable lifelong learners' (Berglund, 2008) (p.142).

Discourses of learning represent and reproduce an interesting juxtaposition of ideologies. They may serve the political and economic interests of neo-liberal self-responsibility and self-reinvention, but they do so by invoking the ideas and language of humanism. Much of the literature on the 'learning organization' is grounded in a deeply humanistic tradition, which is committed to emancipating and supporting human beings to realise their true and full potential. The emotive appeal of the learning discourse thereby hinges on the notion that the learner identity is *empowering* for those human beings who absorb it into their sense of self. Thus, cultures of learning are often associated (both explicitly in corporate rhetoric and implicitly in our 'common-sense' understandings) with notions of employee 'engagement' and 'empowerment'. These are amongst the most attractive messages in the contemporary corporate lexicon.

However, through the prism of Foucauldian analysis, this construction of the empowered, self-challenging, self-improving individual merely exchanges one form of power for another (Lupton, 2018; Siebert and Walsh, 2013). Rather than being disciplined by external force, the neo-liberal learner-subject engages in self-discipline to fashion him/herself into the right kind of worker and the right kind of member of society. The notion of plasticity, which we previously applied to the human brain with its power of self-regeneration, now applies to the whole human being, who must mould him/herself into the type of person required by institution. As Nicoll and Fejes (2008) (p.6) put it:

> The autonomous, self-reflective life does not overcome power relations. Instead, it is a particular kind of historical 'figure of thought' of self-government through which we become traversed by power relations *even as we believe ourselves to be free.* [our emphasis]

We may 'buy in' to the rhetoric of learning as empowering, but from a Foucauldian perspective, seeing ourselves as life-long learners keeps us on a treadmill of endless self-enhancement and reinvention, serving interests which may not truly align with our own. Plasticity is thus self-constitution and self-discipline within relations of power.

Learning discourse produces and rewards committed learners, and pathologizes those who fail to live up to the rhythm and expectations of life-long self-improvement and its various operationalisations in continuous professional development/CPD. For instance, Berglund (2008) highlights the rituals that those who find themselves unemployed have to undergo, suggesting that enrolment at the job centre, and the requirement to provide proof of attendance at re-training and re-skilling programmes, can be seen as a powerful societal punishment. As she explains:

> The unemployed has to show him- or herself to be a sinner and penitent to authority. Following such rituals the unemployed person will be 'forgiven' and restored to a healthy and desired condition through verbal confession, and by showing willingness to become a lifelong learner.
>
> *(Berglund, 2008) (p.146)*

The cost of this neo-liberal self-discipline for the individual human being is guilt and self-blame. The responsibility for one's own employability, self-improvement and hence well-being is not always easy to bear, and a relentless focus on learning can reinforce a sense that one is never quite good enough. Just as the contemporary emphasis on the care of the self (Chapter 3) can lead to feelings of inadequacy in relation to lifestyle, the construction of the self as life- and career-long learner can lead to similar feelings of inadequacy in relation to professional competence, security and employability. The employee-as-learner absorbs responsibility for failures, and if one's health suffers, this is because one is not sufficiently committed to, or skilled in, self-reflection and self-improvement (Vince and Saleem, 2004). This is why many critical scholars argue against popular constructions such as the 'reflective practitioner' (Schön, 2017), which places responsibility for learning and hence well-being firmly with the individual, irrespective of the organizational conditions in which he or she operates. Instead, critical theorists such as Reynolds (2017) and Vince (2002b) shift the terminology of this debate away from the notion of the 'reflective practitioner' towards the more collective notion of 'organizing reflection'. The well-being that learning might inspire thereby becomes a collective endeavour, rather than a stick with which the neo-liberal learner-subject can beat him or herself up.

As suggested in the following vignette (Box 5.3), arguments from this critical perspective cast an interesting light on organizational artefacts such as individual 'personal development plans' (PDPs). These tools have become part of what we take for granted in our understandings of performance management and evaluation at work, and we probably do not often stop to think about the politics of their construction.

---

### BOX 5.3  CASE STUDY: A PERSONAL DEVELOPMENT PLAN (PDP) AT *ANOTHER CONSULTING*

The *AnOther Consulting* core values are: Partnership, Innovation and Diversity

*Section A: Achievements and Successes*
Please refer to the core values to list your main achievements this year against each of these three criteria. Try to provide concrete illustrations for each core value.

_____
_____
_____
_____
_____

*Section B: Areas for Development*
Please refer to the three core values to list your main developmental needs, and what you plan to do to address each of them over the coming year.

_____
_____
_____
_____
_____

---

This mock-up probably feels very familiar. Most of the PDPs (and associated artefacts, such as 'learning contracts') that we have encountered are structured in a similar way to this. Adopting a critical lens prompts us to reflect on the interesting effects of the learning discourse on such performance management procedures, e.g., the fact that achievements and successes are not contrasted with weaknesses or mistakes, but rather, with development needs. The seemingly quite benign message is that one does not have to be *flawless* to have a successful career in this organization, but one does have to be willing to commit to *learning* (see Chapter 4 for a similar point about the significance of 'making an effort'). Confessing to, and taking ownership of, one's development needs is thus a kind of organizational ritual through which the individual employee reaches for learning as a form of contrition or penitence (Berglund, 2008). Constructing oneself as a learner is more positively sanctioned than constructing oneself as a failure. It points to the possibility of future action, rather than dwelling on the mistakes of the past, thus reinforcing that overall sense that learning is, indeed, a very 'good thing'.

As we have highlighted, the yoking of learning and well-being involves a curious mix of ideologies, playing to humanist notions of agency *qua* search for meaning as well as neo-liberal interests of agency *qua* flexibility and innovation in the face of the challenges of market forces and globalisation. However, such yoking is not always successful in the sense of furthering organizational or political aims and objectives, and sometimes its effects can be paradoxical. Advocates of organizational learning emphasise the benefits to organizations of a positive association between learning and well-being (both in the sense that learning enhances well-being, i.e., learn enough to be well, and in the reverse sense that well-being enhances learning, i.e., be well enough to learn). In our experience, however, the relationship is often more complex than this.

Promoting a commitment to learning and reinvention is a powerful organizational strategy if the results of such a commitment are organizationally advantageous, such as encouraging an employee to put more effort into her/his communication skills, or become more skilled at managing relationships, or develop more of a mindset for organizational innovation, etc. But what happens if the results are less organizationally advantageous? As Contu et al. (2003) (p.942) suggest, promoting a love for learning might not automatically create a more flexible, employable workforce, for 'enquiring minds might be led to question the assumptions about economic growth, competition and the economic primacy of the West which permeate these policy promotions'. The outcome of learning might, therefore, be a *disengagement* from organization and/or institution, rather than any deepening of commitment to organizational objectives or to any project of self-improvement geared principally towards employability.

## Final thoughts on learning and health: Shifting the base metaphor

Discourses of learning and reinvention are amongst the most appealing of contemporary organizational concepts, and therefore very easily associated with notions of the good and the well. They create a sense of optimism, because they convey a message that success is something to be worked on, requiring commitment, effort and energy rather than privilege, personality or luck (a variant of the argument that leaders are made, not born). Competitive advantage and cultures of high performance can be learned into existence at an organizational level; and enhanced career prospects, and material and psychological well-being can be learned into existence at an individual employee level. As Senge (2006) (p.4) proposes, the great appeal of the learning organization is that 'the team that became great didn't start off great – it *learned* how to produce extraordinary results'. Learning can convert failure into success; problem into opportunity; redundancy into employability.

As Contu and Willmott (2003) argue, learning was once considered a 'Cinderella topic' in organization studies, and associated in many people's minds simply with training as one of the more formulaic, routine elements of the typical human resources portfolio. But as soon as learning was connected directly with organizational performance, the topic grew to become one of the most powerful concepts in contemporary organizational theory and practice and, along the way, became strongly associated with issues of organizational well-being. The idea of a positive correlation between learning and well-being is extremely ideologically appealing. Whether one approaches this debate through the prism of humanism, with its emphasis on meaning and fulfilment, the prism of psychoanalysis, with its emphasis on the containment of emotions, or the prism of neo-liberalism, with its emphasis on economic responsibility, discourses of learning foreground the notion of agency, and turn well-being into something we can influence through the workings of that agency.

However, with agency comes at least some space for idiosyncrasy and individuality (as opposed to individualism). Thus, we cannot fully predict the effects of learning discourse on individual people, for human 'plasticity' cannot always be controlled. In some cases, promoting a spirit of inquiry, self-improvement and continuous professional development will create ever more 'perfect employees', who hone their skills to align with the needs of current and future employers, and deepen their sense of well-being via this alignment. In other cases, such inquiry may trigger a desire to fashion one's own 'learning journey', and to construct and explore experiences of well-being away from institutional expectations.

In this chapter, we have traced a development from learning as information processing (Oppenheimer and Kelso, 2015) and plasticity of self-organization towards a view of learning as deeply entwined with emotion and politics. This acknowledges the work of scholars such as Vince (2001) (p.1326), who focuses on 'the interaction between emotion and power that creates the social and political context within which both learning and organizing can take place'. If, as we have suggested, notions of emotional and political resilience lie at the heart of the relationship between learning and well-being in organizations, then we may well conclude that the metaphor of the brain is perhaps not best placed to represent this relationship. The brain emphasises spontaneous self-organization and computational efficiency, but it is not so successful at capturing issues of emotional and/or political complexity, in particular, the influences and constraints on self-organization from the wider context.

Thus, despite the power and enduring popularity of the brain metaphor (Broekstra, 1996; Morgan, 2007; Weaver, 2015), we would like to suggest a shift of imagery from brain to school to explore the contextual dynamics of the relationship between learning and well-being. We think the discourse of organization-as-school provides a more striking blueprint for the power dynamics of organizational learning and reinvention, and hence supports a critical engagement with the topic of health and well-being. Unlike the brain, which conjures up notions of individual biology and almost unprompted self-organization, the school is much more clearly associated with practices of authority and power asymmetry in the relations between learners and learning providers, and hence connects more readily with our overall interest in the theme of responsibility for health. Thus, we see learning and well-being as co-constituted within the broader context of institutional power; and we argue that asymmetrical power relations play a vital role in our understandings and expectations of institution, whether in the family (as in Chapter 3) or in the school-room (as we are now suggesting for discourses of learning and reinvention). The subject who learns the right things is the perfect student, and well-being is enveloped in issues of conformity, stability and alignment. The subject who learns the wrong things, on the other hand, is expelled from school, and well-being becomes a matter of resistance and revolt.

# 6

# TECHNOLOGY AND HEALTH

## Discourses of cyberspace

In this chapter, we explore the complex ways in which organization, work and health have become technologized in recent years, and examine how this impacts our understandings and experiences of well-being at work. Specifically, we:

- Introduce the realm of cyberspace, highlighting the ways in which this discourse incorporates the material as well as the textual in framing and enabling particular understandings of health.
- Unpack relationships between technology and 'users' which have exerted a crucial influence on our understandings of workplace health, exposing to scrutiny notions of technological progress and user resistance.
- Examine the ways in which health has been reinforced as individual and physiological via the classic approach of ergonomics.
- Explore relationships between well-being and communication, specifically in the use of technology in the management of communications at work.
- Explicate the health implications embedded in understandings of technology as a means of managing time and space at work.
- Highlight the impact of future developments in technology and its broadening impact on our understandings and expectations of health.

## Technological developments in organizational life

The impact of technological change is writ large across any report on either the current challenges or the future of work (e.g., Deloitte, 2018). Whether the trend highlighted is artificial intelligence (AI), robotics or digitalisation – or indeed a combination of all three – it seems inescapable that all aspects of work are subject to rapid technological development. The effects of modern technology are playing out across all spheres of our lives and, as we will explore in this chapter, we are increasingly turning to more technology to manage the other technology in our lives. The term cyberspace is now commonly used to denote an overall culture that encompasses our immersion in, and integration with, information technology. Since we typically engage with information technology via a range of material devices, there is a physicality to this engagement. This material physicality is implicated in the discourses of cyberspace that we explore in this chapter. That is to say, whilst we examine organization *as if* it were a machine (Chapter 1), or an organism (Chapter 2), or a family (Chapter 3), etc., here there is less *as-if*-ness. With discourses of cyberspace, therefore, the interrelationships between discourse and materiality come sharply into focus.

---

### BOX 6.1 AN ADVERTISING CAMPAIGN FROM *GUILTY PLEASURES!*

Christmas excess?

We can get you back on track with our *Fast-to-Fitness©* app.

Compatible with all leading wearable devices, *Fast-to-Fitness©* will support you at every step of your journey to health and happiness.

Simply by looking across your individual health data we can advise you on when to Fast and which of *Guilty Pleasures!* amazing shakes will provide that much needed pick-me-up when your Fast is over. Linked to automatic payment, we can even place the order for you and deliver it to your door.

Our revolutionary approach to *Fastfasting©* offers you all the benefits of fasting in more intense and enjoyable short *Fastfasting©* bursts.

Our amazing shakes then boost your energy offering a unique *Fast-to-Fitness©* benefit.

If you sign up to our exclusive *Comparafast©* service, we will provide you with valuable benchmark information mapping your *Fastfasting©* progress across the *Guilty Pleasures!* community.

---

As this promotion of the *Fast-to-Fitness©* app suggests (Box 6.1), new technologies are both shaping and reflecting many of our experiences of health, both in and beyond the workplace. New technologies purport to know us better than we know ourselves, not just responding to, but *predicting*, what we need to maintain and enhance our well-being. Relatedly, the positive computing movement suggests that a re-positioning towards well-being at individual, organizational and societal levels is the very future for technology (Calvo and Peters, 2014).

However, not all share an optimistic view of the future of technology and well-being. Where our assumptions of organization were once dominated by allusions to the machinery of industrial-age production, now they are mechanised in the sense of Haraway's (2000) cyborg colonisation, in which technology is so powerful that it blurs human and machine:

> Modern production seems like a dream of cyborg colonization work, a dream that makes the nightmare of Taylorism seem idyllic ... our machines are disturbingly lively and we, ourselves are frighteningly inert.
>
> *(Haraway, 2000) (p.292 and p.294)*

Technology in this context is more than our traditional understanding of software and hardware devices. Firstly, devices are evolving. It is not that long ago that we understood 'a computer' as a physical object and our primary, if not only, contact with cyberspace. We now take mobile devices for granted, and we are getting used to the idea that everyday household objects are computerised as part of the 'Internet of Things' (Greengard, 2015). Secondly, software and associated aspects of technological architecture have also advanced such that the notion of a 'package' seems outdated in these interconnected and data-driven times. Data, particularly of the 'big' variety, is heralded as enabling a management revolution (Brynjolfsson and McAfee, 2014). In this revolution, predictive and real time data takes centre stage in guiding all aspects of organizational decision-making. Significantly, analysis of big data looks forward, and is being embraced across education and health, though not without warnings regarding potential ethical dilemmas related to the use of personal information for potential public good (Andreu-Perez et al., 2015; Mayer-Schönberger and Cukier, 2014).

A future of work, in which machines work alongside, and potentially replace, employees, now seems inevitable in many sectors. McKinsey (Chui et al., 2015) (p.2) suggest that 'as many as 45 percent of the activities individuals are paid to perform can be automated by adapting currently demonstrated technologies'. A new term has emerged – the collaborative robot or 'co-bot' – to highlight the expectations of an integrated human and technological workforce (Wang, 2015). Relatedly, broader discussions of artificial intelligence (AI) highlight the potential of machine learning to transform the use of technology at work: no longer will computing be reliant on our ability to *code* performance, rather, performance will be *learned* (Brougham and Haar, 2018).

Crucially, issues of cyberspace cannot be disconnected (no pun intended) from the global presence of technology companies themselves. These companies (including the likes of Apple, Facebook, and Google) shape our understandings and expectations of our digital selves, both at work and beyond. Their products and services act to normalise certain behaviours at work and have introduced a vocabulary that has spread to other uses. Thus, our understanding of the need to 'upgrade' our phones or tablets every two or three years can extend to our understandings of the need to 'upgrade' employees' capabilities or performance on a similarly regular basis. In this way, how we talk about the 'health' of our technology is now influencing our broader understandings of personal and organizational health. 'My phone has died' is an ever-popular Google search, illustrating the way in which technology and health are now mutually implicated. This is an idea that also informs other volumes in this series, most notably Lupton (2018).

The effects of cyberspace can be seen in many of the ways we think and talk about organizational experience – both healthy and otherwise. Discourses surrounding technological developments are nearly always progressive and emphasise increasing control of time and space. This control is often denoted by terms such as connectivity, accessibility, flexibility, and speed, which support organizational cultures based on busyness (Wajcman, 2015) and immediacy (Kaun, 2015). The ways in which work is coordinated and managed is no longer reliant on physical presence at the same time and in the same place; such control is repositioned as freedom. However, both organizational and individual challenges require speedy, technologically-mediated solutions. The control/freedom rhetoric of technological discourses is replicated in our understandings of health as both technologically managed but freely chosen (Lupton, 2018).

In the context of our overall approach in this book, it is important to note that discourse studies have been somewhat criticised for ignoring the material aspects of work and organization. As a result, there is now lively debate about the ways in which discourse and materiality are ontologically and epistemologically interwoven (e.g., the point-counterpoint series on this topic in the *Journal of Management Studies*; see Editors, 2015). Such debates come sharply into focus when considering technology. Just as there is a blurring of human and non-human (Haraway, 2000), so there is also a blurring of the discursive and the material.

While discussions of cyborgs and co-bots may seem to be heading towards the world of science fiction, the notion of a mechanisation of employee experience is, of course, not new. Here, discourses of industrial-age automation (see Chapter 1) are adapted to a world in which efficiency and speed of data processing become the most sought-after organizational attributes. Where workers were once seen as physically connected cogs in the organizational machine, virtual and digital connectivity is now equally, if not more, prized.

## The 'healthy employee' in cyberspace

The complex interrelation of human and non-human, discourse and material, is critical in unpicking understandings of the construction of the 'healthy employee' in cyberspace. We are often most comfortable when drawing clear lines between these and separating out technology as some 'thing' that impacts health and well-being at work. Seen through this prism, the employee is constructed first and foremost as a 'user' of technology. Many of the theoretical foundations which inform our understandings of technology at work originated at a time when it was relatively straightforward to both physically and conceptually identify 'a technology' and then seek to understand its impact on its intended user and, via that user, on the organization. The technology is objectified and the user must change and adapt to its use. This draws on a perspective called technological determinism whereby 'technological change is the cause of specific and predictable change in demands on workers such that knowledge of the technology is sufficient to understand these changing demands' (Majchrzak and Borys, 1998) (p.310). From this perspective, there are two aspects of health to consider. The first is the ultimate health and well-being implications of the end-technology, and the second is the health and well-being implications of the associated change processes. In both cases, there is a need to minimise health risks and maximise well-being.

If the employee is constructed as a 'user', the healthy employee is a 'super-user'. Super-users make maximum use of technological innovations, and are fully proficient and committed to technological upgrade. Their needs have been considered during technological design, and their views have been sought during 'user consultation', making their endorsement of any new implementation more likely. Securing super-users' acceptance of new technology is thus a key organizational objective in any programme of technological change. Much research has focused on understanding how such acceptance can be ensured, with widespread application of the Technology Acceptance Model (TAM), which emphasises the importance of perceived usefulness and perceived ease of use at an individual level (Laumer and Eckhardt, 2012). These factors often become equated with the likely positive engagement and use of the technology, ensuring individual well-being once the technology is in place.

Interestingly, the construction of the opposite kind of employee is particularly well defined in this discursive framing. Where the healthy employee is cast as proficient, quick, adaptable, supportive, and flexible, the unhealthy employee is cast not only as lacking proficiency, but is often also said to be *resistant*. Thus, it is firmly established in the rhetoric of both theory and practice that user resistance to technological progress is problematic, akin to a virus that must be eradicated. Resistant users must be cured and transformed into acceptant users, and those who urge caution in relation to technological progress risk being labelled as technophobes or luddites (Roszak, 1994). Interestingly, the assumption that such resistant positions lead to negative health outcomes is hotly contested. Rafferty and Jimmieson (2017) suggest, for instance, that the degree to which employees are enabled to voice and discuss their concerns about technology may play a significant role in minimising any negative effects on well-being.

Mostly, however, there is little room for grey areas in cyberspace, with ambiguity, ambivalence or any form of mixed views seemingly side-lined. From this perspective, it is healthy to adopt and accept technology, and unhealthy to question or resist. In the sometimes frenzied rhetoric surrounding the pace and progressiveness of technological change, the unhealthy employee may well be left behind.

Taking this view, progress and technology are inextricably linked, and successful organizations are able to harness these developments. A determinist view is often softened to allow for more agency by managers who can shape the potential of the technology, if they make the right decisions at the right times (Pettigrew et al., 1992). In these process-orientated views, contingency comes into play, as managers must adjust technological change to fit their particular organizational context.

---

**BOX 6.2 PERSONAL REFLECTIONS: HEALTH CHECKS AS BAROMETERS OF ACCEPTANCE AND RESISTANCE**

The assumption of a fundamental link between technology and progress was at the heart of much of our previous work as management consultants. We worked to offer robust change processes and the means by which organizational assessments could be undertaken to support technological implementation.

Discourses of health were readily applied here: organizational 'health checks' of various kinds were a key part of the offering, and were both explicitly and implicitly linked to the issue of user acceptance. Early in our engagement we would undertake such a 'health check' to ascertain (by means of a standardised survey) how employees perceived the forthcoming technology and whether there were any issues that might prevent its adoption.

Our assessment of the organizational context focused on the employees and, largely, the technology was taken for granted. We might uncover issues of technology design during our work, but more often we were tasked with managing user acceptance of what was already well into production. Our job was clearly aligned with management. The overall 'health' of the organization was often said to depend on this new technology, and our job was to design communication and training programmes to ensure that employees adopted the system successfully. Particularly in the early days of any new system, this also required considerable effort in terms of supporting users when things did not work as envisaged. Often this involved identifying workarounds to technological problems, which could be expensive and lengthy to fix. Persuading users to adopt new technology was often a process of ongoing negotiation, particularly if the system itself was perhaps not as 'healthy' as had been promised.

---

The experiences highlighted in Box 6.2 reflect broader issues of organizational leadership, culture and performativity that we do not pursue directly here, and raise questions about discursive power, such as the eliding of 'organizational health' and 'individual health' (see Chapter 7). Our point here is that they illustrate a wide-spread, taken-for-granted organizational message that technological complexity can be managed, suppressed and overcome as long as the correct path is followed, particularly if one is guided by experienced (and expensive) management consultants (Sturdy, 1997). Managing health in this context becomes a matter of effective planning and implementation of appropriate support mechanisms for individuals across an organization.

However, while this perspective is still common amongst organizational practitioners, academics have started to ask themselves, as Grint and Woolgar (1997) (p.37) suggest, 'what happens when you apply the scepticism normally reserved for social relations to technology?' A complex and diverse set of propositions have emerged from adopting this more sceptical approach, which itself is embedded in critical views of scientific knowledge (e.g., Gilbert and Mulkay, 1984). These related social studies of science are often approached from a postmodern perspective with the aim of examining the 'plurality of heterogeneous claims to knowledge' (Giddens, 1990) (p.2), since 'what science or knowledge *is*, is not already determined but is at issue in what scientists and others do' (Rouse, 2001) (p.196, original emphasis).

If the healthy employee is a super-user, and the unhealthy employee is a resistant luddite, there is perhaps room for a discursive middle ground in the notion of the 'sceptical user'. Employee scepticism might even provide useful insight into problems with a particular technological offering, and offer alternative perspectives and solutions for how a particular organizational challenge might be met. However, as with many other pairings, the discursive binary between acceptance and resistance is a difficult one to bridge. From a practical perspective, a sceptical position might be temporally recognised as useful, but in many organizations it will be quickly categorised as resistant. Much empirical work has emerged recently, which has examined the complexity of emotional responses involved in technological change and how these may contribute to individual well-being (Barclay and Kiefer, 2014). Somewhat inevitably, this is a complex area with few straightforward causal connections.

Recently, there has been a shift in academic debates about the best way to conceptualise relationships between humans and technology at work. These views challenge the simplistic positioning of the user and the black box of the technology. Social constructionist perspectives have been critical here. These not only unpack individual identity and technological objects (Symon and Pritchard, 2015), but also apply this lens to the relationships between them. For example, Orlikowski and Scott (2008) (p.45) propose that we should view human and technology as 'a constitutive entanglement that does not presume independent or even interdependent entities with distinct and inherent characteristics'. Rather than health outcomes being attributed to either the technology or the human, they emerge through the interaction between them. The term 'sociomaterial' (Pickering, 1995) is often used to describe this emergence through interaction and the entanglement of the human and technological.

From a social constructionist perspective, technological connectivity at work can be understood as a sociomaterial outcome. That is to say, neither a device nor its user achieves connectivity independently; rather, connectivity is co-produced in practice (Barad, 2003). Symon and Pritchard (2015) suggest that individuals *perform* connection as a means of being identified as a certain type of employee. Sociomaterial performances of connection include being contactable and responsive, being involved and committed, and being in-demand and authoritative. Relating this more explicitly to health, we can therefore say that the health and well-being implications of connectivity are not simply *caused* by the technology, but are tangled up in working practices.

Such situated performances are informed and influenced by broader discourses of technology and its use. Connectivity is positioned as essential to both employee and organizational health, while being 'out of touch' (literally and metaphorically) confers the risk of poor health and performance. Connectivity is thus embedded in an increasingly cybermechanistic framing of organizational experience, in which terms like 'refresh', 'reboot' and 'upgrade' are used in relation to skills, careers, relationships, bodies, moods, and feelings. In contemporary conversations at work, it passes almost unnoticed that health needs the occasional 'reboot' – as if physiological, emotional, relational or existential well-being were a matter of pressing control-alt-delete on the keyboard or holding down the home key on a mobile device.

## Health and the technological management of self

Much of the early work on relations between the health of the employee and technology was design-centred around the physical impact of the technology. Ergonomics is perhaps the best known example of a field of study that adopts this approach, seeking to understand how technology at work can be most effectively designed to ensure both productivity and well-being of the employee. The Chartered Institute of Ergonomics and Human Factors website defines the objective of this approach as 'to ensure that designs complement the strengths and abilities of people and minimise the effects of their limitations' (Chartered Institute of Ergonomics and Human Factors, n.d.).

In many complex technological and safety-critical contexts, such as the cockpit of a passenger plane, ergonomic approaches remain highly relevant, and the use of technology to assist with the complexities of designing such technology is commonplace. Technological solutions are thus increasingly deployed to help with problems that other technologies have created, for instance, in the provision of mindfulness apps on mobile devices to help employees cope with technology overload (Plaza et al., 2013). Moreover, it is important to note that ergonomics continues to play a crucial role in ensuring workplace accessibility for employees with physical, or other forms of, disability (Moody et al., 2017).

However, in everyday work contexts, difficulties in identifying who will be using various interrelated technologies, and how, when and where they are to be used, have presented challenges for this approach. We are probably all familiar with advice regarding the height of our desks and angle of our computer screens. This kind of health message focuses on certain aspects of health such as eyestrain, concern to avoid repetitive strain injury and/or muscular-skeletal problems arising from an employee's sedentary use of the computer (Van Tulder et al., 2007). Such messages are usually delivered in the form of advice and/or training, i.e., they are no guarantee of healthy practice. Thus, contemporary organizing poses considerable challenges for ergonomists. As both technology and work have become more fluid in time and space, so it becomes more problematic to control the ways in which users relate to both (*she [KP] types this sat on a sofa with a cushion under her laptop*). This means that health relies on individual responsibility, self-awareness and self-correction (*KP replaces cushion with laptop tray*).

Relatedly, ergonomic issues continue to be highlighted in relation to the shrinking size of technology devices, which can cause challenges for those inputting data. Terms such as 'blackberry thumb' and 'iPad finger' have entered the vocabulary. The transition to voice control, most recently popularised via the likes of Siri and Alexa, promises to change our modes of interaction with these devices, but this has yet to be fully realised in most organizational contexts. New technologies will undoubtedly pose new challenges. For example, virtual reality technologies are increasingly being applied in a wide range of contexts from the operating theatre (McCloy and Stone, 2001) to understanding consumer reaction to misshapen vegetables (Verhulst et al., 2017), and the full effects on their users and other beneficiaries are yet to emerge.

Sedentary work is a significant emergent concern, hitting the headlines with increasing frequency (Castillo-Retamal and Hinckson, 2011). For example, an article via CNN (Squires, 2018) warns that the average American sits for half the day and that the health risks are similar to smoking. This has prompted a range of new tools such as the standing desk (Reiff et al., 2012), and suggestions such as the walking meeting (Hill et al., 2003a), along with targeted exercise and health promotion advice. However, many of us persist in seeing our work as facilitated by fixed technological means. As academics, we often communicate with students and colleagues via email, working on virtual learning environments and marking electronic submissions. All these require extended periods working at a laptop or tablet, often away from the office. Alongside other developments, such working practices are increasingly highlighted as detrimental to the health and well-being of those working in academia (Butler et al., 2017).

Of interest here is the notion that the use of technology and aspects of physical health are inextricably interlinked. Problems with physical health are then understood to cause broader impacts on well-being in a more psychosocial sense (Farnacio et al., 2017). Thus, emerging health dilemmas include issues such as addiction and 'digital overload' (Van Rooij and Prause, 2014), which can be related to conditions such as 'technostress' or 'digital depression' (Tarafdar et al., 2017). Taking 'technostress' as an example, this is conceived as a particular form of stress that is related to an individual's inability to cope with the increased use of technology in the course of work tasks (Riedl et al., 2012; Tarafdar et al., 2010). Such stress is seen as directly caused by technology (including break-downs *in* technology) and as having a direct impact on individual well-being and performance at work. The medicalisation and definition of disorders related to technology use should not be taken lightly, not least since the health concern becomes individualised (see also Chapter 7). Moreover, much of the research on these issues relates to non-work usage and is predominately conducted with student samples (Kuss and Griffiths, 2011). In short, the ease with which notions of rebooting and refreshing can be applied as a solution to problematic psychosocial experiences with technology is surely cause for concern.

## Health and the technological management of relationships

We have moved into an era where technological communication has become the norm for many people. In 2015, it was estimated that 112.5 billion e-mails were exchanged every day in businesses worldwide, with more detailed analysis suggesting that this translates to '88 e-mails received and 34 e-mails sent per user per day' (Sonnentag et al., 2018) (p.369). This is set within a broader context of an explosion in communications technology. For instance, there were over 2 billion active users of Facebook in 2018, while WhatsApp had 1.5 billion active users in December 2017 (figures available from www.statista.com). In terms of the technological management of relationships, communication – whether by voice, text or image – has been the main focus of research on implications for health. Such research seeks to unpack the ways in which techno-logically-mediated communication might offer some health benefits in terms of facilitating connections, but also has the potential for negative effects on well-being, given the different nature of the interactions.

Email communication has been a dominant topic of research, particularly in comparison with face-to-face communication, where it is generally found to be lacking and therefore has the potential to negatively impact well-being. Early research on the use of email focussed on the weaknesses of text-based communica-tion, particularly the lack of social cues and reduction in communication richness compared to face-to-face interaction (Parlamis and Geiger, 2015). Essentially, rely-ing on the pared down written form of email or other electronic message reduces much of the depth of communication we experience when discussing a topic in person. Indeed, many newer technologies provide an automated 'sent from my …', which appears as an apology in advance for brevity, spelling, and any other error in communication (Carr and Stefaniak, 2012). This lack of depth is said to influence not only the effectiveness of the communications themselves but also the quality of our social relations at work – relations which are seen as crucial for human well-being (Eid and Larsen, 2008).

As senders of emails, we seem to have become more focused on our own agenda, and we lack concern for the perspectives and views of those receiving our communications. It is perhaps not a surprise, therefore, that we tend to assume our written messages are unequivocal, particularly in relation to the intended conveyance of emotion (Butts et al., 2015; Kruger et al., 2005). This line of research suggests that the resulting mis-communication between senders and recipients can both create issues and disrupt their resolution in the workplace. Such communication issues are said to have an adverse effect on the health and well-being of both individuals and teams at work (Eid and Larsen, 2008).

More recent work has argued that the comparison between email and face-to -face communication is unhelpful. Rather than focusing on what is lacking, we should consider the ways in which employees are developing practices of email to enhance communication and hence relationships. Just as there is no single mode of face-to-face communication, emailing encompasses a huge range of socially embedded and technologically-mediated practices. For instance, Pritchard and Symon (2014) investigate how engineers working in the field use photographs to supplement textual communications. Shared visual images provide a potential means of bridging the distance involved in distributed work (Hinds and Mortensen, 2005). However, while sharing images helps to establish facts about a particular engineering scenario, these images also become potentially more valuable than the engineers' own verbal or textual accounts to their managers (Pritchard and Symon, 2014). From this perspective, the complex ways in which communication practices develop at work have significant potential to impact both individual and organizational health.

This research highlights that technologically-mediated communication is situated within particular organizational contexts and, of clear pertinence here, particular socio-political systems. While engineers use images as a means of demonstrating the difficulty of some aspects of their work, this reinforces the value of the image-as-truth in their relationships with their managers (Pritchard and Symon, 2014). Here the digital image becomes an important boundary object (Bechky, 2003) in the power relations between engineers and their managers. The features of the technology (here a smartphone) are implicated in these relations, not least because the engineers often work outside, in challenging physical circumstances, and typing long messages on small devices is difficult (Pritchard and Symon, 2014). The smartphone provides a useful focus for discussing these issues, for it becomes a repository of explanations for wider issues in the organization (Symon and Pritchard, 2015). This research highlights how the implications for health are complex and therefore equally difficult to disentangle; assigning health concerns solely to the impact of the smartphone would only offer limited insights. Rather, understanding what influences well-being in such contexts requires us to unpick carefully the socio-technological context.

The field engineers in Pritchard and Symon's (2014; Symon and Pritchard, 2015) study represent just one form of distributed work. Virtual teams vary enormously, as do the ways in which work is performed across technologies. Given this variation, it is hardly surprising that there is a similar variance in the research evidence surrounding the relationships between virtual working and health. Well-being in such contexts is closely linked to the ways in which virtual teams operate and the levels of social and personal support that are available (Nurmi, 2011). For example, Wadsworth and Blanchard (2015) highlight that the opportunities offered by technology to support virtual working can be positively exploited with benefits for individual well-being; but also, just as importantly, technology offers a means by which communication can also be withheld, and individuals excluded, which can result in negative health outcomes. Their research looks at a variety of influencing tactics used within virtual work, as individuals seek to secure personal positioning and presence within the team.

Wadsworth and Blanchard (2015) also highlight the issue of technological disruption, including the ways in which emails can demand and elicit immediate attention (via classifying a message as urgent, or tactical copying-in of senior staff, for example). Recent research by Sonnentag et al. (2018) highlights the complexity of understanding interruptions in complex, multi-goal settings. On the one hand, they see interruptions as a cause of frustration which can lead to stress. On the other hand, individuals also report a sense of satisfaction in resolving other work issues if they are able to respond to the interruptions successfully. Such examples remind us of the complexity of technology in use and the multiple ways in which such use might influence experiences of well-being. Fundamentally, such research also highlights issues with reducing the challenges of modern working environments to the ills of technology (Barley et al., 2011).

Much of the research discussed above works on an assumption of positive *intent* in the use of technology, particularly for communication. We are only now starting to see issues of technology misuse emerge as a topic for discussion in work contexts. Indeed, D'Cruz and Noronha (2013) highlight that in investigating such 'misuse', far more research has investigated 'cyberslacking' (the personal use of technology during work time) than other forms. This may well be because conflict at work has always been a problematic area of organization studies. The CIPD (2015) (p.2) *Managing Conflict at Work* survey highlights lack of respect as the most commonly reported negative behaviour, defining this as 'failing to relate to each other as individuals in a healthy way'. Others suggest that low-level conflict at work, whether perpetuated via technology or not, may be one of the most serious health issues within contemporary workplaces (Lim et al., 2008).

A particular concern here is the emergence of cyberbullying, with one recent study finding that this may have a more significant negative impact on well-being than more traditional 'offline' bullying (Coyne et al., 2017). Pertinent issues relate to the potential for anonymity and the ability to reach beyond the workplace; for example, broadcasting material publicly or impersonating an individual online, which can result in significant negative consequences for health, particularly due to the difficulty of disconnecting for the individual concerned

(Nocentini et al., 2010). There is a burgeoning body of research related to cyberbullying in childhood and adolescence, particularly in educational contexts. However, as Coyne et al. (2017) highlight, research regarding the impact of cyberbullying on health at work is in its infancy and clearly an area requiring further investigation.

Relatedly, the complexity of technology at work is crucial to debates about technological security and surveillance. Highlighting the potential for anonymous cyberbullying via impersonation (as above) might prompt a reaction that these actions should be traceable and the perpetrator identified. Of course, to some degree or other, organizations have always monitored their employees. However, whereas once observation was direct, contemporary organizations have moved towards systems of technological control. D'Urso's (2006) research suggests that 80% of organizations in the USA use some form of technological surveillance, with 55% of surveyed companies reporting that they retain and review the email messages their employees send and receive. As Gabriel (2008) (p.312) suggests, employees now experience 'camera lenses everywhere, ready to intrude into people's privacy; open-plan offices and glass buildings; a quasi-religious obsession with transparency; audits, reviews, appraisals, feedbacks, lists, and league tables'.

Drawing on determinist arguments, some suggest that these new forms of technological surveillance cause employee stress (Cascio and Montealegre, 2016), while broader perspectives link digital accountability to overall systems of organizational control (McDonald and Thompson, 2016), which in turn are related to negative health outcomes. McDonald and Thompson (2016) cite the figure that 40% of UK organizations have sacked someone for email or internet abuse. An employee's awareness that any use of a digital device might be monitored and recorded requires a constant self-regulation of behaviour, which in turn might be expected to affect feelings of well-being at work.

One argument often invoked is that individuals behaving well and doing their job effectively have nothing to fear from such surveillance. Yet in many organizations and roles, there may not be clear or shared understandings of good or acceptable use of technology. It is the imbalance between the observed and observer that is most commonly highlighted, where the observer might include an employer, an organization providing the surveillance technology and others who acquire or monitor data from them. As Crain observes (2018) (p.92), 'the privacy of those under watch is undermined, while the watchers themselves operate with substantial freedom from scrutiny'. The extent to which data from surveillance flows *into* organizations is not yet well understood, and the complex relations between the monitoring of employees and well-being outcomes are a significant emerging research concern (Marx, 2016).

A final note here relates to debates about whistleblowing, which occurs when one person makes a disclosure or raises concerns about another person's behaviour at work. There is a difficult balance between enabling whistleblowing and placing individual employees in the position of monitoring each other's behaviour (Kenny et al., 2018a and 2018b). Suggesting that these represent two extreme poles of a continuum, Tsahuridu and Vandekerckhove (2008) (p.108) observe that 'whistleblowing legislation and organizational policies either aim to enable individual responsibility and moral autonomy at work, or protect organizations by allowing them to control employees and make them liable for ethics at work'. Outcomes for individual whistle blowers have sometimes been extreme, but research also highlights how health discourses can be used to undermine whistle blowers' actions by positioning them as unstable or mentally ill (Kenny et al., 2018a). With the increasing use of surveillance technology to facilitate whistleblowing, we can see that the increasing cybermechanisation of organizational relationships is complex indeed.

## Health and technological management of time and space at work

In the sections above, we allude to the ways in which technology is implicated in changing understandings of time and space at work. For example, Bosch-Sijtsema et al. (2010) (p.183) suggest that smartphones 'have liberated work from being bound to a particular place and time'. Emergent issues are often presented as a binary between freedom to work anywhere/anytime, and oppression to work everywhere/all the time. These positions are related to notions of 'work/life balance' and correlated with positive and negative impacts on health and well-being. Recent analyses suggest that poor 'work/life balance' has a significant influence on health outcomes across many different occupational sectors, although Lunau et al. (2014) suggest that, in Europe at least, this may vary for men and women, and across different welfare states.

In the midst of this complexity, it is tempting to treat time and space in a naïve objective sense. Both have a taken-for-granted naturalness, which enables us to easily place them outside the reach of organizational or individual control. At the same time, 'managing' space and time is exactly what we are told technology does best, particularly in an international context. Technology, therefore, becomes a convenient scapegoat for concerns related to 'work/life balance'. However, Shove (2009) suggests that we actively construct and perform 'time' through our work, rather than 'it' existing independently. This draws on social constructionist ideas which were considered in relation to individual connectivity (Symon and Pritchard, 2015) and means of communicating (Pritchard and Symon, 2014) earlier in this chapter.

A key discursive tension exists as understandings of time-used-well are related to notions of efficiency and productivity. Many, if not all, contemporary technologies have been directly linked to this 'better' use of time at work and correlated with positive outcomes for organizational health. However, from Shove's (2009) perspective, such understandings of time are not 'caused' by the technology, rather they are enacted in their use. An example of this is the use of mobile devices during commuting and travel time (Axtell et al., 2008). Green

(2002) labels these 'Lazarus devices', whereby previously 'dead time' is reconstructed and repositioned as available for work. Commuters now work, where they might previously have read a newspaper, stared out of the window or even conversed with fellow passengers. Such technologized time could, of course, be used for non-work purposes, such as watching a box-set or listening to music. However, we have seen travel to work emerge as an essential digital preparation time and the journey home as digital wrap up. This time has therefore become re-understood as part of the working day, albeit one which is rarely acknowledged or remunerated in employment contracts. Evidence is mixed regarding the relationship between commuting-work and health, suggesting both positive and negative outcomes in which a wide range of variables must be considered (Voydanoff, 2005).

While predominantly drawing on time, such issues also invoke space and place of work. For many years, being at work required attendance at a specific place of work (and of course, at the correct time). However, as we have seen, technology now provides the basis for new forms of virtual and distributed work. Contemporary technologies allow work to extend to other places, via both the emergence of the gig economy (Petriglieri et al., 2018) and even within more traditional working arrangements, into the home. Graham et al. (2017) (p.136) refer to this as the 'spatial unfixing of work'. For some researchers, individual characteristics determine both the amount and the impact of extending the time and place of work, and indeed, whether this is problematic for individual health and well-being. For example, MacCormick et al. (2012) suggest that the extent to which increased engagement with work offered by smartphones might be taken up is dependent on the centrality of work to the individuals involved, leading them to identify 'dynamic connectors', 'hyperconnectors' and 'hypo-connectors'. They found that 'over-engaged employees risk their personal health and wellbeing' (MacCormick et al., 2012) (p.195), and that those who were more disengaged also reported negative effects on wellbeing. Thus, the 'dynamic connectors' who were able to most effectively balance and adjust their use of technology to both work and personal demands were those who had the most satisfactory health outcomes.

Rosengren (2015) (p.8) suggests that:

> The temporal strategies that the individual formulates in relation to the expectations of their environment can be seen partly as a direct response to contract agreements and the nature of the work task, and partly as a symbolic act performed in relation to surrounding norms.

In a similar vein, Whiting et al. (2015) review an emergent form of digital labour which they call 'digi-housekeeping'. This work, often performed in an individual's own time, includes the tasks which are necessary to maintain an online and connected presence, such as organizing emails, managing calendar invites, updating online profiles, etc. Indeed, as the authors highlight, similar tasks are often performed for both working and personal needs, thus this online space becomes a hybrid or potentially liminal sphere of activity. Whereas previously we looked at the relationship *between* work and life (as in 'work/life balance'), the online world offers a new, potentially more integrative, realm of activity. Whiting et al. (2015) highlight similarities between 'digi-housekeeping' and domestic housekeeping, especially given the invisibility of such tasks, which include clearing, sorting, preparing, provisioning and trouble-shooting. Together these tasks represent the additional work that follows from using digital technologies and which is carried out by individuals to support and sustain flexible working. Further research that examines the impact of this work on well-being is now needed.

Others, such as Wajcman and Rose (2011) and Mazmanian (2013), argue that patterns of spatial and temporal connection are related to organizational culture and practices. As highlighted earlier, Symon and Pritchard (2015) in their research on smartphones discuss how being available – and actively demonstrating this availability through *responding* – has become essential to constructing a credible organizational identity as a committed worker. Their research suggests 'a view of connectivity that is not just about communication (or even work engagement) but also about being *known* and *knowable* – having presence in the organization's life and, through responding, enacting that presence and one's identity as an employee' (Symon and Pritchard, 2015) (p.256). Mazmanian (2013) suggests the norms for such performances might be linked to particular occupational expectations, offering another sphere of influence beyond the organization. All these authors highlight the importance of ongoing re-performance as an essential mechanism through which understandings of time and space are continually reconstructed, but also draw attention to the power mechanisms at work. It is these power mechanisms that become particularly influential when there is some form of breakdown in expected ways of working. Symon and Pritchard (2015) demonstrate that sometimes, employees can invoke an alternative construction in resistance. In their particular empirical context, discourses of 'health and safety' could be invoked to construct both times and spaces that were immune· to the otherwise pervasive understanding of being contactable. In this way, well-being might be retrievable through resistance.

## Final thoughts on technology, cyberspace and health

Underlying assumptions about the use and users of technology are well-established organizational discourses. These are reflected in constructions of the 'healthy employee' as a 'super-user', fully engaged in, and known through, the application of technology at work and at home. However, it is not only an employee's direct engagement with technology that is related to health at work. Rather, it matters how an employee is *perceived* to be engaging with technology, or indeed *feels* he or she is being perceived. An employee who is seen as cyber-resistant might experience work and working relationships in a different and potentially 'less healthy' way than those who are perceived to engage.

Thus, technologized notions of health are increasingly embedded within organizational experiences in ways that are both more and less visible to employees. As technology develops, we move away from being able to identify physically the hardware that shapes our lives, and away from the 'packaged' software that once enabled us to specify, with reasonable confidence, the tools we used in our jobs. As we have argued here, the increasingly invisible ways in which technology is embedded within our working (and indeed, all aspects of our) lives have altered our understandings of time, place and self. It is a question warranting critical scrutiny whether these are liberating and enabling or institutionally, physiologically and/or psychologically repressive (see also Chapter 7).

We should not, however, take a straightforward technologizing trajectory as a given. Recent events suggest that we may have reached a tipping point in relation to how much we will allow our lives to be absorbed into the machinery of artificial intelligence, digitalisation and robotics. Once the icons of industry and epitome of entrepreneurship, the technology mega-companies have experienced several crises of late. The recent scandals involving the now defunct Cambridge Analytica and the previously impervious Facebook, amongst others, have highlighted increasing concerns with the way in which our lives are dominated by a relatively small number of organizations and their products. News stories bring to the fore concern with the surveillance functions of emerging technologies and the disaggregation of jobs via the task-driven economy (Sundararajan, 2016). These issues are having a profound influence on the experiences of 21st century work, both within and beyond the world of formal, employment-based organization. However, they are discourses that can be resisted as well as absorbed. The 'healthy employee' may well be constructed as a 'super-user', whose well-being is both knowable and known, but this is not the only identity position or possibility in play.

Whilst we may be impressed by the sophistication of complex new technologies, we should, at the same time, be wary of objectifying them. For example, it is easy to talk about the web, treating 'it' as uniform and static and 'its' use as a singular experience. We suggest that it is more helpful to consider our experiences of these (and other) technologies and their relationships to health as socially situated and open to multiple possible meanings and deployments. Thus, the question of whether what is possible technologically is also good for our health is one to which we – not the giants of Silicon Valley – must provide the answers.

# 7

# POLITICS AND HEALTH

## Discourses of power

In this chapter, we reflect on the interplay of power, politics and health in organizational and institutional life, which draws together the key critical themes of the book as a whole. Specifically, we:

- Introduce the metaphor of the organization-as-political system, and reflect on how this shifts our gaze towards the dynamics of negotiation, compromise, contingency and inequality.
- Consider some of the most influential elaborations of organizational power, and the patterns of privilege and disadvantage they invoke.
- Linger on the notion of the 'healthy employee' through the prism of Foucauldian bio-power, in which desirable identities are promoted and become absorbed into people's sense of who they are and who they could, want and ought to be.
- Explore how the notion of bio-power throws into sharp relief the question of who (or what) is responsible for health, and the implications of this for individual agency and subjectivity.
- Interrogate the assumption of a mutually beneficial and reinforcing relationship between individual and organizational health, and consider whether individual health is sometimes sacrificed, consciously or otherwise, for the sake of the health of the organization.
- Suggest that popular topics in books on organizational and occupational health, such as the definition of stress and the measurement of effectiveness of health interventions, raise profoundly political as much as scientific questions.

## Organizations as crucibles of power and politics

The preceding chapters have paved the way for an exploration of the politics of organizational health. Although we are following Morgan (2007) in considering the organization-as-political system as a specific metaphor in and of itself, this chapter is also a culmination of many of the themes that we have traced in previous chapters on other discourses. Through this prism of organization as the site of power and politics, the critical aspects of our discussion of health and well-being become most overt and explicit, and we are able to pick up and elaborate some of the trails we laid down earlier. Thus, the organization-as-political system serves as something of a meta-discourse, reflecting the approach and sensibility of the book as a whole.

Power is a central concern for critical scholars of organizational experience. As Clegg et al. (2006) (p.3) suggest:

> Power is to organization as oxygen is to breathing. Politics are at the core of public life and their expression is invariably dependent on organization, be it in government, business, administration, religion, education, or whatever. Formal politics are organized and all organizations are themselves crucibles of political life. The term 'organizational politics' is not a part of the lexicon of everyday speech without good reason.

The everyday lexicon of organizational politics to which Clegg et al. (2006) refer includes common expressions such as: 'it's not what you know, but who you know that counts'; 'it's not a problem, it's an opportunity'; one needs to 'climb the greasy pole to success'; and 'don't shoot the messenger' when trying to 'speak truth to power'. The formal rhetoric of organization may emphasize the importance of rationality, efficiency, evidence-based decision-making, planning and management, but anyone who has ever worked in or with an organization will testify that behind the scenes of such rationality, things get done (or not done) in a range of ways which are more complex; more the result of whim or favouritism, more unfair, more contradictory, more based on compromise and negotiation, in short, more 'political'.

In everyday work practice, different organizational stakeholders will have different perspectives on what matters most, and their range of different goals and concerns will need to be sufficiently aligned to allow work to take place. Thus, in its most obvious guise, power unfolds in the navigation, negotiation, and sometimes conflict, between different interests, especially when there are decisions and choices to be made about the direction an organization should take. As Morgan (2007) argues, through the prism of politics, *all* organizational activities and encounters are based on convergences and disconnects between different interests. Thus, even apparently formal aspects, such as strategy, structure and job design, have a political dimension, as well as the more overt political power plays and conflicts.

In our 'common sense' understandings of organization, power is perhaps most readily associated with what happens at the top of an organizational hierarchy. In theories of leadership, for instance, much emphasis has been placed on the power of personality in constructs such as the charismatic leader (House and Howell, 1992), its close relation, the transformational leader (Bass and Riggio, 2006; Yukl, 1999), and more recently neo-charismatic leadership approaches, such as authentic, ethical and servant leaders (Antonakis, 2017; Ladkin and Spiller, 2013; Spears and Lawrence, 2016; Tomkins and Nicholds, 2017). In their various ways, these approaches all see power as being wielded and reinforced through some aspect of a leader's character and presence. The powerful leader is thus one who possesses exceptional skills of persuasion and motivation, and the ability to embody and communicate some sense of vision and higher purpose which others are inspired to follow.

Different power dynamics can also be traced in the way we categorise various organizational types. The suffix -cracy, from the Greek *kratia*, meaning system of government, is used to indicate the predominant source and nature of power in particular organizational types. So, autocracy means that power is wielded by a single, often dictatorial, ruler. Bureaucracy means that power is located in rules, regulations, procedures and administrative systems. Technocracy suggests that power is exercised through technical knowledge and expertise. Democracy refers to a power which is distributed amongst the people, either directly amongst the people themselves, or indirectly through the election of agents and representatives, such as union representatives in unionised industries or various employee 'champions' in other, more corporate organizational configurations. Elsewhere in this book, we considered the adhocracy (Mintzberg and McHugh, 1985), in which power and control are wielded on a temporary, quasi-spontaneous basis, in order to maximise an organization's ability to respond quickly and flexibly to new opportunities. In short, even when an organization looks less formally and systemically power-orientated than the traditional, top-down hierarchy, power has not disappeared, it has simply metamorphosed into a different dynamic.

In addition to marking particular organizational types, power and politics appear in many guises in organizational life. Power can be 'hard', that is, grounded in force, threats or coercion, or 'soft', that is, exercised through persuasion and appeal (Nye, 1990), the latter often crystallised in the expression 'winning hearts and minds' (King and Walker, 2014). Power can be restrictive or facilitative, as in the distinction between 'power over' and 'power to' (Haugaard, 2012). 'Power over' evokes a more traditional view of the influence that is wielded because of formal role or position at the top of an organizational hierarchy, which requires that subordinates acquiesce and comply. In contrast, 'power to' conjures up a more distributed kind of agency and influence, especially if it is used to mean individuals being pro-active in making things happen, that is, seeing oneself as having the 'power to' make a difference. 'Power to' tends, therefore, to be conceived as a more positive, more creative, and potentially more emancipatory dynamic than 'power over'. Few people in an organization overtly wield 'power over', but many more might be said to have 'power to'. This is why 'power to' feels relevant in our so-called knowledge economy and the flatter, project-based organizational configurations that are deemed more conducive for know-ledge-based work and organizational learning (see also Chapter 5 on the pol-itics of learning and health). 'Power to' seems similar to the idea of 'responsible autonomy', which Fairtlough (2005) sees as an important challenge to the notion that the only viable model of organizational power is hierarchy. It is no surprise, therefore, that the notion of 'power to' is frequently invoked in the context of organizational change to emphasise the importance of stakeholder participation and engagement.

'Power to' can be criticised, of course, for being a neo-liberal ploy to shift responsibility and blame for success and failure onto the individual employee, often under the banner heading of attractive messages about employee 'empowerment' and 'engagement' (Bloom, 2017). In other words, even when responsibly autonomous, participatory and empowered, the contemporary employee is arguably still subject to the sovereignty of organizational leaders and paymasters. It is not usually the 'power to' do whatever one wants, but rather, the 'power to' do whatever is deemed most suitable and appropriate within a particular organizational regime, that is, it is usually the 'power to' ensure that one's own interests are sufficiently aligned with, and supportive of, the interests of the regime.

A concern for issues of power, politics and privilege – and the different advantages and disadvantages they produce and reinforce for different stake-holders – lies at the heart of the discipline of critical organization studies. Much of this scholarship examines the co-constitution of power and know-ledge, such as the ways in which management expertise, including examples of 'best practice' in best-selling management texts or on the curricula of the most prestigious business schools, tends to present ideas and value-propositions as if they were facts and givens, thereby exercising power through legitimising some perspectives as more authoritative than others (Parker, 2015; Rhodes et al., 2018; Willmott, 2015). From a critical perspective, power unfolds in a broad range of everyday actions, conversations, communications, gestures, decisions, inclusions and exclusions, especially those which are considered to represent the 'normal', the 'natural' and the 'taken-for-granted'.

Moreover, power can be at its most potent when it has apparently disappeared or diminished, for instance, when organizational leaders suggest that they are 'powerless' in the face of brutal market conditions to justify the necessity of employee redundancies. This kind of rhetoric can be seen as a political manipu-lation of threat and uncertainty to legitimise a particular course of sometimes pretty unpalatable action. The carefully calculated language of powerlessness seems to be at least partially responsible for the relatively low levels of protest and resistance to such enforced redundancies in contemporary organizations. As

Clegg et al. (2006) (pp.336–337) suggest, 'there is a political paradox lying behind these dynamics, comprising the fact that admitting powerlessness in the face of "external threats" provides business elites with an easy way to refurbish a slightly severed legitimacy'.

In short, power is everywhere. Power takes many different forms, and therefore, invites many conceptualisations, models and labels, but it is always there in some shape or other. As Haugaard (2010) (p.419) suggests, power 'constitutes a "family resemblance concept", with family members forming complex relationships within overlapping language games'. These family members include power to/power over, systemic power, dispositional power, positional power, discursive power, power abuse, etc. Indeed, for Clegg et al. (2006) (p.400), the dynamics of organization are:

> Unthinkable without power because all social relations are relations of various shades of domination, seduction, manipulation, coercion, authority, and so on. Power is; power always will be, and can never not be.

So, power is a, if not, *the* key interest for critical organization and management scholars, and therefore, crucial for a critical exploration of organizational health. It is a topic to which we cannot possibly do full justice in the space we have here in this chapter, so we direct readers to specialist compendia on organizational power, such as Clegg et al. (2006) or Knights and Willmott (1999), for further detail, analysis and provocation. For the purposes of this book, we continue the theme of previous chapters by drawing on mostly Foucauldian motifs of power, occasionally contrasting them with the more functionalist perspective that is represented in most of the practitioner literature. We consider this broadly Foucauldian approach to be especially illuminating for the politics of health and well-being at work.

## The political construction of the 'healthy employee'

The inspiration for much of the most provocative academic work on the politics of health at work is Foucault (e.g., Allender et al., 2006; McGillivray, 2005; Thanem, 2009; Zoller, 2003a, 2003b). In the Introduction to this volume, we grounded our overall approach in the notion of Foucauldian Discourse, referring to the ways in which particular constellations of ideas and assumptions shape the way organization is conceived, and how people come to be defined – and *define themselves* – in relation to these ideas and assumptions about what it means to be well (and unwell) at work. We returned to Foucault in Chapter 3, when we discussed the politics of self-care and suggested that this is helping to turn the healthy life-style into a matter of individual rather than organizational or societal responsibility, and to distort the practice of self-care from a matter of *work*, as it is in Socratic and Platonic philosophy, into a matter of *leisure*, as it tends to be in contemporary popular discourse. We also considered Foucault in Chapter 4 on the connections between age and health, and constructions of health *qua* fitness. And in Chapter 5, we invoked Foucauldian philosophy to reflect on the neo-liberal learner-subject, who disciplines him/herself into becoming a desirable and successful employee through a career- and life-long commitment to skills-development, self-improvement and the project of employability.

Much of the critical scholarship on the politics of well-being draws on a Foucauldian notion of bio-power, which envelops a number of different ideas (Foucault, 1979, 1980). At a macro level, there is the bio-politics of the population, whereby power unfolds in the classification, evaluation and promotion of what is 'normal' and 'acceptable'. Bio-power is also exercised at a micro level, that is, in relation to the individual body, as each of us is moulded into that which it seems most useful or appropriate to be. The success of this moulding lies in its intimacy and personalisation, that is, these expectations of usefulness or appropriateness become absorbed into our most private sense of self, i.e., it is a *self*-moulding, a regulation of one's own insides (Alvesson and Willmott, 2002; Nadesan, 2010).

These two aspects of bio-power construct both categories or types of self, such as 'The Overweight' or 'The Addictive Personality' (Lupton, 1995), and actual, individual selves who absorb such identities into their own sense of who they are, and who they could, want and ought to be. They are co-constitutive, not causal in a linear or unidirectional sense. Individual and population are 'two sides of a global political technology that simultaneously aims at the control of the human as individual body and at the human as species' (Lemke, 2011) (p.38). The notion of bio-power thereby marks a radical departure from traditional theories of power, and perhaps from 'common sense' understandings, too. As Lupton (2018) (p.15, in this series) suggests, 'where once coercion and violence were used to discipline bodies under regimes of sovereign power, more subtle and dispersed forms of power now operate to encourage citizens to conform to expectations and norms'. Thus, bio-power is the very life-blood of organizational politics, because it creates and maintains the template of the 'perfect employee', evaluates and rewards (or penalises) individual employees against this template, and all the while manages to seem as if becoming this ideal self is a matter of individual agency, freedom and choice. Foucauldian scholars on organizational health have developed several angles of criticism from the concept of bio-power (see, for instance, Dale and Burrell, 2014; James and Zoller, 2018), and we use some of these to structure our discussion below.

## The question of responsibility

We have argued throughout this book that health and well-being are increasingly seen as matters of individual responsibility in contemporary Western discourse. The enlightened organization provides opportunities for health maintenance and improvement, but it is down to the individual employee to take proper advantage of them. To illustrate this, we present the vignette below

(Box 7.1), which is paraphrased only very slightly from a 'real-world' example that we encountered recently. In the original, the background on the poster was a reproduction of the famous picture of Lord Kitchener, pointing a large finger towards the viewer (usually accompanied by the words 'your country needs *you!*'). We think the message is unambiguous: what are *you*, the employee, going to do about *your* well-being, given that *we*, the employer, have laid on so many helpful events and initiatives for you?

---

**BOX 7.1 CASE STUDY: POSTER AT *DEPARTMENT X* FOR 'WELLNESS AT WORK WEEK'**

Wellness means much more than just avoiding being sick. It means feeling good about yourself, and energised both at work and at home.

This week, we are offering a range of health activities and services for you to try out. You can sign up for a neck and shoulder massage at your desk, or book one of our taster Yoga and Pilates sessions. Come along to one of our lunchtime lectures on superfoods and anti-oxidants, where there will be lots of tasty, energy-boosting snacks to sample. There'll be a new range of super-smoothies in the cafeteria, and we really want to hear what you think of them. Wellness Champions will be in the atrium all week, happy to talk to you about your wellness goals and provide practical advice on how best to achieve them.

So, what are *you* going to do this week to enhance your wellness?

---

For many critical organizational scholars, this apparent shifting of responsibility for well-being onto the individual is perhaps the greatest issue with health promotion programmes in contemporary workspaces (Cederström and Spicer, 2015; Dale and Burrell, 2014; Maravelias, 2009; McGillivray, 2005; Zoller, 2003a, 2003b). Through rhetorical tactics of personal enlightenment and empowerment, the individual employee is encouraged to see health as the result of lifestyle choices, for which he or she is, to a very large extent, responsible. From this perspective, poor health is a matter of individual fault, whether through laziness or insufficient knowledge or education (which is also a form of laziness, given the multiple resources provided by organizations and other institutions, such as local health and fitness services).

In the UK, where we both live and work, the discourse of self-responsibility is now firmly embedded in the way health is conceptualised amongst policy-makers and promoted across organizations and institutions. For instance, the Chartered Institute of Personnel and Development (CIPD), the foremost professional association for human resources practitioners in the UK, makes it very clear where accountability for health at work really lies: 'Well-being is ultimately an individual's responsibility requiring education and a degree of self-awareness'

(CIPD, 2015, p.4, cited in Dale and Burrell, 2014, p.162). On the global stage, whilst the World Health Organization's *Ottawa Charter* does emphasise social and political accountability for health, it also has a message of personal agency and responsibility at its core. Thus, 'health is created by caring for oneself and others, by being able to take decisions and have control over one's life circumstances, and by ensuring that the society one lives in creates conditions that allow the attainment of health by all its members' (WHO, 1986) (p.2).

Increasingly, therefore, health and well-being are things that organizations and institutions are charged with *facilitating*, rather than delivering or guaranteeing. The primary responsibility for securing and maintaining optimal health, and preventing and treating poor health, seems now to lie with the contemporary employee. Indeed, scholars suggest that there has been a major restructuring of the social contract between individual, organization, state and society over the past few decades. Just as successive government policies have shifted the problem and the cost of absenteeism onto employers (Gründemann and Van Vuuren, 1998), employers have shifted much of the well-being burden onto employees (Cederström and Spicer, 2015; McGillivray, 2005). The emphasis of workplace health has shifted from the industrial-age prevention of accidents (as in the 'fix it!' origins of occupational health) towards contemporary lifestyle scourges, such as obesity, diabetes and a range of chronic back problems. Within the neo-liberal social contract, the organization encourages and enables, but it is the individual who must deliver.

This individualised responsibility does not create an autonomous, fully self-sufficient agent, however. The neo-liberal subject may accept personal responsibility for health management, but simultaneously recognises the importance of seeking expert input and support. Contemporary understandings of health and well-being involve, therefore, an interesting discursive combination of self-discipline and external expertise, that is, a recognition of both the sovereignty and the limitations of personal agency (Maravelias, 2009). From this perspective, the 'healthy employee' is sufficiently self-disciplined to handle the freedom, choice and flexibility available in 21st century life (both in and out of organization), and simultaneously willing to be further educated in issues of lifestyle management (see also the connection between health, politics and learning in Chapter 5). So, the healthy self tends to be middle-class, elitist, respectful of the professional expertise of others, and to possess sufficient emotional, cognitive and financial resources to make good choices about healthy living (Crawford, 2006; Lupton, 1995; Zoller, 2003a, 2003b). The well-being identity, and all the self-control and self-discipline upon which it relies, works through flattery, ambition and aspiration.

Connected to this individualised responsibility for health is a blurring of the boundaries between 'work' and 'home' (Cederström and Spicer, 2015; Holliday and Thompson, 2001). The erasing of once quite clear and rigid boundaries between different domains is often presented in empowering, emancipating terms; for instance, in cutting down travel time, enabling people to work from home more often, and enjoy more flexible working patterns. However, critical organization scholars emphasise the potential cost of this move, in that the blurring of boundaries leaves one permanently 'at work' in one sense or another (see also Chapter 6 on the effects of technological developments on health). As McGillivray (2005) (p.133) puts it, 'the intensification of discourses of wellness seems to indicate the presence of an increasingly omnipresent gaze over the conduct of individuals' lives'. The politics of organization – and hence organizational health – is no longer something one can leave behind at the end of the working day. As we saw in the vignette about *Department X*'s 'Wellness at Work Week', health means feeling energised both at work and at home.

Thanem (2009) suggests that policy initiatives known as New Public Health (NPH) often rely on such individualisation, personalisation and boundary-breaching in campaigns to get the population to eat more fruit and vegetables; for instance, in the slogan that we should all eat 'Five a Day'. The politics of this discourse includes the construction of the Ideal Mother, who leads by example in her own eating habits, and ensures that her children eat healthily both at home and at school. Focusing on the responsibility of the mother is an interesting way to blur the boundary between these two institutions and to subtly shift responsibility for what happens at school, the public organization, into the more private, domestic realm of the home. Such campaigns are often fronted by celebrity mothers, who role-model not only what to eat but, more insidiously, *who to be*. They are reinforced through the provision of tool-kits for self-management, such as diary-templates to record one's progress each day against the healthy eating targets. This is Foucauldian bio-politics for the Celebrity Age.

As well as being committed to health management across both work and domestic spheres, the healthy individual is also well equipped to tackle the best-known, most-discussed health hazard in contemporary organizational life, namely stress. Stress is notoriously problematic to define, being cast sometimes as a stimulus from the environment (e.g., hostile or unpleasant conditions at work), and refined in the notion of stressors; at other times as a personal response or disposition in the face of challenging events or circumstances (e.g., being good – or not good – at handling stress); and in some cases, as an interaction between individual and environmental factors (Kinman and Jones, 2005; Sanders, 2001). Such is the lack of formal consensus about stress that some organizational scholars have questioned its continued usefulness as a construct for empirical research (Briner et al., 2004). In everyday constructions of health and well-being, however, stress remains an extremely powerful concept, probably precisely because of its lack of formal definitional clarity. Its vagueness makes it something that different stakeholders can appropriate for different purposes, in both conscious and unconscious power relations at work. Thus, for the purpose of this chapter, we want to highlight the bio-politics rather than the science of its construction.

Lewig and Dollard (2001) suggest that the social construction of workplace stress – as crystallised in the media – is of something that is largely caused by the organizational environment, yet down to the individual employee to manage. This pattern is replicated in studies of organizational practitioners' understandings of stress, such as Kinman and Jones (2005), who suggest that interpretations based on external, environmental causes outnumber interpretations based on internal personality or disposition factors by approximately 4:1. It is, therefore, not surprising to find that the majority of work-related stress-management interventions, such as training in relaxation techniques or cognitive reframing, appear to be focused on the individual (Hill et al., 2003b). Interestingly, whilst it is increasingly felt to be normal to experience stress at work, it is not usually deemed normal to show it (Harkness et al., 2005). In other words, the neo-liberal employee is not only required to suffer the effects of pressure from work; this suffering must be done in relative silence.

Moreover, the politics of stress may be more complex than simply the unfortunate consequences of ever-increasing workplace demands, which organizational practitioners may have come to accept as 'just the way things are'. Assumptions and interpretations of cause and effect may sometimes be deliberately manipulated to serve particular interests. For instance, Maravelias (2009) cites one of his research participants, an occupational health psychologist, who explains that stress is *deliberately framed* as a problem which is caused by external factors in order to persuade individuals to try to tackle it. Thus, the health practitioners in this particular study are guided by the belief that 'the individual is more likely to accept the problem if he or she does not feel responsible for having caused it. Once the individual has accepted the problem and the fact that change is required, we turn things around' (Maravelias, 2009) (p.199). In this example, responsibility for stress is not a naïve or casual misattribution of causality, but a calculated political manoeuvre, which is designed to make personal accountability more palatable.

Whether the source of stress for a particular person is actually something in the working environment, or just made to seem that way in order to lessen his or her defensiveness and resistance, the politics of responsibility for stress seems to accumulate in one simple meaning. As with Lord Kitchener's finger pointing accusingly towards the viewer, the message is: what are *you,* the individual employee, going to do about *your* stress?

We can, of course, only touch on the issue of stress in this chapter, and give a flavour for how a discursive, political approach to stress can raise questions that scientific and functionalist approaches do not. An enormous amount has been written about stress, both in and beyond the workplace, and readers are referred to works such as Briner and Reynolds (1999), Cooper et al. (2017) and Dewe et al. (2014), for more comprehensive overviews of the literature and the status of current debates.

## Human costs and freedoms

As we have suggested elsewhere in this book, absorbing responsibility for one's health and well-being can be a difficult emotional burden for a person to bear, both within and beyond organizational boundaries. It can lead to feelings of guilt, anxiety and shame when one experiences physical or emotional difficulties, because these mean that one has failed to mould oneself into the perfect specimen (Cederström and Spicer, 2015). The rhetoric of workplace health which encourages self-enhancement and self-improvement depends, at least to some extent, on the individual being made to feel dissatisfied with his or her current or previous self. For instance, Zoller critiques one particular example of a health promotion message, which emphasises that it is 'Time for a New You' (Zoller, 2003b) (p.188). If it *is* time for a 'New You', then this implies that the 'Old You' was therefore inadequate in some way! The manufacturing of personal dissatisfaction is thus a key tactic in health promotion, whether or not it is conscious or deliberate. It highlights that we rarely, if ever, experience organizational messages which tell us that we are fine exactly the way we are!

Much of the contemporary rhetoric of health focuses on creating hyper-awareness of what we put into our mouths. Dissatisfaction with the 'Old You' is thereby linked to an obsession about what we eat. The 'healthy employee' is constructed as a kind of anorexic, terrified of consuming the wrong sort of nutrition and hence becoming the wrong sort of person. As Cederström and Spicer (2015) (p.7) suggest:

> Eating has become a paranoid activity, which is not just intended to bring momentary pleasures through taste. It puts your identity to the test. Eating correctly is thought to be a way to cook up a happy and prosperous life, free from stress and despair. To eat correctly is an achievement, which demonstrates your superior life-skills.

Many of the corporate messages that we have illustrated in the case studies and vignettes in this book suggest that changes in lifestyle will somehow make employees healthier in a much broader sense, that is, according to moral, ethical and existential, not just physiological criteria. This involves a potentially devastating manipulation of employees' emotions, anxieties and dissatisfactions, all under the seemingly benign banner heading of health and well-being. As we suggested earlier, the contingency of this health morality emerges especially powerfully in changing attitudes towards smoking over the past 30 years or so, as an emphasis on the (unhealthy) activity of smoking has given way to moral messages about smokers as (immoral) people (Brewis and Grey, 2008). The employee who fails to attain optimum health is not just physiologically disadvantaged, but morally suspect too.

As Lupton (1995) (p.90) suggests, if health messages are given and health services provided, then those who are vulnerable to poor health 'become the sinners, not the sinned against, because of their apparent *voluntary* courting of risk' [our italics]. Thus, the unhealthy employee can be cast as a wilful outlaw as much as an anxiety-ridden discursive blotting-paper, because discourses can be resisted as well as absorbed. Critical organizational scholars highlight that bio-power is an enmeshment of power and resistance (Foucault, 1980), particularly those who draw on Foucault's later work on the self-constitution of the ethical subject and technologies of subjectivity, such as care of the self (e.g., Crane et al., 2008; Ladkin, 2018) (see also Chapter 3).

In the face of constructions of health at work, resistance can involve the individual employee refusing to recognise particular health assertions ('I refuse to accept that drinking alcohol every evening causes problems'); or can mean that he or she recognises the health risk but decides to engage in the risky behaviour anyway ('I realise that my drinking is causing a problem, but I simply don't care') (McGillivray, 2005). Both refusal (as a form of denial) and rebellion (as a more active form of resistance) may be facilitated through competing discourses or counter-narratives of selfhood, which provide alternative ways of being that do not rely on the self-denial and self-control of the neo-liberal well-being injunction. Health discourses may, therefore, lose out to consumerist discourses, which encourage people to enjoy a vast array of hedonistic pleasures (Rose, 2007), and/or to fantasies of immortality (Schwartz, 1992), which can justify all sorts of risky behaviours if we think we can get away with them and 'dodge a bullet'.

Just as earlier we referenced Ezzamel et al.'s (2001) classic study of resistance to mechanistic, engineered identity positions, so resistance can be directed towards any discourse in play, including the discourses of health and organization that we have used to structure this book. However, resistance does not necessarily involve the construction of strong, authentic maverick selves – a somewhat romantic notion of the rebel or anti-hero who stands firm in the face of corporate pressures and incursions. Instead, the multiple identity possibilities which are said to characterise 21st century lives might be flattering and motivational to some people sometimes, but unsettling and demotivational to other people at other times. Resistance can thereby be seen as part of the insecurity of the contemporary workplace, where people struggle to work out 'who they are' in an ongoing, dialectical project of identification-resistance across subject positions which are fluid, contradictory and ambiguous (Kondo, 2009). The resistant self is thus no more coherent, authentic or powerful than the conformist blotting-paper self (Collinson, 2003).

### Individual versus organizational health: Synergy or antagonism?

At the outset of this book, we said that one of the most interesting debates in workplace health revolves around the assumption of a synergy between individual and organizational health. Before we even explore, let alone accept or reject, such a synergy, it is worth pausing to reflect on the very possibility of one side of this equation; namely, the very notion of 'organizational health'. From a critical perspective, we would do well to reflect on the assumptions upon which such a construction relies, whose interests it best serves, and what tactics are deployed to create and sustain it. Once these have been exposed to critical scrutiny, we can consider whether, and how, organizational health might be related, either positively or negatively, to the health of the individual employee.

In everyday work-talk, as well as in many management and organizational development textbooks, it has become 'common sense' that there is such a thing as 'organizational health'. When we encounter the term, we tend to find it used as a heuristic, which invokes and refers to a range of things that must interact and intersect for the organization to function well. From here, it is easy to accept a basically positive relationship between 'healthy' functioning at individual and organizational levels. In its crudest sense, this relationship refers to the idea that employees who are physically present, fit, able and willing are more likely to do what they are supposed to do, and the organization will therefore function as it is designed to function. In contrast, employees who are sick or absent are not able to function efficiently, if at all, and hence the organization cannot operate at full efficiency either. This tends to cast health in relatively mechanistic and functionalist terms, of course, rather than any broader sense of health as flourishing or good living (see the basic contrast in Chapters 1 and 2); but if individual health is conceptualized in terms of the well-oiled, functioning part, then it is not much of a stretch to accept organizational health conceptualized symbiotically in terms of the well-oiled, functioning whole.

As we have sought to demonstrate throughout this book, however, as soon as we broaden the metaphorical field to incorporate discourses of organization as organism, family, brain, school, competitive sporting arena, etc., and discourses of humanity as growth, meaning-making, self-care, quality of relationship, life purpose, desire for belonging, etc., we find that this functionalist notion of health as the absence of sickness or repair of breakdown is only one way to understand health at work. We have suggested that the workplace is rife with clashes of construction – or mixed metaphors – that is, different concepts or images being paired or combined which do not always mesh easily, and which can have a profound effect on how we understand and promote health (as in the example of 'experience architect' for the contemporary human resources practitioner, or 're-engineering' through yoga or mindfulness).

In a sense, the very notion of 'organizational health' is a construction clash or mixed metaphor, because it pairs something that is fundamentally associated with being alive (health) with something which is pretty much 'dead' (organization), i.e., only 'human' by virtue of the fact that human beings work in and for it. The idea of 'organizational health' is therefore similar to the notion of 'institutional feelings' (or for that matter, 'experience architecture'), i.e., something which is clearly juxtaposing different *kinds* of things – not even apples versus oranges, but something like apples versus pencils. Indeed, the more one reflects upon this sort of pairing, the odder it probably seems. Institutions clearly do not have feelings (the people who work in them do, but the institutions themselves cannot); so how on earth could an organization experience 'health'?

Attributes of health help to anthropomorphise and civilise organization, because health is so unimpeachably a 'good thing' (Haunschild, 2003), that is, both human and humane. The very construction of 'organizational health' serves to maximise the positive valence of organization, and thereby usually serves the interests of leaders and other powerful stakeholders. It can be deployed, whether consciously or unconsciously, to distract attention away from the sometimes dehumanising effects of working life and leadership decisions. It is, after all, much easier for stakeholders, especially the relatively powerless, to 'buy in' to an initiative associated with 'health' than it is to accept one labelled as being about 'efficiency' or 'productivity' or 'competitive positioning'; and yet the contents and objectives of such organizational initiatives may well be quite similar.

The rhetoric of 'organizational health' can therefore be a potent legitimizing strategy, serving to make difficult decisions easier to implement, and not necessarily having anything to do with 'health' as we would normally understand it at the level of the individual human being. As Stein (2001) suggests, such legitimising strategies are effectively an assault on meaning, which privileges the logic of the bottom-line and clothes it in the most palatable language available. Labelling an initiative with the language of organizational health as opposed to, say, organizational redundancies, is akin to using the language of 'rightsizing' as opposed to 'downsizing', or calling the approach to employee relations 'counselling out' as opposed to 'firing'. Thus, the concept and construct of 'organizational health' is perhaps the most formidable example of a mixed metaphor in contemporary organizational practice. That the idea of an organization experiencing 'health' can pass by us in everyday organizational talk relatively unremarked is a phenomenal discursive and ideological achievement. From a critical perspective, therefore, we should maintain a certain scepticism about the very possibility of 'organizational health' in any analysis of the relationship between individual and organizational health.

In most of the practitioner literature, however, the concept of 'organizational health' is accepted relatively unchallenged. This acceptance sets the scene for the possibility of a synergy between individual and organizational health, that is, that what is good for the organization ought to be good for the individual, and vice versa (Bennis, 1962; Brache, 2001; Herzberg, 1974). For instance, Rosen and Berger (1991) discuss the 'healthy company', and posit a range of criteria which must be satisfied from both an overall organizational perspective and an individual employee perspective for a company to enjoy good organizational health. Thus, practices of open communication, employee involvement, learning and renewal, fairness and diversity, *inter alia,* bring about both individual and collective well-being (Rosen and Berger, 1991). In a related vein, Cox and Leiter (1992) see organizational health as unfolding in the degree of consistency between the 'objective organization', that is, how the organization really is, and the 'subjective organization', that is, how practitioners and other stakeholders perceive it to be. Organizational health may therefore be 'in the eye of the beholder', at least in part, but the possibility of its attainment is not really in question.

This assumption of synergy between individual and organizational health has helped to stoke the enormous popularity of workplace health and well-being initiatives over the past few decades, because it helps to create a sense of 'win-win'. Both organization and employee 'win' when health is good, that is, allocated its rightful place on our lists of priorities. Where a perfect symbiosis of the two levels of health may not be possible, that is, where a potential difference in interests and/or levels of analysis between organization and individual *is* acknowledged, the language of synergy and equivalence often morphs into the language of *balance* (MacIntosh et al., 2007). Thus, the factors which create good organizational health may not always be identical to those associated with good individual health, but in models based on balance, there is a sense of compromise or 'give and take'. The overall idea of health becomes a hybrid, in which both human and non-human, both powerful and relatively powerless, have their needs addressed at least some of the time.

Whether cast as symbiosis (co-constructive and mutually dependent) or balance (co-existing but in some form of compromise and negotiation), the idea that the relationship between individual and organizational health is basically a positive one is fuelled by the language used to represent health. When looking at the language of organizational health, in particular, we find a huge range of meanings and connotations, often very vague and more aspirational than descriptive. This vagueness allows notions of health to be blended with a range of other descriptors of successful organizational functioning. For example, in the vignette below (Box 7.2), organizational health is equated with a range of attributes that would strike one as very odd if they really *were* applied to issues of human health.

---

## BOX 7.2 CASE STUDY: THE *ANOTHER CONSULTING* ORGANIZATIONAL HEALTH MAP© (OHM©)

Our Organizational Health Map© (OHM©) provides a simple but effective road map for leaders to drive enhanced performance. You can use the map to benchmark your own organizational health against the health of your competitors, both public and private sector. Tracking your health against these metrics will help you to identify priority action areas for health check-ups and design interventions to catch health issues early.

The OHM© is evidence-based, and endorsed by world-class behavioural scientists. It is founded on proven links between the four dimensions of health and performance:

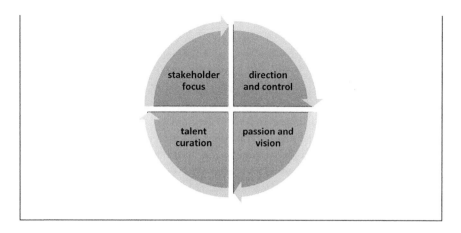

This example may seem to represent the worst possible corporate jargon, but it is not unusual for organizational strategy and consultancy work. Although we have mocked up this vignette in order to preserve the anonymity of the organization from which it derives, it is neither too far removed from the original, nor all that unusual in contemporary organizational practice. What is noteworthy for present purposes, of course, is the way in which it suborns understandings of health by equating health with key issues of organizational performance, such as vision, values and processes of talent management. The components of organizational health are thus morphed with those of organizational delivery and success. We wager that the more readers pause to reflect on this, the odder it will seem to have health operationalised in terms of, say, 'stakeholder focus'. If one asked a fellow human being about the state of their health, would they ever really answer by referencing 'stakeholder focus'?!

At the level of individual health, there is a similar linguistic and conceptual blurring. In the vignette about *Department X*'s 'Wellness at Work Week' earlier in this chapter, we found health being equated with feeling energised. This dovetails with arguments from Dale and Burrell (2014), who propose that organizational messages often elide 'wellness' and 'willingness', that is, being well means being fully committed to participating in organizational activities, in furtherance of organizational goals. Maravelias (2009) notes a similar elision between well-being and flexibility, wherein organizational messages present a picture of flexibility as a positive for employees (teeing up notions of choice, agency, variety, etc.), whilst subtly reinforcing flexibility as an organizational benefit (i.e., related to cost control, the provision of insecure employment models, such as zero-hour contracts, etc.). Through a conflation of notions of well-being and flexibility, health promotion programmes 'subtly distinguish those employees who have career potential from those who do not, and they contribute to making up self-governing subjects who flexibly adapt their lifestyles to the criteria of health, well-being and professional success' (Maravelias, 2009) (p.194).

Whilst the practitioner literature tends to assume a positive correlation between individual and organizational health (at least as an objective, if not as a given), scholars writing from more critical perspectives have challenged such an assumption. For instance, MacIntosh et al. (2007) suggest that efforts to improve organizational health can have inadvertently detrimental effects on individual health. They highlight a particular tension when organizational health is conceived in terms of an organization's ability to cope with change and complexity, but individual health is compromised by the chaos and uncertainty that accompany such change and complexity-management initiatives. With a clash between an organization's need for agility and flexibility and an individual's need for at least a degree of stability, organizational health may improve whilst individual health deteriorates.

In a further twist, investments and initiatives designed to improve individual health may not always have the desired effect on organizational health. In a consultancy project one of us recently undertook, we found that 'sports hours' that were scheduled during employees' lunchtimes, and which they were actively encouraged to attend, often overestimated employees' physical fitness levels and therefore pushed them to do far too much, far too quickly. As a result, many employees would be distracted from work during the afternoon, because they were suffering with aches, pains and exhaustion! They may well have been on a 'journey towards wellness' (as the promotional blurb promised), but in the short term, at least, it was the organization's 'health' that suffered!

Whether organizational health compromises individual health or, vice versa, individual health compromises organizational health; there is perhaps an assumption that this disconnect is usually inadvertent, that is, simply one of those unfortunate consequences of the complexities of organizational life. For Gabriel (2012), however, organizational well-being is not just *inadvertently* incompatible with individual well-being, it may at times be *necessarily* so. Writing from a psychodynamic perspective, he elaborates the notion of miasma as a way of reflecting a toxic state of organizational affairs, especially during periods of transformational change. In one particular (and, in our view, very typical) case study, organizational health is associated with a glossy new image and the rhetoric of being excellent, world-leading, cutting-edge, vibrant, etc., and with a marketing campaign which included a vilification of the past and fetishization of the future. Against this backdrop of ambition, individual employees were made to feel inadequate and depressed, as criticism from outside (including from so-called 'change agents') morphed into self-criticism and feelings of personal disgust, uncleanliness and worthlessness. For such a radical revamping of the organization to be necessary, their previous work and their previous contributions must surely have been dreadfully inadequate.

Gabriel (2012) suggests that this dynamic reflects and reproduces a conceptualisation of organizational health which *requires* a certain amount of individual unhealth. He connects with Stein (2001) in suggesting that organizations require human sacrifice, and the removal of 'sick' employees is part of a ritual of cleansing and purification. Comparing corporate cleansing with ethnic cleansing, he explains that 'the religion of the "bottom line" requires sacrifices to purify the body of the organization from the ineffective and those who fail to add value' (Gabriel, 2012) (p.1144). The health of the organization is thus associated with making tough decisions about who adds value and who does not. As a result, employees are made to feel increasingly depressed, inadequate and unclean, and the 'sickest' of them will probably leave, thereby helping to purify and decontaminate the organization they leave behind. This construction of unhealth as a failure to add value bears a certain resemblance to Riach and Kelly's (2015) elaboration of the organization-as-vampire, with its incessant need for fresh blood and its creation of sacrificial victims – usually older workers – to allow the organization to regenerate (see also Chapter 4 on connections between age and health).

Ultimately, such purification efforts are probably counterproductive. The more an organization attempts to self-cleanse by excising its pollutants, the 'sicker' it becomes. Scapegoating, defensiveness and the emergence of a blame culture are the usual and understandable consequences when the needs of the organization are set so diametrically at odds with those of the human beings within it, and individual sacrifices are required to purify and cleanse the whole. What is so startling about this line of argument is that disconnects between individual and organizational health are no longer seen as accidental, innocent or simply unfortunate; the construction and expulsion of 'unhealthy' employees is now part of the strategy of the organization.

## Concluding thoughts: Politics as meta-discourse

At the start of this chapter, we explained that we were following Morgan (2007) in considering the organization-as-political system as a specific metaphor in and of itself, but that this exploration of the political dimension of organizational health was also a culmination of the themes discussed in other chapters and therefore a crystallisation of our approach overall. In this sense, we are treating the organization-as-political system as something of a meta-discourse, in that it is not just these *particular* organizational discourses (machine, organism, family, brain, school, competition, etc.) that effect the conceptualisation of health, but the politics of *discourses per se*. In Morgan's (2007) language, we have moved through metaphors (i.e., specific frames or prisms through which to view organization) to metaphor (i.e., a way of thinking about organization which is by definition critical, because it recognises that any perspective is partial, foregrounding and privileging some understandings over others).

From this broader perspective, the partiality and contingency of *any* elaboration of health can be seen as a political manoeuvre. Our view of health is contingent on the prism through which we are looking, and our choice of prism (or the choice made for us by writers and speakers on organization) involves privileging some interests over others. Where these interests seem to intersect or mesh easily, the language we use to describe and promote health tends to go unnoticed. Where they diverge, however, the result can be overt mixed messages or more covert feelings of disjunction or discomfort that something is odd about the way a particular health question or initiative is being framed.

Whether overt or covert, this contest over meaning constitutes much of the fabric of our everyday understandings of the workplace and what it means to operate and/or thrive there. We have seen how discourses of mechanistic efficiency often jostle with those of effectiveness, adaptability, growth and meaning-making in our constructions of health at work, in the same way as popular sayings such as 'if it ain't broke, don't fix it' clearly come from a different metaphorical lexicon to expressions such as 'just go with the flow', 'it's time to raise your game', or success means having 'skin in the game'. Indeed, we have suggested that even the well-worn expression 'health and safety' contains an inherent construction-clash between different underlying metaphors, and that this is highlighted when one juxtaposes the notions of health-as-safety and health-as-lifestyle (Allender et al., 2006).

Clashes of construction operate not only between different metaphors or images, such as the machine versus the organism in our 'fix it!' versus 'flourish!' comparison (Chapters 1 and 2). They also produce and expose the workings of power, that is, different ways of conceptualising health can serve different stakeholders' interests. Thus, as we have suggested in this chapter, the very idea of 'organizational health' might be said to comprise a mixed metaphor, that is, a contradiction between something human and something non-human. It is perhaps also a clash between different interests or levels of analysis, in the sense of a tension between the relatively powerful and the relatively powerless.

From the perspective of politics as meta-discourse, therefore, we see the question of the definition of health and well-being as a political as much as a scientific issue. We sympathise with those who are frustrated with the lack of definitional clarity of well-being in particular, but suggest that efforts to pin down an exact definition which is 'simple, universal in application, optimistic and a basis for measurement' (Dodge et al., 2012) (p.222), are necessarily reductionist and, as such, contribute only superficially to any sustained efforts to understand, let alone improve, people's working lives. Understandings of health are contingent on perspective, and we see that not as a failure of scientific definition, but as a reminder that health and well-being have a very considerable subjective element. What feels healthy for you might not feel so healthy for me. One person's stress is another person's adrenalin rush. One person's mindfulness and self-care is another person's failure to roll up their sleeves and get on with it.

This also applies to efforts to clarify any distinctions between health and well-being. At the outset, we suggested that well-being was probably associated in most people's minds with a sense of health beyond the purely physical or physiological, incorporating psychological, emotional, even existential factors.

Now, through the prism of organization-as-political system, we would also suggest that a good question would be: who benefits from this apparent shift of language and focus from health to well-being, that is, from the prevention of illness and accidents to the promotion and fostering of lifestyle? If one looks around the contemporary workplace, it is hard to avoid the army of lifestyle consultants, fitness gurus, personal trainers, yoga masters and mindfulness practitioners, etc., all of whom owe their financial success to the construction of well-being as a serious issue to address, rather than a more physiological understanding of health. Well-being is big business, covering a broader range of services than a purely physiological approach to the prevention or treatment of illness.

Just as we seek to politicise rather than fix issues of definition, we also want to suggest that the question of effectiveness is a political issue too. A large body of work is focused on the attempt to evaluate the effectiveness of organizational health interventions (e.g., Nielsen and Randall, 2015; Richardson and Rothstein, 2008), but we believe that many of these efforts would benefit from a more critical sensibility. With such a sensibility, the answer to the question 'does this health initiative work?' is: 'it depends what you mean by health', and for that matter, 'it also depends on what you mean by work'. In other words, how can we evaluate the success of an initiative or intervention unless or until we understand the assumptions of both organization and health which underpin it? If we ask, for instance, whether *Department X*'s 'Wellness at Work Week' has actually 'worked', what do we really mean? By which criteria are we assessing wellness? In whose interests would any such wellness improvements actually lie? And whom would we blame if we concluded that the initiative had not been a success?

In problematizing the desire to standardise and measure workplace health initiatives, we are not saying that we should abandon all efforts to enhance health at work, or that there is no point in trying to approach health issues systematically or methodically, or with the hope of spending corporate money wisely. We are simply sharing the reflections from our own experience that we should not rely too much on 'tool-kits' or the latest fad or gimmick, because these tend to imply that there is a uniformly-accepted set of desirable health outcomes and a tried and tested recipe for achieving them. We believe that the best investments in health at work come not from hankering after definitional exactitude or one-size-fits-all solutions, but from inspiring critical reflection and conversation, and surfacing the tensions and challenges that *any* focus on human health will probably evoke.

In sum, therefore, we see health and well-being as chameleons, which shift according to perspective, interest, language and level of analysis. On the whole, we would suggest that this linguistic slipperiness and lack of conceptual clarity tends to serve institutional over individual interests, that is, it suggests the workings of asymmetrical power relations. Whichever metaphor of organization we use, therefore, the questions we pose about the construction of health are profoundly political ones.

# 8

# CONCLUSIONS AND CONSEQUENCES

In this chapter, we summarise the key metaphors and other discursive framing devices we have explored in this book, and crystallise their implications for health and well-being in organizational life. Specifically, we:

- Review the effects of discourses of machine, organism, family, competition, reinvention, cyberspace, and power on understandings of the healthy and unhealthy employee.
- Summarise the implications of these discourses for the design of well-being interventions, and the assumptions of successful organizational functioning which they create, reflect, and legitimise.
- Consider how the more concrete and well-established metaphors have an enduring power and visual immediacy, which may clash with emergent, looser organizational affiliations and configurations.
- Argue for the practical value of increased awareness of metaphor in general, and mixed metaphor in particular, so that we can challenge those taken-for-granted ideas and expressions which may have unfortunate or unintended consequences for how we treat both ourselves and each other in all domains of institutional life.

## Implications of metaphors for health

For decades, organizational scholars have engaged in debate about whether metaphors and other devices of analogy and association are a tool of creativity and liberation, or a means of manipulation and oppression. Some warn against the seductive power of metaphors to obfuscate the true rationale and impact of organizational change initiatives, especially those that will result in less advantageous and/or less secure employment. Thus, even in the early, relatively innocent, days of the change management movement, Sinclair (1994) warns against the rhetorical skill of management consultants to manipulate employees into embracing the latest change initiative through judicious use of metaphors of organizational correctness, e.g., through the concept of 'rightsizing'. Such discourses of correctness help to reify organizational strategies, decisions, and processes, so that an initiative starts to feel inevitable; and such inevitability makes it possible to persuade people that change is for their own good, even when it clearly is not (Sinclair, 1994). Indeed, Tinker (1986) famously argues that metaphors create a 'false consciousness' which inoculates organizations against critique and locks employees in a permanent state of disadvantage, and hence unhealth.

Others emphasise the productive power of metaphor to generate and test out new ways of seeing things (e.g., Bolman and Deal, 1991; Morgan, 2007; Örtenblad et al., 2016; Tsoukas, 1991). For instance, Jermier and Forbes (2016) use Morgan's organization as an instrument of domination metaphor to problematize the relationship between humans, institutions, and water. They highlight the politics and the limitations of our taken-for-granted assumption that 'water management' organizations are there to harness water and control water distribution, suggesting that this reflects the workings of the instrument of domination metaphor and casts both suppliers and their customers as 'water exploiters'. They suggest an alternative notion of 'water keeper' to highlight the possibility of a different, non-exploitative and less anthropocentric relationship with water, which 'brings needed attention to water problems and invites further research on activist organizations (businesses and others) seeking to change thinking and practice related to environmental sustainability' (Jermier and Forbes, 2016) (p.1001). Notwithstanding that even 'water keeper' sustains a kind of soft anthropocentrism that still sees humans and their organizations as both separate and superior to nature, the authors suggest that a shift, indeed, *any* shift, in the discursive repertoire will surely mark the beginnings of a change in attitudes and behaviours towards the environment.

Over the course of this book, we hope to have persuaded readers that discourses of organization can operate in both senses. They can be both a spur to rethink and reframe the possibilities of organization and a means of manipulating people into accepting, even believing, what they otherwise might not. We think that becoming aware of their power and presence is an important aspect of organizational experience and an important part of the mission of critical organizational scholarship. This applies both to those discourses with a strong material element, such as the developments in cyberspace we explored in Chapter 6, and to those with a stronger visual, conceptual and/or analogical aspect, such as those which derive from Morgan's (2007) eight images of organization, and from other classic works on metaphor, e.g., Lakoff and Johnson (2003). We hope to have captured the potential of metaphor to be both productive and restrictive in the table below (Box 8.1), which summarises the implications of the core discourses of this book for our constructions, understandings and meanings of health.

## BOX 8.1 DISCOURSES OF ORGANIZATION AND THEIR CONSEQUENCES FOR HEALTH

| Discourse of organization | Construction of the healthy employee | Construction of the unhealthy employee | Construction of employee well-being interventions | Assumptions about organizational health |
|---|---|---|---|---|
| **Machine** | Cog in the wheel; fully operational & maximally efficient; physically interconnected | Broken; not fit for purpose | Fix & repair breakdowns & restore functioning; replace with better models; deal with sickness (diagnostic expertise) | Organizational health is equated with efficiency, predictability, delivery & measurable output |
| **Organism** | Living creature with needs & potential; health means growth & flourishing | Stunted; soon to be extinct | Cultivate growth, development & adjustment to new ways & ideas; cure sickness (healing) | Organizational health is equated with flexibility, effectiveness, adaptability to changing environment |
| **Family** | Cherished child who belongs & feels wanted; young adult preparing to become self-sufficient | Outcast; waif | Foster feelings of belonging; balance strict guardianship with a softer version which addresses people's needs, especially in times of trouble | Organizational health is equated with ability to recognise when human needs come before business needs; discourses of self-care let organizations off the hook |
| **Competition** | Corporate athlete; fit & primed to perform; young | Unfit or unenergetic; uncompetitive in multiple senses; old | Coach & motivate for performance; offer opportunities to fix the unhealthy body, but within the constraints of age-related stereotypes; encourage people to embrace activity to avoid decline in performance | Organizational health is equated with being the winning team; high individual & collective performance is celebrated, but the older or unfit employee is problematic |
| **Reinvention** | Learner engaged in continuous self-renewal; agent of | Uncommitted to self- | Promote learning as the route to well-being as | Organizational health is equated with continuous |

| | | | | |
|---|---|---|---|---|
| | his/her own well-being | improvement; unruly pupil | (a) self-fulfilment, (b) relief from anxiety & fear of blame, & (c) material & psychological security via employability | innovation, self-renewal and self-improvement; the healthy organization is co-constructed with the learning organization |
| **Cyberspace** | Super-user; accessible & contactable; completely & continually known & knowable; digitally interconnected | Disconnected; resistant luddite; out of touch | Reboot, upgrade & refresh; provide technological support to improve health; predict individual needs via big data analytics; eradicate resistance to new technology | Organizational health is equated with progressive technological innovation & technologized capabilities |
| **Power** | Neo-liberal self-disciplining subject, able to make good lifestyle choices, & manage accompanying guilt & self-blame | Anarchist or sinner | Facilitate well-being opportunities, which an employee is free to choose or ignore; promote personal responsibility & choice for lifestyle enhancement; encourage the dissolution of boundaries between home & work | Organizational health and individual health are co-constructed so that what seems good for the individual is also good for the organization; health is strongly associated with lifestyle choices |

Like Marshak (1996), we argue that greater sensitivity to the discourses 'in play' in the workplace does not have to mean a radical overthrow of an organization's meaning system; simply that such sensitivity will allow us to recognise their sources and their effects, and hence create the possibility of reframing how we think and talk both about work in general and about health at work in particular. As Latusek and Vlaar (2015) suggest, exploring the ways in which people capture, visualise, and crystallise their experiences of organization, e.g., through the taken-for-granted language of playing games, fighting and winning battles, and performing acts, is a useful way to bridge an apparent scholar-practitioner gap, allowing academics to 'translate abstract constructs and variables into specific acts or behaviours that practitioners can take hold of and change in the real world' (Latusek and Vlaar, 2015) (p.16).

At the outset of this book, we explained that we were grounding our discussion in discourses of organization, and focusing our attention on the different ways in which the meanings of, and priorities for, employee health (and unhealth) emerge, depending on which of these contrasting constructions of organization is in play. This meant that our key framing mechanism was the relatively concrete 'organization', rather than the somewhat more abstract notions of 'work', 'employment', 'career', etc. This was despite the fact that not everyone works as an employee for an employer (as traditionally understood), and new technologies are enabling new patterns of work and new possibilities for the economic and psychological relationship between individual and institution, including various forms of self-employment.

Concrete notions of organization lend themselves particularly well to the more concrete metaphors (machine, brain, etc.), which are relatively simple to grasp and therefore have phenomenal heuristic value. However, as the world of organized work changes, the metaphorical lexicon is changing with it (see also Lupton, 2018, in this series). Thus, it may well be that the solidity and concreteness of the machine or the brain is giving way to more fluid ways of representing organizational life. For instance, Morgan's (2007) own attempt to condense organizational change via the metaphor of flux and transformation is much less vivid and successful as a metaphor, but is perhaps a more resonant reflection of a world of *organizing* rather than *organization* (Robichaud and Cooren, 2013; Weick, 1979). Many theorists highlight the risk of strongly concrete metaphors, because they foster a 'taken-for-granted tangibility' (Boud and Hager, 2012) (p.18) which, in the case of the association of the brain with organizational learning, for instance, makes learning a thing that is acquired and transferred rather than more emergent, relational notions of learning experiences, relationships, processes, struggles, etc.

The concrete metaphors of organization persist, however, in part because they are easier to *visualise*. The significance of the visual for constructing, as well as representing, working experience is attracting increasing attention in organization studies (see, for instance, Bell et al., 2014; Meyer et al., 2013). Visuals can be approached archeologically, that is, as artefacts that contain and store collective understandings of a particular community or institution; they can be used strategically, that is, as symbolic devices that are deployed to manipulate stakeholders' responses to particular events or decisions; and they can be seen as dialogical, that is, as prompts for collective sense-making, communication, and the creation of mutual understanding about health and the myriad ways in which our experiences of organization seem to foster, inhibit or ignore it.

Crucially for our discussion of concrete versus more fluid metaphors, visuals seem to capture a central message more readily than linguistic text, which can be interpreted in multiple different ways. Thus, the visual:

> Implies greater facticity, eliminating predication and logical conjunction, disguising itself as information, rather than argument, and as an accurate

map of the world rather than a construction of reality, thus enhancing its coerciveness (even though such coerciveness is never made explicit).

*(Meyer et al., 2013) (p.6)*

From this perspective, metaphors such as the machine and brain persist, in part, because their concreteness and visual immediacy give them this semblance of accuracy and facticity. As we said at the start, how often do we really pause to reflect on the metaphorical basis of mechanistic expressions such as 'blowing a fuse' or 'running out of steam'? And yet we all seem to know exactly and unambiguously what they mean and how they feel.

The most pragmatic reason for our emphasis on concrete 'organization' over more abstract notions of, say, 'work', is that we wanted to address the 'so what?' question by suggesting the relevance of these ideas for health practice and policy, especially in the domain of human resources and organization develop-ment. Thus, foregrounding organization as our central unit of analysis allows us to relate these discussions to the domain where such practices and policies are most likely to be developed and applied, namely the world of organization-based employment, which we have attempted to bring to life in part through our three case studies in this book.

We think it is a priority for both theorists and practitioners to develop an alertness to the discursive underpinnings of so much of our talk about health at work. We would all do well, for instance, to pause and reflect when we reach *automatically* for words such as 'tool-kit' or 'fix', and thereby both invoke and reinforce mechanistic notions of both health and selfhood. If we talk about 'fixing things', we are surely less likely to be sensitive to people's emotions or quest for meaning than if we use concepts from other, more humanistic registers. Similarly, the idea of a 'skills refresh' now feels an almost axiomatic way of describing and promoting a new training pro-gramme, but it both reflects and reinforces a digitisation of our life-worlds, in which human well-being becomes a matter of reboot and control-alt-delete. Or, when the word 'performance' trips off the tongue as a taken-for-granted organizational objective, it feels genuinely helpful to stop and reflect on the assumptions of competitive excellence and rivalry that underpin meta-phors of competition and sport, as well as the other discursive framings in which 'performance' is vital, such as the theatre, with its requirement for play-acting and make-believe. Words like 'tool-kit', 'refresh', and 'perform-ance' are part of the fabric of everyday work-talk, but they carry a deeper set of connotations that can have a profound effect on how we see the possi-bilities for, and constraints on, human welfare.

To support such a critical and constructive engagement with health at work, we offer some ideas for discussions that readers might have with their col-leagues and their sources of health expertise, both in and beyond organization (Box 8.2).

---

## BOX 8.2 QUESTIONS FOR CRITICAL CONVERSATIONS ABOUT HEALTH AT WORK

- When considering a particular health message, what base metaphor or image is being invoked in this particular description, or injunction, of health?
- How does this base metaphor or image make you feel about your health?
- Whose interests are best served through this prism or framing?
- Whose interests are therefore relegated?
- What are the effects of such privileging and prioritising on the people who encounter these constructions, arguments, and the material practicalities that stem from them?
- What linguistic tactics and techniques are used to give life and legitimacy to these ways of viewing the world of work and the experiences of health? How do they gain their 'taken for granted' or 'common sense' status?
- Whose interests (including financial interests) are served by using the language of 'well-being' as opposed to 'health'?
- What are the results of this shift of language? Does it shift the locus of responsibility?
- What other words are being associated with health (both as 'organizational health' and as 'individual health'), and what are the effects of these associations on our understanding of health (and/or its absence)?
- When health is said to refer to the organization as a whole, what is the relationship between this kind of health and health as something experienced by the individual human being?

---

As we have argued and sought to illustrate throughout this book, organizations are the space for multiple clashes of construction and for mismatches between organizational discourse, health intervention, and health experience. When health initiatives are designed and promoted based on a mixing of metaphors, such as a mingling of re-engineering with personal growth, fixing with flourishing, or performance with belonging, it is no wonder they attract ridicule (as in the idea of human resources professionals as 'experience architects', or firing someone being framed as 'counselling out'); or at least fail to gain the traction for which their designers had hoped (Grant and Marshak, 2011). As we suggested in Chapter 7 on politics and health, construction clash can be part of an organization's legitimising strategy for unpleasant, even unethical actions, and thus represent what Stein (2001) sees as an assault on meaning. Readers will have drawn their own conclusions, of course, about how consciously or unconsciously construction clash is deployed in the organizational settings which they themselves encounter.

Whether you are an organizational health practitioner, human resources professional, leader, employee, scholar or student, or indeed, all or none of the above, we hope that this book has encouraged you to interrogate your own assumptions about health and well-being – both your own and that of the people with whom you work. The next time you come across a piece of organizational communication such as the one below (Box 8.3), perhaps you will feel inspired to unpack its web of construction, and explore any discursive tensions which might have implications for what we mean by health and how we might go about improving it. In this case, two different notions of space (or rather, a shortage of it) reflect very different assumptions about the priorities for action. In a single missive, organization both opens up and closes down the space for health!

---

## BOX 8.3  CASE STUDY: A POSTING ON THE INTERNAL WEBSITE AT *DEPARTMENT X*

Worried about your mental health? Finding it difficult to carve out space for some 'me-time', and get things back into perspective?

Come along to one of our seminars on emotional resilience and well-being. There you will learn techniques for stress management, and be introduced to tools to help you manage your stress levels.

The seminars are free to *Department X* employees, and attendance will be strictly confidential.

To book a place, please go to the *Department X* Wellness portal.
Hurry! Spaces are limited and filling up fast!

---

# REFERENCES

Acemoglu, D. & Restrepo, P. (2017). Robots and jobs: Evidence from US labor markets. NBER Working Paper No. w23285. Available at SSRN: https://ssrn.com/abstract=2941263.

Aguiar, L.L. & Herod, A. (Eds.) (2006). *The dirty work of neoliberalism: Cleaners in the global economy.* Oxford: Blackwell.

Allender, S., Colquhoun, D. & Kelly, P. (2006). Competing discourses of workplace health. *Health, 10*(1), 75–93.

Alqithami, S. & Hexmoor, H. (2014). Plasticity in network organizations. *JACIII, 18*(4), 567–572.

Alvesson, M. & Karreman, D. (2000). Varieties of discourse: On the study of organizations through discourse analysis. *Human Relations, 53*(9), 1125–1149.

Alvesson, M. & Spicer, A. (Eds.) (2010) *Metaphors we lead by: Understanding leadership in the real world.* Abingdon: Routledge.

Alvesson, M. & Willmott, H. (2002). Identity regulation as organizational control: Producing the appropriate individual. *Journal of Management Studies, 39*(5), 619–644.

Alwin, D.F. (2012). Integrating varieties of life course concepts. *The Journals of Gerontology: Series B, 67B*(2), 206–220.

Andreu-Perez, J., Poon, C.C., Merrifield, R.D., Wong, S.T. & Yang, G.Z. (2015). Big data for health. *IEEE J Biomed Health Inform, 19*(4), 1193–1208.

Antonakis, J. (2017). Charisma and the "new leadership". In J. Antonakis & D.V. Day (Eds.) *The Nature of Leadership* (pp. 56–81). Los Angeles, CA: SAGE.

Argyris, C. (1992). *On organizational learning.* Oxford: Blackwell.

Argyris, C. & Schön, D.A. (1978). *Organizational learning: A theory of action perspective.* London: Addison-Wesley.

Axtell, C., Hislop, D. & Whittaker, S. (2008). Mobile technologies in mobile spaces: Findings from the context of train travel. *International Journal of Human-Computer Studies, 66*(12), 902–915.

Bakker, A.B. & Schaufeli, W.B. (2008). Positive organizational behavior: Engaged employees in flourishing organizations. *Journal of Organizational Behavior: the International Journal of Industrial, Occupational and Organizational Psychology and Behavior, 29*(2), 147–154.

Bapuji, H. & Crossan, M. (2004). From questions to answers: Reviewing organizational learning research. *Management Learning, 35*(4), 397–417.

Barad, K. (2003). Posthumanist performativity: Toward an understanding of how matter comes to matter. *Signs, 28*, 801–831.

Barclay, L.J. & Kiefer, T. (2014). Approach or avoid? Exploring overall justice and the differential effects of positive and negative emotions. *Journal of Management, 40*(7), 1857–1898.

Barley, S.R., Meyerson, D.E. & Grodal, S. (2011). E-mail as a source and symbol of stress. *Organization Science, 22*(4), 887–906.

Barnes, M. (2006). *Caring and social justice.* Basingstoke: Palgrave Macmillan.

Bass, B.M. & Riggio, R.E. (2006). *Transformational leadership.* Mahwah, NJ: Lawrence Erlbaum.

Bauman, Z. & May, T. (2014). *Thinking sociologically.* Oxford: Blackwell.

BBC (2018). Deputy Governor sorry for calling economy 'menopausal'. Available from: www.bbc.co.uk/news/business-44138229.

Bechky, B.A. (2003). Object lessons: Workplace artifacts as representations of occupational jurisdiction. *American Journal of Sociology, 109*(3), 720–752.

Belk, R.W. (1990). Me and thee versus mine and thine: How perceptions of the body influence organ donation and transplantation. In J. Shanteau & R. Harris (Eds.) *Organ donation and transplantation: Psychological and behavioral factors* (pp. 139–149). Washington, DC: APA.

Bell, E., Warren, S. & Schroeder, J.E. (Eds.) (2014). *The Routledge companion to visual organization.* Abingdon: Routledge.

Bennis, W.G. (1962). Towards a 'truly' scientific management: The concept of organization health. *General Systems Yearbook, 7*, 269–282.

Bennis, W.G. (1967). The coming death of bureaucracy. *Journal of Occupational and Environmental Medicine, 9*(7), 380.

Berglund, G. (2008). Pathologizing and medicalizing lifelong learning: A deconstruction. In A. Fejes & K. Nicoll (Eds.) *Foucault and lifelong learning: Governing the subject* (pp. 138–150). Abingdon: Routledge.

Bianchi, E.C. (2011). *Elder wisdom: Crafting your own elderhood.* Eugene, OR: Wipf and Stock Publishers.

Bloom, P. (2016). Work as the contemporary limit of life: Capitalism, the death drive, and the lethal fantasy of 'work–life balance'. *Organization, 23*(4), 588–606.

Bloom, P. (2017). *The Ethics of Neoliberalism: The Business of Making Capitalism Moral.* Abingdon: Routledge.

Bolman, L.G. & Deal, T.E. (1991). *Reframing organizations: Artistry, choice, and leadership.* San Francisco, CA: Jossey-Bass.

Börsch-Supan, A. (2013). Myths, scientific evidence and economic policy in an aging world. *The Journal of the Economics of Ageing, 1*, 3–15.

Bosch-Sijtsema, P.M., Ruohomäki, V. & Vartiainen, M. (2010). Multi-locational knowledge workers in the office: Navigation, disturbances and effectiveness. *New Technology, Work and Employment, 25*(3), 183–195.

Boud, D. & Hager, P. (2012). Re-thinking continuing professional development through changing metaphors and location in professional practices. *Studies in Continuing Education, 34*(1), 17–30.

Bourdieu, P. (1993). *Sociology in question.* London: Sage.

Boyatzis, R.E., Smith, M.L. & Blaize, N. (2006). Developing sustainable leaders through coaching and compassion. *Academy of Management Learning & Education, 5*(1), 8–24.

Boyle, B. (2012). Foucault among the classicists, again. *Foucault Studies, 13*, 138–156.

Brache, A.P. (2001). Prescription for improving organizational health. *ASQ World Conference on Quality and Improvement Proceedings, American Society for Quality*, 720–725.

Braedley, S. & Luxton, M. (2010). Competing philosophies. In S. Braedley & M. Luxton (Eds.) *Neoliberalism and everyday life* (pp. 3–21). Montreal, Canada and Kingston, ON: McGill-Queen's University Press.

Brewis, J., Davies, A., Matheson, J. & Beck, V. (2017). Three reasons employers need to recognise the menopause at work. Available from: http://theconversation.com/three-reasons-employers-need-to-recognise-the-menopause-at-work-82543.

Brewis, J. & Grey, C. (2008). The regulation of smoking at work. *Human Relations, 61*(7), 965–987.

Briner, R.B., Harris, C. & Daniels, K. (2004). How do work stress and coping work? Toward a fundamental theoretical reappraisal. *British Journal of Guidance & Counselling, 32*, 223–234.

Briner, R.B. & Reynolds, S. (1999). The costs, benefits, and limitations of organizational level stress interventions. *Journal of Organizational Behavior, 20*(5), 647–664.

Broekstra, G. (1996). The triune-brain metaphor: The evolution of the living organization. In D. Grant & C. Oswick (Eds.) *Metaphor and organizations* (pp. 53–73). London: Sage.

Bromwich, J.E. (2018). Tell us what to call the generation after millennials (please). Available from: www.nytimes.com/2018/01/23/style/generation-names.html.

Brookfield, S. (2012). The impact of lifelong learning on communities. In D.N. Aspin, J. Chapman, K. Evans & R. Bagnell (Eds.) *Second International Handbook of Lifelong Learning* (pp. 875–886). Dordrecht: Springer.

Brougham, D. & Haar, J. (2018). Smart Technology, Artificial Intelligence, Robotics, and Algorithms (STARA): Employees' perceptions of our future workplace. *Journal of Management & Organization, 24*(2), 239–257.

Brown, A.D. (2017). Identity work and organizational identification. *International Journal of Management Reviews, 19*(3), 296–317.

Brown, P. (1995). Cultural capital and social exclusion: Some observations on recent trends in education, employment and the labour market. *Work, Employment and Society, 9*(1), 29–51.

Bruce, K. (2006). Henry S. Dennison, Elton Mayo, and human relations historiography. *Management & Organizational History, 1*(2), 177–199.

Bryan, L. (2008). Enduring ideas: The 7-S framework. www.mckinsey.com/business-functions/strategy-and-corporate-finance/our-insights/enduring-ideas-the-7-s-framework.

Brydsten, A., Gustafsson, P.E., Hammarström, A. & San Sebastian, M. (2016). Does contextual unemployment matter for health status across the life course? *The European Journal of Public Health, 26*(1), 167–189.

Brynjolfsson, E. & McAfee, A. (2014). *The second machine age: Work, progress, and prosperity in a time of brilliant technologies*. New York: W.W. Norton & Company.

Burgoyne, J., Pedler, M. & Boydell, T. (1994). *Towards the learning company: Concepts and practices*. London: McGraw-Hill.

Burns, T.E. & Stalker, G.M. (1961). *The management of innovation*. London: Tavistock.

Burrell, G. (1988). Modernism, post modernism and organizational analysis 2: The contribution of Michel Foucault. *Organization Studies, 9*(2), 221–235.

Butler, N., Delaney, H. & Śliwa, M. (2017). The labour of academia. *Ephemera, 17*(3), 467–480.

Butts, M., Becker, W.J. & Boswell, W.R. (2015). Hot buttons and time sinks: The effects of electronic communication during nonwork time on emotions and work-nonwork conflict. *Academy of Management Journal, 58*(3), 763–788.

Bytheway, B. (1994). *Ageism*. Buckingham: McGraw-Hill Education.

Calvo, R.A. & Peters, D. (2014). *Positive computing: Technology for wellbeing and human potential*. Cambridge MA: MIT Press.

Cameron, K.S. & Caza, A. (2004). Contributions to the discipline of positive organizational scholarship. *American Behavioral Scientist, 47*, 731–739.

Cameron, K.S., Dutton, J.E. & Quinn, R.E. (2003). *Positive Organizational Scholarship: Foundations of a New Discipline*. San Francisco, CA: Berrett-Koehler.

Campion, M.A. & Palmer, D.K. (1996). Discovering corporate consciousness. *Journal of Business and Psychology, 10*(4), 389–400.

Carr, C.T. & Stefaniak, C. (2012). Sent from my iPhone: The medium and message as cues of sender professionalism in mobile telephony. *Journal of Applied Communication Research, 40*(4), 403–424.

Cascio, W.F. & Montealegre, R. (2016). How technology is changing work and organizations. *Annual Review of Organizational Psychology and Organizational Behavior, 3*, 349–375.

Castillo-Retamal, M. & Hinckson, E.A. (2011). Measuring physical activity and sedentary behaviour at work: A review. *Work, 40*(4), 345–357.

Cederström, C. & Spicer, A. (2015). *The wellness syndrome*. Cambridge: Polity Press.

Cederström, C. & Spicer, A. (2017). *Desperately Seeking Self-Improvement: A Year Inside the Optimization Movement*. New York: OR Books.

Chartered Institute of Ergonomics and Human Factors (n.d.). What is ergonomics? Available from: www.ergonomics.org.uk/Public/Resources/What_is_Ergonomics.aspx. Last accessed, 7/11/18.

Chartered Institute of Personnel and Development (CIPD) (2015). *Managing Conflict at Work*. Available from: www.cipd.co.uk/knowledge/fundamentals/relations/disputes/conflict-management-report. Last accessed, 7/11/18.

Chui, M., Manyika, J. & Miremadi, M. (2015). Four fundamentals of workplace automation. *McKinsey Quarterly, 29*(3), 1–9.

Cieslik, M. & Pollock, G. (2017). *Young People in Risk Society: The Restructuring of Youth Identities and Transitions in Late Modernity*. Abingdon: Routledge.

Ciulla, J.B. (2004). *Ethics, the Heart of Leadership*. Westport, CT: Praeger Publishers.

Ciulla, J.B. (2009). Leadership and the ethics of care. *Journal of Business Ethics, 88*(1), 3–4.

Clancy, A., Vince, R. & Gabriel, Y. (2012). That unwanted feeling: A psychodynamic study of disappointment in organizations. *British Journal of Management, 23*(4), 518–531.

Claxton, G., Owen, D. & Sadler-Smith, E. (2015). Hubris in leadership: A peril of unbridled intuition? *Leadership, 11*(1), 57–78.

Clegg, S.R., Courpasson, D. & Phillips, N. (2006). *Power and organizations*. London: Sage.

Cogin, J. (2012). Are generational differences in work values fact or fiction? Multi-country evidence and implications. *International Journal of Human Resource Management, 23*(11), 2268–2294.

Colley, L. (2013). Not codgers in Cardigans! Female workforce participation and ageing public services. *Gender, Work & Organization, 20*(3), 327–348.

Collinson, D., Smolović Jones, O. & Grint, K. (2018). 'No more heroes': Critical perspectives on leadership romanticism. *Organization Studies, 39*(11), 1625–1647.

Collinson, D.L. (2003). Identities and insecurities: Selves at work. *Organization, 10*(3), 527–547.

Contu, A., Grey, C. & Örtenblad, A. (2003). Against learning. *Human Relations, 56*(8), 931–952.

Contu, A. & Willmott, H. (2003). Re-embedding situatedness: The importance of power relations in learning theory. *Organization Science, 14*(3), 283–296.

Cooper, C.L. & Quick, J.C. (Eds.) (2017). *The Handbook of stress and health: A guide to research and practice.* Chichester: John Wiley & Sons.

Cornelissen, J.P. (2004). What are we playing at? Theatre, organization, and the use of metaphor. *Organization Studies, 25*(5), 705–726.

Cornelissen, J.P., Oswick, C., Thøger Christensen, L. & Phillips, N. (2008). Metaphor in organizational research: Context, modalities and implications for research. *Organization Studies, 29*(1), 7–22.

Costas, J., Blagoev, B. & Kärreman, D. (2016). The arena of the professional body: Sport, autonomy and ambition in professional service firms. *Scandinavian Journal of Management, 32*(1), 10–19.

Coupland, C. (2015). Organizing masculine bodies in rugby league football: Groomed to fail. *Organization, 22*(6), 793–809.

Cox, T. & Leiter, M. (1992). The health of health care organizations. *Work & Stress, 6*(3), 219–227.

Coyne, I., Farley, S., Axtell, C., Sprigg, C., Best, L. & Kwok, O. (2017). Understanding the relationship between experiencing workplace cyberbullying, employee mental strain and job satisfaction: A dysempowerment approach. *The International Journal of Human Resource Management, 28*(7), 945–972.

Crain, M. (2018). The limits of transparency: Data brokers and commodification. *New Media & Society, 20*(1), 88–104.

Crane, A., Knights, D. & Starkey, K. (2008). The conditions of our freedom: Foucault, organization, and ethics. *Business Ethics Quarterly, 18*(3), 299–320.

Crawford, R. (2006). Health as a meaningful social practice. *Health, 10*(4), 401–420.

Cudd, A.E. (2007). Sporting metaphors: Competition and the ethos of capitalism. *Journal of the Philosophy of Sport, 34*(1), 52–67.

Cutcliffe, J.R. (2000). Fit for purpose? Promoting the human side of mental health nursing. *British Journal of Nursing, 9*(10), 632–637.

Cycling Weekly (n.d.). Doping. Available from: www.cyclingweekly.com/tag/doping.

Czarniawska, B. & Gustavsson, E. (2008). The (D)evolution of the Cyberwoman? *Organization, 15*(5), 665–683.

D'Cruz, P. & Noronha, E. (2013). Navigating the extended reach: Target experiences of cyberbullying at work. *Information and Organization, 23*(4), 324–343.

D'Urso, S.C. (2006). Who's watching us at work? Toward a structural–Perceptual model of electronic monitoring and surveillance in organizations. *Communication Theory, 16*(3), 281–303.

Dale, K. & Burrell, G. (2014). Being occupied: An embodied re-reading of organizational 'wellness'. *Organization, 21*(2), 159–177.

Dalley, G. (1996). *Ideologies of caring: Rethinking community and collectivism.* London: Macmillan.

Deal, J.J., Altman, D.G. & Rogelberg, S.G. (2010). Millennials at work: What we know and what we need to do (if anything). *Journal of Business and Psychology, 25*(2), 191–199.

Deloitte (2018). Global capital trends. Available from: www2.deloitte.com/content/dam/insights/us/articles/HCTrends2018/2018-HCtrends_Rise-of-the-social-enterprise.pdf

Descartes, R. (1641). *Meditations and other metaphysical writings* (D.Clarke, trans, 1998). London: Penguin.

Dewe, P., Cox, T. & Leiter, M. (2014). *Coping, health and organizations.* London: Taylor & Francis.

Dodge, R., Daly, A.P., Huyton, J. & Sanders, L.D. (2012). The challenge of defining wellbeing. *International Journal of Wellbeing, 2*(3), 222–235.

Doughty, H.A. & Rinehart, J.W. (2004). Employee empowerment: Democracy or delusion. *The Innovation Journal: The Public Sector Innovation Journal, 9*(1), 1–24.

Dreyfus, H. & Rabinow, P. (1983). *Michel Foucault: Beyond structuralism and hermeneutics.* Chicago, IL: University of Chicago Press.

Du Gay, P. (2000). *In praise of bureaucracy: Weber-organization-ethics.* London: Sage.

Duncan, C. & Loretto, W. (2004). Never the right age? Gender and age-based discrimination in employment. *Gender, Work & Organization, 11*(1), 95–115.

Dutton, J.E., Frost, P., Worline, M.C., Lilius, J.M. & Kanov, J.M. (2002). Leading in times of trauma. *Harvard Business Review, 80*(1), 54–61.

Dutton, J.E., Worline, M.C., Frost, P.J. & Lilius, J.M. (2006). Explaining compassion organizing. *Administrative Science Quarterly, 51*(1), 59–96.

Easterby-Smith, M. & Lyles, M.A. (Eds.) (2011). *Handbook of organizational learning and knowledge management.* Chichester: John Wiley & Sons.

Eaves, S., Gyi, D.E. & Gibb, A.G. (2016). Building healthy construction workers: Their views on health, wellbeing and better workplace design. *Applied Ergonomics, 54*, 10–18.

Editors (2015). New directions in studying discourse and materiality. *Journal of Management Studies, 52*(5), 678–679. doi:10.1111/joms.12117

Edmondson, A.C. (2011). Strategies for learning from failure. *Harvard Business Review, 89*(4), 48–55.

Eid, M. & Larsen, R.J. (Eds.) (2008). *The science of subjective well-being.* New York: Guilford Press.

Engster, D. & Hamington, M. (2015). *Care ethics and political theory.* Oxford: Oxford University Press.

Ernst Kossek, E., Lewis, S. & Hammer, L.B. (2010). Work-life initiatives and organizational change: Overcoming mixed messages to move from the margin to the mainstream. *Human Relations, 63*(1), 3–19.

Ezzamel, M., Willmott, H. & Worthington, F. (2001). Power, control and resistance in 'the factory that time forgot'. *Journal of Management Studies, 38*(8), 1053–1079.

Fairhurst, G.T. & Putnam, L. (2004). Organizations as discursive constructions. *Communication Theory, 14*(1), 5–26.

Fairtlough, G. (2005). *The three ways of getting things done: Hierarchy, heterarchy and responsible autonomy.* Axminster: Triarchy Press Limited.

Farnacio, Y., Pratt, M.E., Marshall, E.G. & Graber, J.M. (2017). Are workplace psychosocial factors associated with work-related injury in the US workforce?: National Health Interview Survey, 2010. *Journal of Occupational and Environmental Medicine, 59*(10), e164-e171.

Feldman, D.C. (1994). The decision to retire early: A review and conceptualization. *Academy of Management Review, 19*(2), 285–311.

Field, J. (2009). Good for your soul? Adult learning and mental well-being. *International Journal of Lifelong Education, 28*(2), 175–191.

Fineman, S. (2004). Getting the measure of emotion-and the cautionary tale of emotional intelligence. *Human Relations, 57*(6), 719–740.

Fineman, S. (2006). On being positive: Concerns and counterpoints. *Academy of Management Review, 31*(2), 270–291.

Ford, C.M. & Gioia, D.A. (2000). Factors influencing creativity in the domain of managerial decision making. *Journal of Management, 26*(4), 705–732.

Forgeard, M.J.C., Jayawickreme, E., Kern, M. & Seligman, M.E.P. (2011). Doing the right thing: Measuring wellbeing for public policy. *International Journal of Wellbeing, 1*(1), 79–106.

Foster, P.A. (2016). *The open organization: A new era of leadership and organizational development*. Abingdon: Routledge.

Foucault, M. (1979). *Discipline and punish* (A. Sheridan trans.). New York: Vintage.

Foucault, M. (1980). *The history of sexuality, Volume 1, An introduction* (R. Hurley, trans.). Harmondsworth: Penguin.

Foucault, M. (1986). *The history of sexuality, Volume 3, The care of the self* (R. Hurley, trans.). New York: Pantheon.

Foucault, M. (1989a). *The birth of the clinic* (A.M. Sheridan, trans.). Abingdon: Routledge.

Foucault, M. (1989b). *Madness and civilisation* (R. Howard, trans.). Abingdon: Routledge.

Foucault, M. (1997a). *The hermeneutic of the subject* (R. Hurley & J. Faubion, trans.). New York: The New Press.

Foucault, M. (1997b). Technologies of the self (R. Hurley & J. Faubion, trans.). In P. Rabinow (Ed.) *Ethics: Subjectivity and truth* (pp. 223–251). London: Penguin.

Foucault, M. (1997c). On the genealogy of ethics: An overview of work in progress (R. Hurley & J. Faubion, trans.). In P. Rabinow (Ed.) *Ethics: Subjectivity and truth* (pp. 253–280). London: Penguin.

Frank, A.W. (1998). Stories of illness as care of the self: A Foucauldian dialogue. *Health, 2*(3), 329–348.

Franklin, B. (2018). Does ageing matter when it comes to workforce productivity? ILCUK Publication. Available from: https://ilcuk.org.uk/wp-content/uploads/2018/10/09_Does_ageing_matter.pdf.

Frederick, J. & Lessin, N. (2000). Blame the worker: The rise of behavioral-based safety programs. *Multinational Monitor, 21*(11), 10–14.

Friends Life & The Future Foundation (2011). *Visions of Britain 2020: Pensions: Crisis and reforms*. London: Friends Life.

Furlong, A. (2006). Not a very NEET solution: Representing problematic labour market transitions among early school-leavers. *Work, Employment & Society, 20*(3), 553–569.

Gabriel, Y. (1995). The unmanaged organization: Stories, fantasies and subjectivity. *Organization Studies, 16*(3), 477–501.

Gabriel, Y. (1997). Meeting god: When organizational members come face to face with the supreme leader. *Human Relations, 50*(4), 315–342.

Gabriel, Y. (1999). *Organizations in depth: The psychoanalysis of organizations*. London: Sage.

Gabriel, Y. (2008). Spectacles of resistance and resistance of spectacles. *Management Communication Quarterly, 21*(3), 310–326.

Gabriel, Y. (2012). Organizations in a state of darkness: Towards a theory of organizational miasma. *Organization Studies, 33*(9), 1137–1152.

Gabriel, Y. (2015). The caring leader – What followers expect of their leaders and why? *Leadership, 11*(3), 316–334.

Gabriel, Y. & Griffiths, D.S. (2002). Emotion, learning and organizing. *The Learning Organization, 9*(5), 214–221.

Gallagher, S. & Zahavi, D. (2008). *The phenomenological mind: An introduction to philosophy of mind and cognitive science*. Abingdon: Routledge.

Gardiner, R.A. (2018). Ethical responsibility: An Arendtian turn. *Business Ethics Quarterly, 28*(1), 31–50.

Garud, R. & Kotha, S. (1994). Using the brain as a metaphor to model flexible production systems. *Academy of Management Review, 19*(4), 671–698.

Generations Working Together. https://generationsworkingtogether.org/resources/health-wellbeing/.

Gergen, K.J. (1992). Organization theory in the postmodern era. In M.D. Hughes & M. Reed (Eds.) *Rethinking organization: New directions in organization theory and analysis* (pp. 207–226). London: Sage Publications.

Giddens, A. (1990). *The consequences of modernity*. Cambridge: Cambridge University Press.

Gilbert, G.N. & Mulkay, M. (1984). Experiments are the key: Participants' histories and historians' histories of science. *Isis, 75*(1), 105–125.

Gill, R. (2008). Empowerment/sexism: Figuring female sexual agency in contemporary advertising. *Feminism & Psychology, 18*(1), 35–60.

Gilligan, C. (1982). *In a different voice: Psychological theory and women's development*. Cambridge, MA: Harvard University Press.

Goleman, D., Boyatzis, R.E. & McKee, A. (2013). *Primal leadership: Unleashing the power of emotional intelligence*. Boston, MA: Harvard Business Press.

Graeber, D. (2015). *The utopia of rules: On technology, stupidity, and the secret joys of bureaucracy*. Brooklyn, NY: Melville House.

Graham, M., Hjorth, I. & Lehdonvirta, V. (2017). Digital labour and development: Impacts of global digital labour platforms and the gig economy on worker livelihoods. *Transfer: European Review of Labour and Research, 23*(2), 135–162.

Grant, A.M., Christianson, M.K. & Price, R.H. (2007). Happiness, health, or relationships? Managerial practices and employee well-being trade-offs. *Academy of Management Perspectives, 21*(3), 51–63.

Grant, D. & Marshak, R.J. (2011). Toward a discourse-centered understanding of organizational change. *The Journal of Applied Behavioral Science, 47*(2), 204–235.

Grant, D. & Oswick, C. (1996). *Metaphor and organizations*. London: Sage.

Green, N. (2002). On the move: Technology, mobility and the mediation of social time and space. *The Information Society, 18*(4), 281–292.

Greengard, S. (2015). *The internet of things*. Cambridge, MA: MIT Press.

Grint, K. & Woolgar, S. (1997). *The machine at work: Technology, work and society*. Cambridge: Polity Press.

Gründemann, R.W. & Van Vuuren, C.V. (1998). *Preventing absenteeism at the workplace: A European portfolio of case studies*. Dublin: European Foundation for the Improvement of Living and Working Conditions.

Gustavsson, E. & Czarniawska, B. (2004). Web woman: The on-line construction of corporate and gender images. *Organization, 11*(5), 651–670.

Hager, P. & Hodkinson, P. (2009). Moving beyond the metaphor of transfer of learning. *British Educational Research Journal, 35*(4), 619–638.

Hamel, G. (2014). Bureaucracy must die. *Harvard Business Review*, 4. https://hbr.org/2014/11/bureaucracy-must-die.

Hamel, G. & Prahalad, C.K. (1991). Corporate imagination and expeditionary marketing. *Harvard Business Review, 69*(4), 81–92.

Hampden-Turner, C. (1990). *Charting the corporate mind: From dilemma to strategy*. Oxford: Blackwell.

Hanlon, G. (2016). Total bureaucratisation, neo-liberalism, and Weberian oligarchy. *Ephemera, 16*(1), 179–191.

Haraway, D. (2000). Science, technology, and socialist-feminism in the late twentieth century. In D. Bell & B.M. Kennedy (Eds.) *The cybercultures reader* (pp. 291–324). Abingdon: Routledge.

Harkness, A.M., Long, B.C., Bermbach, N., Patterson, K., Jordan, S. & Kahn, H. (2005). Talking about work stress: Discourse analysis and implications for stress interventions. *Work & Stress, 19*(2), 121–136.

Haugaard, M. (2010). Power: A 'family resemblance' concept. *European Journal of Cultural Studies*, *13*(4), 419–438.

Haugaard, M. (2012). Reflections upon power over, power to, power with, and the four dimensions of power. *Journal of Political Power*, *5*(3), 353–358.

Haunschild, A. (2003). Humanization through discipline? Foucault and the goodness of employee health programmes. *Tamara Journal of Critical Organization Inquiry*, *2*(3), 46–59.

Hauser, D.J., Nesse, R.M. & Schwarz, N. (2017). Lay theories and metaphors of health and illness. In *The science of lay theories* (pp. 341–354). Cham: Springer. doi:https://doi.org/10.1007/978-3-319-57306-9_14.

Hayes, S. (2016). The hospital library – Extinct dinosaur or phoenix rising? *Journal of Hospital Librarianship*, *16*(4), 352–357.

Hayward, C. & Madill, A. (2003). The meanings of organ donation: Muslims of Pakistani origin and white English nationals living in North England. *Social Science & Medicine*, *57*(3), 389–401.

Heidegger, M. (1962). *Being and time* (J. Macquarrie & E. Robinson, trans.). Oxford: Blackwell.

Held, V. (2018). *Justice and care: Essential readings in feminist ethics*. Abingdon: Routledge.

Hendry, C. & Pettigrew, A. (1990). Human resource management: An agenda for the 1990s. *International Journal of Human Resource Management*, *1*(1), 17–43.

Henkens, K., van Solinge, H. & Gallo, W.T. (2008). Effects of retirement voluntariness on changes in smoking, drinking and physical activity among Dutch older workers. *The European Journal of Public Health*, *18*(6), 644–649.

Heracleous, L. & Jacobs, C.D. (2008). Understanding organizations through embodied metaphors. *Organization Studies*, *29*(1), 45–78.

Herrmann, N. & Herrmann-Nehdi, A. (2015). *The whole brain business book: Unlocking the power of whole brain thinking in organizations, teams, and individuals*. New York: McGraw-Hill Education.

Herzberg, F. (1974). Wise Old Turk. *Harvard Business Review*, *52*(5), 70–80.

Hill, J.O., Wyatt, H.R., Reed, G.W. & Peters, J.C. (2003a). Obesity and the environment: Where do we go from here? *Science*, *299*(5608), 853–855.

Hill, R.G., Rinaldi, M., Gilleard, C. & Babbs, M. (2003b). Connecting the individual to the organisation: Employers' response to stress in the workplace. *International Journal of Mental Health Promotion*, *5*(1), 23–30.

Hinds, P. & Mortensen, M. (2005). Understanding conflict in geographically distributed teams: An empirical investigation. *Organization Science*, *16*(3), 290–307.

Holliday, R. & Thompson, G. (2001). A body of work. In J. Hassard & R. Holliday (Eds.) *Contested bodies* (pp. 117–134). Abingdon: Routledge.

House, R.J. & Howell, J.M. (1992). Personality and charismatic leadership. *The Leadership Quarterly*, *3*(2), 81–108.

Huber, G. & Brown, A.D. (2017). Identity work, humour and disciplinary power. *Organization Studies*, *38*(8), 1107–1126.

Hughes, C. & Tight, M. (1995). The myth of the learning society. *British Journal of Educational Studies*, *43*(3), 290–304.

Hugill, K., Sullivan, J. & Ezpeleta, M.L. (2018). Team coaching and rounding as a framework to enhance organizational wellbeing & team performance. *Journal of Neonatal Nursing*, *24*(3), 148–153.

Huzzard, T. & Spoelstra, S. (2011). Leaders as gardeners: Leadership through facilitating growth. In M. Alvesson & A. Spicer (Eds.) *Metaphors we lead by: Understanding leadership in the real world* (pp. 76–95). Abingdon: Routledge.

Ingle, S. (2018). IOC bans athletes from marching under Russian flag in closing ceremony. Available from: www.theguardian.com/sport/2018/feb/25/ioc-bans-russia-from-marching-under-countrys-flag-in-closing-ceremony.

Issac, A. (2018). Bank of England deputy warns UK economy entering 'menopausal' phase. Available from: www.telegraph.co.uk/business/2018/05/15/menopausal-uk-economy-risks-once-in-a-century-slump-warns-deputy/?WT.mc_id=tmg_share_tw.

Jack, G., Riach, K., Bariola, E., Pitts, M., Schapper, J. & Sarrel, P. (2016). Menopause in the workplace: What employers should be doing. *Maturitas, 85*, 88–95.

James, E.P. & Zoller, H.M. (2018). Resistance training: (Re)shaping extreme forms of workplace health promotion. *Management Communication Quarterly, 32*(1), 60–89.

Japan Times (2018). Japan population declines at fastest pace yet, with only Tokyo seeing significant growth. Available from: www.japantimes.co.jp/news/2018/07/12/national/japan-population-declines-fastest-pace-yet-125-2-million-government/#.W5z7IehKg2w.

Jenkins, A. & Mostafa, T. (2015). The effects of learning on wellbeing for older adults in England. *Ageing & Society, 35*(10), 2053–2070.

Jermier, J.M. & Forbes, L.C. (2016). Metaphors, organizations and water: Generating new images for environmental sustainability. *Human Relations, 69*(4), 1001–1027.

Kabat-Zinn, J. (2015). Mindfulness. *Mindfulness, 6*(6), 1481–1483.

Kahn, W.A. (2015). The practice of organizational diagnosis: Theory and methods. *Academy of Management Learning & Education, 14*(1), 147–149.

Kaun, A. (2015). Regimes of time: Media practices of the dispossessed. *Time & Society, 24*(2), 221–243.

Kelly, J. & Cameron, K. (2017). Applying positive organizational scholarship to produce extraordinary performance. In C. Proctor (Ed.) *Positive psychology interventions in practice* (pp. 207–217). Cham: Springer.

Kelly, P., Allender, S. & Colquhoun, D. (2007). New work ethics? The corporate athlete's back end index and organizational performance. *Organization, 14*(2), 267–285.

Kennedy, A. (2014). Understanding continuing professional development: The need for theory to impact on policy and practice. *Professional Development in Education, 40*(5), 688–697.

Kenny, K., Fotaki, M. & Scriver, S. (2018a). Mental health as a weapon: Whistleblower retaliation and normative violence. *Journal of Business Ethics.* doi:doi.org/10.1007/s10551-018-3868-4

Kenny, K., Fotaki, M. & Vandekerckhove, W. (2018b). Whistleblower subjectivities: Organization and passionate attachment. *Organization Studies.* https://doi.org/10.1177/0170840618814558.

King, B.G. & Walker, E.T. (2014). Winning hearts and minds: Field theory and the three dimensions of strategy. *Strategic Organization, 12*(2), 134–141.

King, D.D., Newman, A. & Luthans, F. (2016). Not if, but when we need resilience in the workplace. *Journal of Organizational Behavior, 37*(5), 782–786.

Kinman, G. & Jones, F. (2005). Lay representations of workplace stress: What do people really mean when they say they are stressed? *Work & Stress, 19*(2), 101–120.

Kittay, E. & Feder, E.K. (2002). *The subject of care: Feminist perspectives on dependency.* Lanham, MD: Rowman and Littlefield.

Klein, R. (2010). What is health and how do you get it? In J.M. Metzl & A. Kirkland (Eds.) *Against health: How health became the new morality* (pp. 15–25). New York: NYU Press.

Knight, R. (2014). Managing people from 5 generations. *Harvard Business Review.* Available from: https://hbr.org/2014/09/managing-people-from-5-generations.

Knights, D. & Clarke, C. (2017). Pushing the boundaries of amnesia and myopia: A critical review of the literature on identity in management and organization studies. *International Journal of Management Reviews*, *19*(3), 337–356.

Knights, D. & Willmott, H. (1989). Power and subjectivity at work: From degradation to subjugation in social relations. *Sociology*, *23*(4), 535–558.

Knights, D. & Willmott, H. (1999). *Management lives: Power and identity in work organizations*. London: Sage.

Knoppers, A. (2011). Giving meaning to sport involvement in managerial work. *Gender, Work & Organization*, *18*(s1), s1–s22.

Koch, S. & Deetz, S. (1981). Metaphor analysis of social reality in organizations. *Journal of Applied Communication Research*, *9*(1), 1–15.

Kofman, F. & Senge, P.M. (1993). Communities of commitment: The heart of learning organizations. *Organizational Dynamics*, *22*(2), 5–23.

Kolb, D.A. (2014). *Experiential learning: Experience as the source of learning and development*. Upper Saddle River, NJ: Pearson.

Kondo, D.K. (2009). *Crafting selves: Power, gender, and discourses of identity in a Japanese workplace*. Chicago, IL: University of Chicago Press.

Koutsoumari, M. & Antoniou, A.S. (2016). Self-efficacy as a central psychological capacity within the construct of positive organizational behavior: Its impact on work. In A. S. Antoniou & C. Cooper (Eds.) *New directions in organizational psychology and behavioral medicine* (pp. 147–168). Abingdon: Routledge.

Kroth, M. & Keeler, C. (2009). Caring as a managerial strategy. *Human Resource Development Review*, *8*(4), 506–531.

Kruger, J., Epley, N., Parker, J. & Ng, Z.W. (2005). Egocentrism over e-mail: Can we communicate as well as we think? *Journal of Personality and Social Psychology*, *89*(6), 925–936.

Kuss, D.J. & Griffiths, M.D. (2011). Online social networking and addiction – a review of the psychological literature. *International Journal of Environmental Research and Public Health*, *8*(9), 3528–3552.

Ladkin, D. (2018). Self-constitution as the foundation for leading ethically: A Foucauldian possibility. *Business Ethics Quarterly*, *28*(3), 301–323.

Ladkin, D. & Spiller, C. (2013). *Authentic leadership: Clashes, convergences and coalescences*. Cheltenham: Edward Elgar Publishing.

Lakoff, G. & Johnson, M. (2003). *Metaphors we live by*. Chicago, IL: University of Chicago Press.

Latusek, D. & Vlaar, P.W. (2015). Exploring managerial talk through metaphor: An opportunity to bridge rigour and relevance? *Management Learning*, *46*(2), 211–232.

Laumer, S. & Eckhardt, A. (2012). Why do people reject technologies: A review of user resistance theories. In Y.K. Dwivedi, M.R. Wade & S.L. Schneberger (Eds.) *Information systems theory: Explaining and predicting our digital society* (pp. 63–86). New York: Springer.

Lauri, M.A. (2009). Metaphors of organ donation, social representations of the body and the opt-out system. *British Journal of Health Psychology*, *14*(4), 647–666.

Lawler, III, E.E. & Galbraith, J.R. (1994). Avoiding the corporate dinosaur syndrome. *Organizational Dynamics*, *23*(2), 5–17.

Lawrence, P.R. & Lorsch, J.W. (1967). Managing differentiation and integration. *Organization and Environment*, *2*(2), 267–274.

Lawrence, T.B. & Maitlis, S. (2012). Care and possibility: Enacting an ethic of care through narrative practice. *Academy of Management Review*, *37*(4), 641–663.

Lemke, T. (2011). *Biopolitics: An advanced introduction* (E.F. Trump trans.). New York: NYU Press.

Leonard, D. & Straus, S. (1997). Putting your company's whole brain to work. *Harvard Business Review, 75*, 110–122.

Levinthal, D.A. & Marino, A. (2015). Three facets of organizational adaptation: Selection, variety, and plasticity. *Organization Science, 26*(3), 743–755.

Levitt, B. & March, J.G. (1988). Organizational learning. *Annual Review of Sociology, 14*(1), 319–338.

Lewig, K.A. & Dollard, M.F. (2001). Social construction of work stress: Australian newsprint media portrayal of stress at work, 1997–98. *Work & Stress, 15*(2), 179–190.

Liebowitz, J. (1999). *Building organizational intelligence: A knowledge management primer* (Vol. 1). Boca Raton, FL: CRC Press.

Liedtka, J.M. (1996). Feminist morality and competitive reality: A role for an ethic of care? *Business Ethics Quarterly, 6*, 179–200.

Lilius, J.M., Kanov, J.M., Dutton, J.E., Worline, M.C. & Maitlis, S. (2012). Compassion revealed: What we know about compassion at work (and where we need to know more). In K.S. Cameron & G.M. Spreitzer (Eds.) *Oxford handbook of positive organization scholarship* (pp. 273–287). Oxford: Oxford University Press.

Lim, S., Cortina, L.M. & Magley, V.J. (2008). Personal and workgroup incivility: Impact on work and health outcomes. *Journal of Applied Psychology, 93*(1), 95–107.

Lloyd, L. (2006). Call us carers: Limitations and risks in campaigning for recognition and exclusivity. *Critical Social Policy, 26*(4), 945–960.

Loehr, J. & Schwartz, T. (2001). The making of a corporate athlete. *Harvard Business Review, 79*(1), 120–129.

Lofthouse, R. & Thomas, U. (2017). Concerning collaboration: Teachers' perspectives on working in partnerships to develop teaching practices. *Professional Development in Education, 43*(1), 36–56.

Logan, G. (2008). Anatomy of a Gen y-er. *Personnel Today, 16*, 24–25.

Lucas, R. (1987). Organizational diagnostics: Translating the political into the technical. *Journal of Management, 13*(1), 135–148.

Lunau, T., Bambra, C., Eikemo, T.A., van Der Wel, K.A. & Dragano, N. (2014). A balancing act? Work-life balance, health and well-being in European welfare states. *The European Journal of Public Health, 24*(3), 422–427.

Lundvall, B.Ä. & Johnson, B. (1994). The learning economy. *Journal of Industry Studies, 1* (2), 23–42.

Lupton, D. (1995). *The imperative of health: Public health and the regulated body.* London: Sage.

Lupton, D. (2018). *Digital health: Critical and cross-disciplinary perspectives.* Abingdon: Routledge.

MacCormick, J.S., Dery, K. & Kolb, D.G. (2012). Engaged or just connected? Smartphones and employee engagement. *Organizational Dynamics, 41*(3), 194–201.

Macik-Frey, M., Quick, J.C. & Nelson, D.L. (2007). Advances in occupational health: From a stressful beginning to a positive future. *Journal of Management, 33*(6), 809–840.

MacIntosh, R., MacLean, D. & Burns, H. (2007). Health in organization: Towards a process-based view. *Journal of Management Studies, 44*(2), 206–221.

Mackay, M. (2017). Identity formation: Professional development in practice strengthens a sense of self. *Studies in Higher Education, 42*(6), 1056–1070.

Madden, L.T., Duchon, D., Madden, T.M. & Plowman, D.A. (2012). Emergent organizational capacity for compassion. *Academy of Management Review, 37*(4), 689–708.

Majchrzak, A. & Borys, B. (1998). Computer-aided technology and work: Moving the field forward. *International Review of Industrial and Organizational Psychology, 13*, 305–354.

Mannheim, K. (1927/1952). *Essays on the sociology of knowledge.* London: RKP.

Mantie, R. (2012). Learners or participants? The pros and cons of 'lifelong learning'. *International Journal of Community Music, 5*(3), 217–235.

Maravelias, C. (2009). Health promotion and flexibility: Extending and obscuring power in organizations. *British Journal of Management, 20*, S194–S203.

Marshak, R.J. (1996). Metaphors, metaphoric fields and organizational change. In D. Grant & C. Oswick (Eds.) *Metaphor and organizations* (pp. 147–165). London: Sage.

Marx, G.T. (2016). *Windows into the soul: Surveillance and society in an age of high technology.* Chicago, IL: University of Chicago Press.

Maslow, A.H. (1943). A theory of human motivation. *Psychological Review, 50*(4), 370.

Maturana, H.R. & Varela, F.J. (1980). *Autopoiesis and cognition: The realization of the living.* Dordrecht, Holland: D. Reidel Publishing.

Mayer-Schönberger, V. & Cukier, K. (2014). *Learning with big data: The future of education.* New York: Houghton Mifflin Harcourt.

Mayo, E. (1949). Hawthorne and the western electric company. In D.S. Pugh (Ed.) *Organization theory* (pp. 345–357). London: Penguin.

Mazmanian, M. (2013). Avoiding the trap of constant connectivity: When congruent frames allow for heterogeneous practices. *Academy of Management Journal, 56*(5), 1225–1250.

McAllister, D.J. & Bigley, G.A. (2002). Work context and the definition of self: How organizational care influences organization-based self-esteem. *Academy of Management Journal, 45*(5), 894–904.

McCabe, D. (2016). 'Curiouser and curiouser!': Organizations as wonderland – A metaphorical alternative to the rational model. *Human Relations, 69*(4), 945–973.

McCartney, M. (2016). The prurient interest in Trump and Clinton's health. *BMJ, 354*, i4940.

McClendon, M.E., Faries, M. & Jones, E. (2016). Destroying God's temple? Physical inactivity, poor diet, obesity, and other 'Sin' behaviors. *International Journal of Exercise Science: Conference Proceedings, 2*(8), 52. Available from: https://digitalcommons.wku. edu/ijesab/vol2/iss8/52.

McCloy, R. & Stone, R. (2001). Science, medicine, and the future: Virtual reality in surgery. *British Medical Journal, 323*(7318), 912–915.

McDonald, P. & Thompson, P. (2016). Social media(tion) and the reshaping of public/private boundaries in employment relations. *International Journal of Management Reviews, 18*(1), 69–84.

McGillivray, D. (2005). Fitter, happier, more productive: Governing working bodies through wellness. *Culture and Organization, 11*(2), 125–138.

McGranahan, C. (2017). An anthropology of lying: Trump and the political sociality of moral outrage. *American Ethnologist, 44*(2), 243–248.

Mehdawi, A. (2017). www.theguardian.com/lifeandstyle/2017/jan/12/self-care-problems-solange-knowles.

Meriac, J.P., Woehr, D.J. & Banister, C. (2010). Generational differences in work ethic: An examination of measurement equivalence across three cohorts. *Journal of Business and Psychology, 25*(2), 315–324.

Merleau-Ponty, M. (1945/1962). *Phenomenology of perception* (C. Smith, trans.). London: Routledge and Kegan Paul.

Merriam, S.B. & Kee, Y. (2014). Promoting community wellbeing: The case for lifelong learning for older adults. *Adult Education Quarterly, 64*(2), 128–144.

Metzl, J.M. (2010). Why against health? In J.M. Metzl & A. Kirkland (Eds.) *Against health: How health became the new morality* (pp. 1–11). New York: NYU Press.

Meyer, R.E., Höllerer, M.A., Jancsary, D. & Van Leeuwen, T. (2013). The visual dimension in organizing, organization, and organization research: Core ideas, current developments, and promising avenues. *Academy of Management Annals*, 7(1), 489–555.

Mintzberg, H. (1976). Planning on the left side and managing on the right. *Harvard Business Review*, 54, 49–58.

Mintzberg, H. & McHugh, A. (1985). Strategy formation in an adhocracy. *Administrative Science Quarterly*, 30, 160–197.

Mishler, E.G. (1981). The social construction of illness. In E. Mishler, L. Amarasingham, S. Osherson, S. Hauser, N. Waxler & R. Liem (Eds.) *Social contexts of health, illness and patient care* (pp. 141–168). Cambridge: Cambridge University Press.

Moody, L., Saunders, J., Rebernik, N., Leber, M., Čurin, A., Wójcik-Augustyniak, M. & Szajczyk, M. (2017). Tackling barriers to the inclusion of disabled people in the European workplace through ergonomics. In J.I. Kantola, T. Barath, S. Nazir & T. Andre (Eds.) *Advances in human factors, business management, training and education* (pp. 841–849). Cham: Springer.

Moran, D. (2010). Husserl, Sartre and Merleau-Ponty on embodiment, touch and the 'double sensation'. In K. Morris (Ed.) *Sartre on the body* (pp. 41–66). London: Palgrave Macmillan.

Morgan, G. (2007). *Images of organization*. London: Sage.

Morris, K. (2010). Introduction: Sartre on the body. In K. Morris (Ed.) *Sartre on the body* (pp. 1–22). London: Palgrave Macmillan.

Mortimer, J.T. (2009). Changing experiences of work. In A. Furlong (Ed.) *Handbook of youth and young adulthood: New perspectives and agendas* (pp. 149–156). Abingdon: Routledge.

Muhr, S.L. (2011). Leaders as cyborgs: Leadership through mechanistic superiority. In M. Alvesson & A. Spicer (Eds.) *Metaphors we lead by: Understanding leadership in the real world* (pp. 138–161). Abingdon: Routledge.

Mulvey, R. (2013). How to be a good professional: Existentialist continuing professional development (CPD). *British Journal of Guidance and Counselling*, 41(3), 267–276.

Munro, I. & Thanem, T. (2018). The ethics of affective leadership: Organizing good encounters without leaders. *Business Ethics Quarterly*, 28(1), 51–69.

Murphy, L.R. & Cooper, C. (Eds.) (2003). *Healthy and productive work: An international perspective*. London: Taylor & Francis.

Nadesan, M.H. (2010). *Governmentality, biopower, and everyday life*. Abingdon: Routledge.

Nehamas, A. (1998). *The art of living: Socratic reflections from Plato to Foucault*. Berkeley, CA: University of California Press.

Nelson, D. & Cooper, C.L. (Eds.) (2007). *Positive organizational behavior*. London: Sage.

Nicoll, K. & Fejes, A. (2008). Mobilizing Foucault in studies of lifelong learning. In A. Fejes & K. Nicoll (Eds.) *Foucault and lifelong learning: Governing the subject* (pp. 1–18). Abingdon: Routledge.

Nielsen, K. & Randall, R. (2015). Assessing and addressing the fit of planned interventions to the organizational context. In M. Karanika-Murray & C. Biron (Eds.) *Derailed organizational interventions for stress and well-being* (pp. 107–113). Dordrecht: Springer.

Nilsson, W. (2015). Positive institutional work: Exploring institutional work through the lens of positive organizational scholarship. *Academy of Management Review*, 40(3), 370–398.

Nocentini, A., Calmaestra, J., Schultze-Krumbholz, A., Scheithauer, H., Ortega, R. & Menesini, E. (2010). Cyberbullying: Labels, behaviours and definition in three European countries. *Journal of Psychologists and Counsellors in Schools*, 20(2), 129–142.

Noddings, N. (2003). *Caring: A feminine approach to ethics and moral education*. Berkeley, CA: University of California Press.

Nolan, A. (2015). Not fit for purpose? Human rights in times of financial and economic crisis. *European Human Rights Law Review, 4*, 358–369.

Nurmi, N. (2011). Coping with coping strategies: How distributed teams and their members deal with the stress of distance, time zones and culture. *Stress and Health, 27*(2), 123–143.

Nyberg, D. (2009). Computers, customer service operatives and cyborgs: Intra-actions in call centres. *Organization Studies, 30*(11), 1181–1199.

Nye, J.S. (1990). Soft power. *Foreign Policy, Autumn, 80*, 153–171.

Nystrom, P.C. & Starbuck, W.H. (1984). To avoid organizational crises, unlearn. *Organizational Dynamics, Spring*, 53–65.

Oppenheimer, D.M. & Kelso, E. (2015). Information processing as a paradigm for decision making. *Annual Review of Psychology, 66*, 277–294.

Orlikowski, W.J. & Scott, S.V. (2008). Sociomateriality: Challenging the separation of technology, work and organization. *Academy of Management Annals, 2*(1), 433–474.

Örtenblad, A., Putnam, L.L. & Trehan, K. (2016). Beyond Morgan's eight metaphors: Adding to and developing organization theory. *Human Relations, 69*(4), 875–889.

Osherson, S. & AmaraSingham, L. (1981). The machine metaphor in medicine. In E. Mishler, L. Amarasingham, S. Osherson, S. Hauser, N. Waxler & R. Liem (Eds.) *Social contexts of health, illness and patient care* (pp. 218–249). Cambridge: Cambridge University Press.

Ostrom, E. (1990). An institutional approach to the study of self-organization and self-governance. In J.M. Shafritz, J.S. Ott & Y.S. Jang (Eds.) *Classics of organization theory, 8th Edition* (pp. 224–244). Boston, MA: Cengage Learning.

Parikh, M. (2016). Move over Mintzberg, let adhocracy give way to ambidexterity. *Management Decision, 54*(5), 1047–1058.

Parker, M. (1998). Judgment Day: Cyborganization, humanism and postmodern ethics. *Organization, 5*(4), 503–518.

Parker, M. (2015). Between sociology and the business school: Critical studies of work, employment and organization in the UK. *The Sociological Review, 63*(1), 162–180.

Parlamis, J.D. & Geiger, I. (2015). Mind the medium: A qualitative analysis of email negotiation. *Group Decision and Negotiation, 24*(2), 359–381.

Parry, E. & Urwin, P. (2011). Generational differences in work values: A review of theory and evidence. *International Journal of Management Reviews, 13*(1), 79–96.

Perreira, K.M. & Sloan, F.A. (2002). Excess alcohol consumption and health outcomes: A 6-year follow-up of men over age 50 from the health and retirement study. *Addiction, 97*(3), 301–331.

Petriglieri, G., Ashford, S.J. & Wrzesniewski, A. (2018). Agony and ecstasy in the gig economy: Cultivating holding environments for precarious and personalized work identities. *Administrative Science Quarterly, 64*, 124–170.

Pettigrew, A.M., Ferlie, E. & McKee, L. (1992). *Shaping strategic change*. London: Sage.

Pickering, A. (1995). *The mangle of practice*. Chicago, IL: Chicago University Press.

Pinto, J. (2016). 'Wow! That's so cool!' The icehotel as organizational trope. *Human Relations, 69*(4), 891–914.

Plaza, I., Demarzo, M.M.P., Herrera-Mercadal, P. & García-Campayo, J. (2013). Mindfulness-based mobile applications: Literature review and analysis of current features. *JMIR mHealth and uHealth, 1*(2), e24.

POSTNOTE (2011). An ageing workforce. Parliamentary Office of Science and Technology, Houses of Parliament. Number 391. October 2011. Available from: www.parliament.uk/pagefiles/504/postpn391_Ageing-Workforce.pdf.

Price, R. & McDonald, P. (2016). The good, the bad and the ugly: The health and safety of young workers. In R. Price, P. McDonald, J. Bailey & B. Pini (Eds.) *Young people and work* (pp. 105–122). Abingdon: Routledge.

Pritchard, K. & Symon, G. (2014). Picture perfect? Exploring the use of smartphone photography in a distributed work practice. *Management Learning, 45*(5), 561–576.

Pritchard, K. & Whiting, R. (2014). Baby boomers and the lost generation: On the discursive construction of generations at work. *Organization Studies, 35*(11), 1605–1626.

Pritchard, K. & Whiting, R. (2015). Taking stock: A visual analysis of gendered ageing. *Gender, Work & Organization, 22*(5), 510–528.

Purser, R.E. & Milillo, J. (2015). Mindfulness revisited: A Buddhist-based conceptualization. *Journal of Management Inquiry, 24*(1), 3–24.

Pylypa, J. (1998). Power and bodily practice: Applying the work of Foucault to an anthropology of the body. *Arizona Anthropologist, 13*, 21–36.

Quick, J.C., Macik-Frey, M. & Cooper, C.L. (2007). Managerial dimensions of organizational health: The healthy leader at work. *Journal of Management Studies, 44*(2), 189–205.

Rafferty, A.E. & Jimmieson, N.L. (2017). Subjective perceptions of organizational change and employee resistance to change: Direct and mediated relationships with employee well-being. *British Journal of Management, 28*(2), 248–264.

Reiff, C., Marlatt, K. & Dengel, D.R. (2012). Difference in caloric expenditure in sitting versus standing desks. *Journal of Physical Activity and Health, 9*(7), 1009–1011.

Resodihardjo, S.L., Carroll, B.J., Van Eijk, C.J. & Maris, S. (2016). Why traditional responses to blame games fail: The importance of context, rituals, and sub-blame games in the face of raves gone wrong. *Public Administration, 94*(2), 350–363.

Reynolds, M. (2017). *Organizing reflection.* Abingdon: Routledge.

Rhodes, C., Wright, C. & Pullen, A. (2018). Changing the world? The politics of activism and impact in the neoliberal university. *Organization, 25*(1), 139–147.

Riach, K. & Kelly, S. (2015). The need for fresh blood: Understanding organizational age inequality through a vampiric lens. *Organization, 22*(3), 287–305.

Richardson, K.M. & Rothstein, H.R. (2008). Effects of occupational stress management intervention programs: A meta-analysis. *Journal of Occupational Health Psychology, 13*(1), 69–93.

Riedl, R., Kindermann, H., Auinger, A. & Javor, A. (2012). Technostress from a neurobiological perspective. *Business & Information Systems Engineering, 4*(2), 61–69.

Robichaud, D. & Cooren, F. (Eds.) (2013). *Organization and organizing: Materiality, agency, and discourse.* New York: Routledge.

Rose, N. (2007). *The politics of life itself: Biomedicine, power, and subjectivity in the twenty-first century.* Princeton, NJ: Princeton University Press.

Rosen, R.H. & Berger, L.L. (1991). *The healthy company: Eight strategies to develop people, productivity, and profits.* New York: GP Putnam.

Rosenblatt, P.C. & Albert, S. (1990). Management and succession: Intergenerational relationships in fact and metaphor. *Marriage & Family Review, 15*(3-4), 161–170.

Rosengren, C. (2015). Performing work: The drama of everyday working life. *Time & Society.* Epub ahead of print. doi: 0961463X15620983.

Rost, K.A. & Alvero, A.M. (2018). Participatory approaches to workplace safety management: Bridging the gap between behavioral safety and participatory ergonomics. *International Journal of Occupational Safety and Ergonomics.* (in press). doi: 10.1080/10803548.2018.1438221.

Roszak, T. (1994). *The cult of information: A neo-Luddite treatise on high-tech, artificial intelligence, and the true art of thinking.* Berkeley, CA: University of California Press.

Rouse, J. (2001). Two concepts of practice. In T.R. Schatzki, K. Knorr-Cetina & E. Van Savigny (Eds.) *The practice turn in contemporary theory* (pp. 189–198). London: Routledge.

Rudman, D.L. & Molke, D. (2009). Forever productive: The discursive shaping of later life workers in contemporary Canadian newspapers. *Work: A Journal of Prevention Assessment & Rehabilitation, 32*(4), 377–389.

Sackmann, S. (1989). The role of metaphors in organization transformation. *Human Relations, 42*(6), 463–485.

Sadler-Smith, E. (2016). 'What happens when you intuit?': Understanding human resource practitioners' subjective experience of intuition through a novel linguistic method. *Human Relations, 69*(5), 1069–1093.

Sandberg, S. (2013). *Lean in: Women, work, and the will to lead.* New York: Random House.

Sanders, M.A. (2001). Minimizing stress in the workplace: Whose responsibility is it? *Work, 17*(3), 263–265.

Sartre, J.P. (2003). *Being and nothingness* (H.E. Barnes trans.). London: Routledge Classics.

Scheuer, C.L. & Mills, A.J. (2017). Reifying age-related employment problems through the constructions of the 'problematic' older and younger worker. In I. Aaltio, A. Mills & J. Mills (Eds.) *Ageing, organisations and management* (pp. 41–63). Cham: Palgrave Macmillan.

Schön, D.A. (2017). *The reflective practitioner: How professionals think in action.* Abingdon: Routledge.

Schultz, A.B. & Edington, D.W. (2007). Employee health and presenteeism: A systematic review. *Journal of Occupational Rehabilitation, 17*(3), 547–579.

Schwartz, H.S. (1992). *Narcissistic process and corporate decay: The theory of the organizational ideal.* New York: NYU Press.

Seligman, M.E. & Csikszentmihalyi, M. (2000). Positive psychology: An introduction. *The American Psychologist, 55*(1), 5–14.

Senge, P. (2006). *The fifth discipline: The art and practice of organizational learning.* New York: Doubleday.

Sewell, G. & Wilkinson, B. (1992). Someone to watch over me: Surveillance, discipline and just-in-time labour process. *Sociology, 26*(2), 271–291.

Shaw, I. & Kauppinen, K. (Eds.) (2017). *Constructions of health and illness: European perspectives.* Abingdon: Routledge.

Shildrick, T. & MacDonald, R. (2007). Biographies of exclusion: Poor work and poor transitions. *International Journal of Lifelong Education, 26*(5), 589–604.

Shove, E. (2009). Everyday practice and the production and consumption of time. In E. Shove, F. Trentmann & R. Wilk (Eds.) *Time, consumption and everyday life: Practice, materiality and culture* (pp. 17–34). Oxford: Berg.

Shraga, O. & Shirom, A. (2009). The construct validity of vigor and its antecedents: A qualitative study. *Human Relations, 62*(2), 271–291.

Siebert, S. & Walsh, A. (2013). Reflection in work-based learning: Self-regulation or self-liberation? *Teaching in Higher Education, 18*(2), 167–178.

Simpson, P.F., French, R. & Harvey, C.E. (2002). Leadership and negative capability. *Human Relations, 55*(10), 1209–1226.

Sinclair, J. (1994). Reacting to what? *Journal of Organizational Change Management, 7*(5), 32–40.

Smedley, J., Dick, F. & Sadhra, S. (Eds.) (2013). *Oxford Handbook of Occupational Health.* Oxford: Oxford University Press.

Smith, A. & Pitt, M. (2009). Sustainable workplaces: Improving staff health and well-being using plants. *Journal of Corporate Real Estate, 11*(1), 52–63.

Smith, R.C. & Eisenberg, E.M. (1987). Conflict at Disneyland: A root-metaphor analysis. *Communications Monographs, 54*(4), 367–380.

Sonnentag, S., Reinecke, L., Mata, J. & Vorderer, P. (2018). Feeling interrupted – Being responsive: How online messages relate to affect at work. *Journal of Organizational Behavior, 39*(3), 369–383.

Sontag, S. (1978). *Illness as metaphor.* New York: Farrar, Straus and Giroux.

Spears, L.C. & Lawrence, M. (Eds.) (2016). *Practicing servant-leadership: Succeeding through trust, bravery, and forgiveness.* San Francisco, CA: John Wiley & Sons.

Spedale, S. (2018). Deconstructing the 'older worker': Exploring the complexities of subject positioning at the intersection of multiple discourses. *Organization.* doi:1350508418768072

Squires, B. (2018). Standing desk recommendations based on weak science. Available from: https://edition.cnn.com/2018/10/03/health/standing-desk-trutv/index.html.

Stein, H.F. (2001). *Nothing personal, just business: A guided journey into organizational darkness.* Westport, CT: Greenwood Publishing Group.

Stein, M. (2016). 'Fantasy of fusion' as a response to trauma: European leaders and the origins of the Eurozone crisis. *Organization Studies, 37*(7), 919–937.

Stenholm, S., Pulakka, A., Kawachi, I., Oksanen, T., Halonen, J.I., Aalto, V. & Vahtera, J. (2016). Changes in physical activity during transition to retirement: A cohort study. *International Journal of Behavioral Nutrition and Physical Activity, 13*(1), 51–58.

Stephens, C. & Breheny, M. (2018). *Healthy ageing: A capability approach to inclusive policy and practice.* Abingdon: Routledge.

Storey, J. & Barnett, E. (2000). Knowledge management initiatives: Learning from failure. *Journal of Knowledge Management, 4*(2), 145–156.

Strati, A. (2007). Sensible knowledge and practice-based learning. *Management Learning, 38* (1), 61–77.

Sturdy, A. (1997). The consultancy process – an insecure business? *Journal of Management Studies, 34*(3), 389–413.

Sullivan, S.E., Forret, M.L., Carraher, S.M. & Mainiero, L.A. (2009). Using the kaleidoscope career model to examine generational differences in work attitudes. *Career Development International, 14*(2-3), 284–302.

Sundararajan, A. (2016). *The sharing economy. The end of employment and the rise of crowd-based capitalism.* Cambridge, MA: MIT Press.

Syed, M. (2015). *Black box thinking: Marginal gains and the secrets of high performance.* London: John Murray Publishing.

Symon, G. & Pritchard, K. (2015). Performing the responsive and committed employee through the sociomaterial mangle of connection. *Organization Studies, 36*(2), 241–263.

Synnott, A. (1992). Tomb, temple, machine and self: The social construction of the body. *British Journal of Sociology, 43*, 79–110.

Tang, Y.Y., Hölzel, B.K. & Posner, M.I. (2015). The neuroscience of mindfulness meditation. *Nature Reviews Neuroscience, 16*(4), 1–13.

Tarafdar, M., Cooper, C.L. & Stich, J.F. (2017). The technostress trifecta–Techno eustress, techno distress and design: An agenda for research. *Information Systems Journal.* doi: https://doi.org/10.1111/isj.12169.

Tarafdar, M., Tu, Q. & Ragu-Nathan, T.S. (2010). Impact of technostress on end-user satisfaction and performance. *Journal of Management Information Systems, 27* (3), 303–334.

Taylor, F.W. (1914). Scientific management. *The Sociological Review, 7*(3), 266–269.

Taylor, P., Brooke, L., McLoughlin, C. & Di Biase, T. (2010). Older workers and organizational change: Corporate memory versus potentiality. *International Journal of Manpower, 31*, 374–386.

Thanem, T. (2009). 'There's no limit to how much you can consume': The New Public Health and the struggle to manage healthy bodies. *Culture and Organization*, *15*(1), 59–74.

Tilleczek, W. (2014). The connection of the care for self and other in Plato's Laches. *Pseudo-Dionysius*, *16*(1), 1–7.

Tinker, T. (1986). Metaphor or reification: Are radical humanists really libertarian anarchists? *Journal of Management Studies*, *23*(4), 363–384.

Tomkins, L. & Eatough, V. (2013). The feel of experience: Phenomenological ideas for organizational research. *Qualitative Research in Organizations and Management*, *8*(3), 258–275.

Tomkins, L. & Eatough, V. (2014). Stop 'helping' me! Identity, recognition and agency in the nexus of work and care. *Organization*, *21*(1), 3–21.

Tomkins, L. & Nicholds, A. (2017). Make me authentic, but not here: Reflexive struggles with academic identity and authentic leadership. *Management Learning*, *48* (3), 253–270.

Tomkins, L. & Simpson, P. (2015). Caring leadership: A Heideggerian perspective. *Organization Studies*, *36*(8), 1013–1031.

Tomkins, L. & Simpson, P. (2018). An ethic of care: Reconnecting the private and the public. In C. Mabey & D. Knights (Eds.) *Leadership matters? Finding voice, connection and meaning in the 21ˢᵗ century* (pp. 89–101). Abingdon: Routledge.

Tomkins, L. & Ulus, E. (2016). 'Oh, was *that* experiential learning?!' Spaces, synergies and surprises with Kolb's learning cycle. *Management Learning*, *47*(2), 158–178.

Tourish, D. (2013). *The dark side of transformational leadership: A critical perspective*. Hove: Routledge.

Townley, B. (1993). Foucault, power/ knowledge, and its relevance for human resource management. *Academy of Management Review*, *18*(3), 518–546.

Tronto, J.C. (1993). *Moral boundaries: A political argument for an ethic of care*. New York: Routledge.

Tsahuridu, E.E. & Vandekerckhove, W. (2008). Organisational whistleblowing policies: Making employees responsible or liable? *Journal of Business Ethics*, *82*(1), 107–118.

Tsang, E.W. (1997). Organizational learning and the learning organization: A dichotomy between descriptive and prescriptive research. *Human Relations*, *50*(1), 73–89.

Tsoukas, H. (1991). The missing link: A transformational view of metaphors in organizational science. *Academy of Management Review*, *16*(3), 566–585.

Twenge, J.M. (2013). The evidence for generation me and against generation we. *Emerging Adulthood*, *1*, 11–16.

Twenge, J.M. (2014). *Generation me, revised and updated: Why today's young Americans are more confident, assertive, entitled – and more miserable than ever before*. New York: Simon & Schuster.

Twenge, J.M. & Campbell, W.K. (2010). Birth cohort differences in the monitoring the future dataset and elsewhere: Further evidence for generation me – Commentary on Trzesniewski & Donnellan (2010). *Perspectives on Psychological Science*, *5*(1), 81–88.

van der Heide, I., Uiters, E., Sørensen, K., Röthlin, F., Pelikan, J., Rademakers, J. & Boshuizen, H. EPHORT consortium (2016). Health literacy in Europe: The development and validation of health literacy prediction models. *The European Journal of Public Health*, *26*(6), 906–911.

Van Der Velden, A.M. & Roepstorff, A. (2015). Neural mechanisms of mindfulness meditation: Bridging clinical and neuroscience investigations. *Nature Reviews Neuroscience*, *16*(7), 439.

Van Rooij, A. & Prause, N. (2014). A critical review of 'Internet addiction' criteria with suggestions for the future. *Journal of Behavioral Addictions, 3*(4), 203–213.

Van Tulder, M., Malmivaara, A. & Koes, B. (2007). Repetitive strain injury. *The Lancet, 369*(9575), 1815–1822.

Veitch, J.A. (2011). Workplace design contributions to mental health and well-being. *Healthcare Papers, 11*(Special Issue), 38–46.

Verhulst, A., Normand, J.M., Lombart, C. & Moreau, G. (2017). A study on the use of an immersive Virtual Reality store to investigate consumer perceptions and purchase behavior toward non-standard fruits and vegetables. *IEEE Virtual Reality, March*, 55–63.

Vince, R. (2001). Power and emotion in organizational learning. *Human Relations, 54*(10), 1325–1351.

Vince, R. (2002a). The politics of imagined stability: A psychodynamic understanding of change at Hyder plc. *Human Relations, 55*(10), 1189–1208.

Vince, R. (2002b). Organizing reflection. *Management Learning, 33*(1), 63–78.

Vince, R. & Martin, L. (1993). Inside action learning: An exploration of the psychology and politics of the action learning model. *Management Education and Development, 24*(3), 205–215.

Vince, R. & Saleem, T. (2004). The impact of caution and blame on organizational learning. *Management Learning, 35*(2), 133–154.

Virtanen, P., Hammarström, A. & Janlert, U. (2016). Children of boom and recession and the scars to the mental health–A comparative study on the long term effects of youth unemployment. *International Journal for Equity in Health, 15*(1), 14–19.

Voydanoff, P. (2005). Consequences of boundary-spanning demands and resources for work-to-family conflict and perceived stress. *Journal of Occupational Health Psychology, 10* (4), 491–503.

Wadsworth, M.B. & Blanchard, A.L. (2015). Influence tactics in virtual teams. *Computers in Human Behavior, 44*, 386–393.

Wajcman, J. (2015). *Pressed for time: The acceleration of life in digital capitalism*. Chicago, IL: University of Chicago Press.

Wajcman, J. & Rose, E. (2011). Constant connectivity: Rethinking interruptions at work. *Organization Studies, 32*(7), 941–961.

Walmsley, J. (1993). Contradictions in caring: Reciprocity and interdependence. *Disability, Handicap & Society, 8*(2), 129–141.

Wang, L. (2015). Collaborative robot monitoring and control for enhanced sustainability. *The International Journal of Advanced Manufacturing Technology, 81*(9-12), 1433–1445.

Watson, T.J. (2008). Managing identity: Identity work, personal predicaments and structural circumstances. *Organization, 15*(1), 121–143.

Weaver, R. (2015). Metaphors impact daily decisions by managers and leaders. *Global Journal of Business Research, 9*(4), 1–16.

Weaver, R.K. (1986). The politics of blame avoidance. *Journal of Public Policy, 6*(4), 371–398.

Weber, M. (1946). *From Max Weber: Essays in sociology* (H.Gerth & C.W.Mills Eds.). New York: Oxford University Press.

Weick, K. (1979). *The social psychology of organizing*. Reading, MA: Addison-Wesley.

Weinberg, R. & McDermott, M. (2002). A comparative analysis of sport and business organizations: Factors perceived critical for organizational success. *Journal of Applied Sport Psychology, 14*(4), 282–298.

Weisbord, M.R. (1976). Organizational diagnosis: Six places to look for trouble with or without a theory. *Group & Organization Studies, 1*(4), 430–447.

Whiting, R. & Pritchard, K. (2018). Re-constructing retirement as an enterprising endeavour. *Journal of Management Inquiry*. in press. doi: https://doi.org/10.1177/1056492618818773.

Whiting, R., Roby, H., Symon, G. & Chamakiotis, P. (2015). Digi-housekeeping: A new form of digital labour? Presented at the *WORK 2015: New Meanings of Work Stream: 'Reconceptualizing Work'*, Turku, Finland.

WHO (1986). *Ottawa Charter for health promotion*. Copenhagen: World Health Organisation.

WHO (2018a). Global health observatory data: Life expectancy. Available from: www.who.int/gho/mortality_burden_disease/life_tables/situation_trends/en/.

WHO (2018b). Global health observatory data: Healthy life expectancy (HALE) at birth. Available from: www.who.int/gho/mortality_burden_disease/life_tables/hale_text/en/.

Willetts, D. (2010). *The pinch: How the baby boomers took their children's future – And how they can give it back*. London: Atlantic Books.

Willmott, H. (2015). Why institutional theory cannot be critical. *Journal of Management Inquiry*, *24*(1), 105–111.

World Bank (2014). Sedentary lives, the other global epidemic. Available from: www.worldbank.org/en/news/feature/2014/10/15/vidas-sedentarias-la-otra-epidemia-global.

Wright, T.A. (2003). Positive organizational behavior: An idea whose time has truly come. *Journal of Organizational Behavior*, *24*, 437–442.

Wynne Evans, C. & Zarb, E. (2018). How menopause policies can help to reduce employment tribunal risk. *Personnel Today*. Available from: www.personneltoday.com/hr/how-menopause-policies-can-help-to-reduce-employment-tribunal-risk/.

Yukl, G. (1999). An evaluation of conceptual weaknesses in transformational and charismatic leadership theories. *The Leadership Quarterly*, *10*(2), 285–305.

Zack, M.H. (2000). Jazz improvisation and organizing: Once more from the top. *Organization Science*, *11*(2), 227–234.

Zoller, H.M. (2003a). Health on the line: Identity and disciplinary control in employee occupational health and safety discourse. *Journal of Applied Communication Research*, *31*(2), 118–139.

Zoller, H.M. (2003b). Working out: Managerialism in workplace health promotion. *Management Communication Quarterly*, *17*(2), 171–205.

Zwetsloot, G. & Pot, F. (2004). The business value of health management. *Journal of Business Ethics*, *55*(2), 115–124.

# INDEX

Page numbers in **bold** refer to tables.